Night Whispers

'The Shades of Jesus'

Volume 01-Q4

October-November-December

Edition 01-Revision 05

Victor Robert Farrell

Night Whispers
All current
Contact & Sales Information
Can be found at
www.NightWhispers.com

Night Whispers
'The Shades of Jesus'
Volume 01–Q4
October-November-December

Copyright © Rev. Victor Robert Farrell

2019

All Rights Reserved

No part of this book may be reproduced in any form, by photocopying or by any electronic or mechanical means, including information storage or retrieval systems, without permission in writing from both the copyright owner and the publisher of this book.

ISBN Number 978-1-910686-06-5

First published in this format September 2015 by Whispering Word

All current contact and sales information can be found at

www.NightWhispers.com

Printed in The United Kingdom

for

WhisperingWord Ltd.

Night Whispers
'The Shades of Jesus'
Volume 01-Q4
October-November-December

Dedication

This book is dedicated, very simply,

To the now four most important people

In the whole wide world to me.

My daughter Gemma,

My son Jonathan,

My grandaughter Ellie May,

And of course,

My wife

Bridget.

PREFACE

I am Pastor, Rev. Victor Robert Farrell, and these everyday Bible insights called 'NightWhispers' have long since been a global endeavor to communicate the God of the WHOLE Bible in very raw terms to very real people. This is my passion and the reason why I founded The 66 Books Ministry, which through the grace of God and according to His will and favor, shall be preaching consecutively from each of the 66 Books of the Holy Bible, the Gospel of the Lord Jesus Christ in 16,500 of the most influential cities of the world on an annual and ongoing basis! We shall plant, 'City Simple' Churches (see www.CitySimple.Church). In this regard, these NightWhispers accompany our endeavors by providing Every Day Bible Insights into the whole Bible, for all of our members and anyone who wants to know the God of the whole Bible.

These NightWhispers are presented in such a way as to be read each day. They are produced on a regular basis, and the 366 daily readings for each year are presented with a unique volume number. That 'Volume' year is then divided into four Quarters. For example:

Year 01= Volume 01-Q1 | January-February-March
Year 01= Volume 01-Q2 | April-May-June
Year 01= Volume 01-Q3 | July-August-September
Year 01= Volume 01-Q4 | October-November-December
Year 02= Volume 02-Q1 | January-February-March
Followed by Volume 3, 4, 5, 6 etc., and the associate four Quarters for the consecutive years. I am sure you get the picture!

The point is, that you can start any volume of NightWhispers IN ANY YEAR you wish, and AT ANY TIME you choose, because whilst these Everyday Bible Insights are fresh and relevant to each day, they are not interconnected in a way which means you have to read one volume before another. Indeed, NightWhispers are produced as stand-alone products rather than connected volumes. Therefore, if you wish, you can also consecutively read any Quarter from any Volume you choose! For example: Volume 02-Q3 might easily be followed by Volume 05-Q4, because each book is a standalone product. May I say that along with the team at The 66 Books Ministry and Whispering Word, I do hope and pray that these particular *NightWhispers,* will be an enormous blessing to you in *revealing just a little more to you of the God of the WHOLE BIBLE.*

Rev. Victor Robert Farrell, June 2019, Scotland.

INTRODUCTION TO NIGHTWHISPERS

VOL 01-Q4- 'The Shades of Jesus'

This is our fourth standalone quarterly volume of NightWhispers and we hope that these Every Day Bible Insights will be as mighty in all the various shades of Jesus which we seek to present here

Autumn time is my own favorite time of year, it is a time of reaping and enjoying the harvest, preparing to hunker on down for winter, dark nights of gifts and preparations for the Newness of the coming year. The focus of the December in this volume is just that, a focus of preparation for the coming year.

As usual, all we earnestly desire is that you especially check the Scriptures to see if these things are so, and also to do your own digging both there in particular and elsewhere in general. May God the Holy Spirit truly guide you in this.

Bible in very raw and very real terms and also challenge you to think very differently about the coming years on planet earth. Therefore, as you find us pursuing and applying Biblically correct truth to our current cultural and geo-political and technocratic context, you will find that not only are we not politically correct, but some of the things I might suggest for your immediate consideration, well, you might find to be just a little 'out there.' However, your children of now, and the up and coming 'Alpha' generation (those born from AD 2010 onwards) will find them to be the norm. Remember, I am a Bible believing Christian, and thus part of the biggest and most solid 'conspiracy theory' ever revealed to man, and if you are a Christian, so are you! It is your responsibility to know the unfolding of the times and seasons according to God's Holy Word for never has morality been engulfed by the selfish application of the sciences like they are today. This, is being done with purpose by the great enemy of our souls both to destroy the image of God and set up his anti-God kingdom upon this earth. 'Contextual Tilting' will attempt to address just a few of those 'inroads of our enemy.' That we might be prepared to protect the image of God and rightly proclaim the Name and claims of His so Great Son, Jesus Christ our Lord.

As usual, all we earnestly desire is that you especially check the Scriptures to see if these things are so, and also to do your own digging both there in particular and elsewhere in general. May God the Holy Spirit truly guide you in this.

Some global historical acknowledgements

Now then, I have been writing these Bible Insights for many years and I have gleaned in a multitude of fine meadows and otherwise. For me to give credit where credit is due then, would not only increase the size of this quarterly volume many, many times, but I would undoubtedly miss many more people out of that massive list of those which I tried to give credit to. It is Solomon who said that *"there is nothing new under the sun"* and I believe it! Therefore, please then take it for granted that when someone like myself, who almost sees 'cut and paste' as an unspoken gift of the Holy Spirit, says he might have gleaned from another person's work, in someplace, somewhere, and at some point in time without giving appropriate credit where credit is due, that I probably have! If this is the case, it was not my intention to rob you of any glory, but if I have, then please inform me of the same and the necessary changes and/or credits will be made. Remember, I have borrowed from everywhere, I have taken from everyone. 'Everywhere' and 'everyone;' there you go, that should have you covered!

US, UK or elsewhere-or, "How do you spell that?"

To be British, is to be somewhat like 'the last of the Mohicans.' The Britain, that is, the United Kingdom I grew up in is breaking apart. No, sadly, it is broken and never to be repaired. Even so, I am of Irish & Scottish great-grandparents, grandparents and parents, and I was also born in England. Therefore, I am British and a Celt at that. In addition to this, I love North America and the South in particular, so much so, that I feel like a British Red-Neck. Does this make me a Yankophile, or loving the South in particular (and its battle flag) does it make me more especially a Dixiophile? Alternatively, maybe I could be an Americophile or a Canameriphile? Who knows? Suffice to say, that as our nations were once only divided by a common 'English' language, (America still being the residence of the majority of our English readers,) I have tried to adopt the spelling and grammar of the Americas. In this, I have no doubt failed, and in the so doing, both mixed and matched the UK and US spelling and English grammatical styles. In doing this, I confess that I am a double-minded man, and unstable in all my editorial ways. The purists, either side of the pond, I am sure will never forgive me. The rest do not care. Either way, I need your help. So, if you spot any 'howlers,' do let me know. Email me your corrections on,

getyouracttogetherman@whisperingword.com

BIBLE VERSIONS

Ah, the Bible. The true meta-narrative of the real world and therefore all things meta-physical. Well, preferring the 'Textus Receptus' or the 'Majority Text,' I have tried to use the New Separatist Bible (NSB), which is a confluence Bible based on the 1560 Geneva Bible and the 1611 Authorized version, (Pure Cambridge Edition) when I have referenced the Bible, though where necessary, for mere contemporary clarity of course, when I have I have deviated from this norm, at that time I have clearly indicated which other Bible Version has been referenced.

NIGHTWHISPERS ARE WRITTEN FOR……..

There is so much 'devotional' material available nowadays for the Christian that a great part of me says that no more should be written. Yet I do believe that we are moving speedily to the time of the end. What devotionals are written to truly address the needs of Christians living in the approach to this period, or in this period? In my opinion, there are none. NightWhispers then, are written for those people of this darkening time in particular. Therefore, you will find that NightWhispers are battle rations that demand your time, attention, study and consideration. If you need a little ear tickler folks, a quick little cuddle before you go to bed at night, a sleeping pill even, indeed, if you have sold out the truth, your calling and your very self for ten shekels and a shirt, then these Bible Insights are NOT for you. They demand your thoughtful consideration and further investigation and ardent application. They need your time! NightWhispers are written for those seekers who are looking for the God of the whole Bible. They are written for those who hate the color grey but love black and white. They are written for those who want to know the truth, even if it is unpalatable to them. They are written for the awakened; that is, for those people who know that the darkness is alive and like a black incoming tide, is infiltrating every area of present life. They are written for those people who know that a Night is coming when no man can work. They are written for those people who refuse to be spoon-fed. They are written for Bible hungry people. They are written for those who are done with distractions. They are written for those people who have not sold out to cultural compromise and refuse to sell themselves to social niceness and religious self-righteousness. They are written for those who want to cease being unpaid social workers for the unthankful and want to love and arm the saints. They are therefore written for fighters, even that growing band of brothers who are no ragged or rag-tag remnant, but rather, are the released people of 'The Revolution,' that back to the Bible, boots on the ground, present movement of God, who are done with everything that has silenced the one true church and with the removal of its voice, have killed our nations. They are written for the sold out the followers of Christ who have at last found their proclamation voice. They are written for the rooted, fruited and flowering stump. Therefore, to all you great and holy people then, who, even in this darkness might just turn the world right ways up once more, I say then this to you this very night: *"Welcome to NightWhispers, Volume 01-Q4- 'The Shades of Jesus.'*
"Be strong and keep looking up for your salvation draweth nigh."

JUST A HUCKSTER

Some young preacher will study until he has to get thick glasses to take care of his failing eyesight because he has an idea he wants to become a famous preacher. HE'S JUST A HUCKSTER buying selling and getting gain. They will ordain him and he will be known as Reverend and if he writes a book, they will make him a doctor. And he will be known as Doctor; but he's still a huckster buying and selling and getting gain.

And when the Lord comes back, HE will drive him out of the temple along with the other cattle.

A.W. Tozer

(from 'Tozer on Christian Leadership,' compiled by Ron Eggert)

John 3:30 He must increase *but I must decrease.*

STILL LOOKING

Wise men speak of trees
From the Cedar to the Hyssop
Springing from the wall
From the Aspen to the Alder
Beside the water fall

Wise men speak of animals of creeping things and fish
Of birds and bees and smooth black cats
That lap the dainty dish

Wise men sing of love and capture moments in a jar
Wise men suck the juice of days
Wise men shop at Spar

Wise men count the fallen ticks
Of old clocks running down
Wise men number muscles
That help create the frown

Wise men follow after
Wise men follow far
Wise men seek the Savior still
Beneath the wandering star

1 Kings 4:33 Also he spoke of trees, from the cedar tree of Lebanon even to the hyssop that springs out of the wall; he spoke also of animals, of birds, of creeping things, and of fish. (NKJV)

The Old 100th!

All people that on earth do dwell,
Sing to the Lord with cheerful voice.
Him serve with fear, His praise forth tell;
Come ye before Him and rejoice.

The Lord, ye know, is God indeed;
Without our aid He did us make;
We are His folk, He doth us feed,
And for His sheep He doth us take.

O enter then His gates with praise;
Approach with joy His courts unto;
Praise, laud, and bless His name always,
For it is seemly so to do.

For why? the Lord our God is good;
His mercy is for ever sure;
His truth at all times firmly stood,
And shall from age to age endure.

To Father, Son and Holy Ghost,
The God whom Heaven and earth adore,
From men and from the angel host
Be praise and glory evermore.

From 'Fourscore and Seven Psalms of David'
(Geneva, Switzerland: 1561); attributed to William Kethe

CONTENTS

Dedication vii

PREFACE ix

INTRODUCTION TO NIGHTWHISPERS xi
VOL 01-Q4- 'The Shades of Jesus' xi
Some global historical acknowledgements xii
US, UK or elsewhere-or, "How do you spell that?" xiii

NIGHTWHISPERS ARE WRITTEN FOR............................... xv

JUST A HUCKSTER xvii

STILL LOOKING xix

The Old 100th! xxi

| Vol 01 | Q4 | NW00275 | October 01st | 1
   NIGHT-WHISPER | **SERVE** 1
The Shades of 'Jesus' 1
   Proverbs 18:10 .... *1*

| Vol 01 | Q4 | NW00276 | October 02nd | 3
   NIGHT-WHISPER | **RESCUE** 3
The Breaker 3
   Micah 2:13 .... *3*

| Vol 01 | Q4 | NW00277 | October 03rd | 6
   NIGHT-WHISPER | **DISCERN** 6
Giant monkey business 6
   Genesis 6:4a *6*

| Vol 01 | Q4 | NW00278 | October 04th | 9
   NIGHT-WHISPER | **COURAGE** 9
The land of "might's and maybe's" 9

Psalm 23:4 .... *9*

| Vol 01 | Q4 | NW00279 | October 05th | 12
NIGHT-WHISPER | SACRIFICE 12
Heavenly abduction 12
Genesis 5:24 .... *12*

| Vol 01 | Q4 | NW00280 | October 06th | 15
NIGHT-WHISPER | LIVE 15
Laugh, love, live and leave the rest to God 15
Ecclesiastes 7:2 .... *15*

| Vol 01 | Q4 | NW00281 | October 07th | 19
NIGHT-WHISPER | CHOOSE 19
Seeing and sailing 19
Numbers 11;29,30 .... *19*

| Vol 01 | Q4 | NW00282 | October 08th | 22
NIGHT-WHISPER | BECOME 22
Disco balls 22
1 Corinthians 15:41 .... *22*

| Vol 01 | Q4 | NW00283 | October 09th | 25
NIGHT-WHISPER | DIFFERENT 25
Some new math & The great equation 25
1 Peter 3:8-10 .... *25*

| Vol 01 | Q4 | NW00284 | October 10th | 29
NIGHT-WHISPER | WISDOM 29
Flying Rowans and The Whispering Word 29
Luke 21:25-28 .... *29*

| Vol 01 | Q4 | NW00285 | October 11th | 32
NIGHT-WHISPER | COURAGE 32
"Hurry now for today…" 32
1 Samuel 9:12,13 .... *32*

| Vol 01 | Q4 | NW00286 | October 12th | 34

NIGHT-WHISPER | **HOPE** 34
Dream insurance 34
    Genesis 37:9-11 34

| Vol 01 | Q4 | NW00287 | October 13th | 37
    NIGHT-WHISPER | **MERRY** 37
The pessimist mug 37
    Proverbs 15:15 37

| Vol 01 | Q4 | NW00288 | October 14th | 39
    NIGHT-WHISPER | **RETURN** 39
Two little tomcats 39
    Jonah 4:6 39

| Vol 01 | Q4 | NW00289 | October 15th | 43
    NIGHT-WHISPER | **CHANGE** 43
Divine dental floss and its present need 43
    Amos 4:6 43

| Vol 01 | Q4 | NW00290 | October 16th | 46
    NIGHT-WHISPER | **PREPARE** 46
The evocations of Bagpipe music and other weird skirling! ... 46
    Jeremiah 18:15a 46

| Vol 01 | Q4 | NW00291 | October 17th | 48
    NIGHT-WHISPER | **DESIRE** 48
Replacing your dry wall dust with the vigor of Rhino! 48
    Genesis 30:14-16 48

| Vol 01 | Q4 | NW00292 | October 18th | 52
    NIGHT-WHISPER | **ACTION** 52
Two agendas but only one game. Be prepared. Preach The Gospel. 52
    2 Kings 18:28-32 52

| Vol 01 | Q4 | NW00293 | October 19th | 57
    NIGHT-WHISPER | **PRAISE** 57

Building chantries 57
    Ephesians 5:19 57

| Vol 01 | Q4 | NW00294 | October 20th | 60
    NIGHT-WHISPER | **CONSIDER** 60
Angel delight 60
    Psalms 8:3-4 60

| Vol 01 | Q4 | NW00295 | October 21st | 62
    NIGHT-WHISPER | WORRY 62
Nasal drips 62
    Ezekiel 8:17,18 62

| Vol 01 | Q4 | NW00296 | October 22nd | 65
    NIGHT-WHISPER | **CONFIDENCE** 65
Of blow holes in the barley corn 65
    Ruth 2:2-4 65

| Vol 01 | Q4 | NW00297 | October 23rd | 68
    NIGHT-WHISPER | GOODNESS 68
Non loquimur sed vivimus 68
    Acts 9:36-37 68

| Vol 01 | Q4 | NW00298 | October 24th | 71
    NIGHT-WHISPER | **CONTINUE** 71
A kicker with a gun 'til heaven doth come 71
    Luke 3:7,8 71

| Vol 01 | Q4 | NW00299 | October 25th | 75
    NIGHT-WHISPER | **CHARACTER** 75
The deal of death 75
    Luke 3:7 75

| Vol 01 | Q4 | NW00300 | October 26th | 79
    NIGHT-WHISPER | **GIVE** 79
The real road show 79
    2 Samuel 24:24,25 79

| Vol 01 | Q4 | NW00301 | October 27th | 82
    NIGHT-WHISPER | **POWER** 82
What to do with this old house 82
    James 3:11,12 .... *82*

| Vol 01 | Q4 | NW00302 | October 28th | 85
    NIGHT-WHISPER | **CLEAN** 85
Remembering the hidden rock piles of redemption 85
    Joshua 4:4-7 .... *85*

| Vol 01 | Q4 | NW00303 | October 29th | 88
    NIGHT-WHISPER | **BECOME** 88
God's Russian dolls are always opened in reverse 88
    Psalm 47:1-4 .... *88*

| Vol 01 | Q4 | NW00304 | October 30th | 90
    NIGHT-WHISPER | **ACTION** 90
Decisive of Tunbridge Wells 90
    Matthew 9:11-13a *90*

| Vol 01 | Q4 | NW00305 | October 31st | 92
    NIGHT-WHISPER | **CHANGE** 92
The dark billions and the baptism at Bellarmine 92
    Romans 1:21,23 .... *92*

PAUSE FOR PRAYER | 66CITIES 95

| Vol 01 | Q4 | NW00306 | November 01st | 97
    NIGHT-WHISPER | **COURAGE** 97
Beware this flower's power 97
    Numbers 14:31 .... *97*

| Vol 01 | Q4 | NW00307 | November 02nd | 99
    NIGHT-WHISPER | **CHOOSE** 99
The undertone of the overtone, or the rat in the scat 99
    Psalms 29:3 .... *99*

| Vol 01 | Q4 | NW00308 | November 03rd | 101
    NIGHT-WHISPER | **TRUST** 101
Of jennels, jiggers, snickleways and twittens 101
    Isaiah 35:4-6 ...... *101*

| Vol 01 | Q4 | NW00309 | November 04th | 103
    NIGHT-WHISPER | **TRUST** 103
The antidote to Christian cannibalism 103
    1 Samuel 1:9-11 ...... *103*

| Vol 01 | Q4 | NW00310 | November 05th | 105
    NIGHT-WHISPER | **LOVE** 105
Spontaneity and the sizzle of the Spirit of God 105
    Acts 8:26-40 ...... *105*

| Vol 01 | Q4 | NW00311 | November 06th | 110
    NIGHT-WHISPER | **ACTION** 110
Are you a 'Faith Leader' and are you on a 'little list?' 110
    Luke 2:3-5 ...... *110*

| Vol 01 | Q4 | NW00312 | November 07th | 113
    NIGHT-WHISPER | **TRUST** 113
How to get high by not believing a lie! 113
    Psalms 107:25-32 ...... *113*

| Vol 01 | Q4 | NW00313 | November 08th | 117
    NIGHT-WHISPER | **TRUST** 117
Scattered, covered and smothered 117
    Acts 8:1b-5 ...... *117*

| Vol 01 | Q4 | NW00314 | November 09th | 119
    NIGHT-WHISPER | **COURAGE** 119
Loving on Len 119

| Vol 01 | Q4 | NW00315 | November 10th | 121
    NIGHT-WHISPER | **FIGHT** 121
Of Gurkhas and gherkins 121

2 Samuel 21:15-17a *121*

| Vol 01 | Q4 | NW00316 | November 11th | 124
   NIGHT-WHISPER | **REMEMBER** 124
Of bread and blood red wine, ...124
   Revelation 19:11-16 ....*124*

| Vol 01 | Q4 | NW00317 | November 12th | 127
   NIGHT-WHISPER | **PASSION** 127
Where are the Ogres? 127
   Ezekiel 23:17-21 ....*127*

| Vol 01 | Q4 | NW00318 | November 13th | 131
   NIGHT-WHISPER | **CONTINUE** 131
The six measurements of a real man 131
   1 Timothy 5:8 ....*131*

| Vol 01 | Q4 | NW00319 | November 14th | 135
   NIGHT-WHISPER | **FOCUS** 135
The 'Category 12 Demographic' of the modern day legacy church......135
   James 1:23-25 ....*135*

| Vol 01 | Q4 | NW00320 | November 15th | 140
   NIGHT-WHISPER | CONTINUE 140
Of suicidal spit and the true signs of salvation 140
   1 Samuel 19:18-21 ....*140*

| Vol 01 | Q4 | NW00321 | November 16th | 142
   NIGHT-WHISPER | **REST** 142
Quiet Querencias 142
   Psalm 27:4 ....*142*

| Vol 01 | Q4 | NW00322 | November 17th | 144
   NIGHT-WHISPER | **FAITHFUL** 144
God the Grandfather and N.O.M.A.N. 144
   Malachi 2:13-16 ....*144*

| Vol 01 | Q4 | NW00323 | November 18th | 148
    NIGHT-WHISPER | **REPENT** 148
Of silver foxes and the strangulation of all our secret sins 148
    Luke 13:32a 148

| Vol 01 | Q4 | NW00324 | November 19th | 150
    NIGHT-WHISPER | **ACTION** 150
The soon coming 'Wonders of The Lord' 150
    Job 14:7-9 NKJV 150

| Vol 01 | Q4 | NW00325 | November 20th | 153
    NIGHT-WHISPER | **TOUGH** 153
Praying Until You Taste The Blood 153
    John 7:38-39 153

| Vol 01 | Q4 | NW00326 | November 21st | 155
    NIGHT-WHISPER | **COMMIT** 155
Sweet smiles and sheer lies 155
    Hosea 10:2a 155

| Vol 01 | Q4 | NW00327 | November 22nd | 157
    NIGHT-WHISPER | **PREPARE** 157
Suited, booted and ready. Having no sympathy for the Devil. 157
    Revelation 19:19-20 157

| Vol 01 | Q4 | NW00328 | November 23rd | 159
    NIGHT-WHISPER | **WATCH** 159
Destroying distraction 159
    1 Corinthians 16:13-14 159

| Vol 01 | Q4 | NW00329 | November 24th | 161
    NIGHT-WHISPER | **CONSIDER** 161
Shocking Roman Catholics and the problem of pain 161
    1 Corinthians 10:13 161

| Vol 01 | Q4 | NW00330 | November 25th | 164
    NIGHT-WHISPER | **HOPE** 164

One foot in the grave..164
    Genesis 3:19..*164*

| Vol 01 | Q4 | NW00331| November 26th | 167
    NIGHT-WHISPER | **PREPARE** 167
The dagger men..167
    Luke 22:35-38 ....*167*

| Vol 01 | Q4 | NW00332| November 27th | 171
    NIGHT-WHISPER | **PREPARE** 171
Avoiding the disappointment at the end of a gushing tap 171
    Luke 9:62...*171*

| Vol 01 | Q4 | NW00333 | November 28th | 173
    NIGHT-WHISPER | **TRUTH** 173
Flick, click, crush 173
    Ephesians 5:11a...*173*

| Vol 01 | Q4 | NW00334 | November 29th | 175
    NIGHT-WHISPER | **CLEAN** 175
The plays, and all the picture painting of redemption..........................175
    2 Samuel 12:1-4 ....*175*

| Vol 01 | Q4 | NW00335 | November 30th | 177
    NIGHT-WHISPER | **COST** 177
A time of true thanksgiving..177
    Luke 14:26-28 ....*177*

It's time to order your next Quarter of 181

| Vol 01 | Q4 | NW00336 | December 01st | 183
    NIGHT-WHISPER | **CONSIDER** 183
Gestation times 183
    Luke 14:28-31 ....*183*

| Vol 01 | Q4 | NW00337 | December 02nd | 185
    NIGHT-WHISPER | **CONTINUE** 185

Right declarations of death **185**
Joshua 1:1,2a *185*

| Vol 01 | Q4 | NW00338 | December 3rd | **188**
NIGHT-WHISPER | **BELIEVE** 188
Miracle aid **188**
John 2:11 .... *188*

| Vol 01 | Q4 | NW00339 | December 04th | **191**
NIGHT-WHISPER | DESTINY 191
Chocolate, churches and Christ **191**
Colossians 3:16 .... *191*

| Vol 01 | Q4 | NW00340| December 05th | **194**
NIGHT-WHISPER | **OBEY** 194
Chocolate pockets and Ripples of goodness **194**
1 Corinthians 1:27-29 .... *194*

| Vol 01 | Q4 | NW00341 | December 06th | **197**
NIGHT-WHISPER | **CONSIDER** 197
The bat out of hell **197**
1 Thessalonians 1:6-8 .... *197*

| Vol 01 | Q4 | NW00342 | December 07th | **201**
NIGHT-WHISPER | **HOPE** 201
A chocolate pearl, from the fiery harbor **201**
1 Corinthians 6:9-11 .... *201*

| Vol 01 | Q4 | NW00343 | December 08th | **204**
NIGHT-WHISPER | **TRUST** 204
Oh me, oh life **204**
Romans 8:28 .... *204*

| Vol 01 | Q4 | NW00344 | December 09th | **207**
NIGHT-WHISPER | **LIVE** 207
The real new man's bones **207**
2 Kings 13:20-21 .... *207*

| Vol 01 | Q4 | NW00345 | December 10th | 210
    NIGHT-WHISPER | **CONTINUE** 210
Merry makrothumia and happy hupomonee 210
    Romans 15:5-6 .... *210*

| Vol 01 | Q4 | NW00346 | December 11th | 213
    NIGHT-WHISPER | **CONSIDER** 213
God's bloody hands 213
    Joshua 10:40-42 .... *213*

| Vol 01 | Q4 | NW00347 | December 12th | 216
    NIGHT-WHISPER | **EXAMINE** 216
Are there fairies at the bottom of your garden? 216
    2 Corinthians 13:5 .... *216*

| Vol 01 | Q4 | NW00348 | December 13th | 218
    NIGHT-WHISPER | **DESIRE** 218
Of hot lips, curvy hips and lovely eyes? 218
    Genesis 29:16-17 .... *218*

| Vol 01 | Q4 | NW00349 | December 14th | 220
    NIGHT-WHISPER | **INTEGRITY** 220
Mizpah monuments 220
    Genesis 31:48-50 .... *220*

| Vol 01 | Q4 | NW00350 | December 15th | 222
    NIGHT-WHISPER | **EXAMINE** 222
Avoiding substance abuse 222
    Luke 15:13 .... *222*

| Vol 01 | Q4 | NW00351 | December 16th | 224
    NIGHT-WHISPER | **JEWELS** 224
Singing sapphires 224
    Jude 24 224

| Vol 01 | Q4 | NW00352 | December 17th | 228

NIGHT-WHISPER | **PRAISE** 228
The elixir of life **228**
   Romans 1:21-22 ...... *228*

| Vol 01 | Q4 | NW00353 | December 18th | 230
NIGHT-WHISPER | **BELIEVE** 230
Clouds of glory **230**
   Matthew 13:58 ...... *230*

| Vol 01 | Q4 | NW00354 | December 19th | 233
NIGHT-WHISPER | **CONTINUE** 233
Completing circles **233**
   Exodus 4:19-20 ...... *233*

| Vol 01 | Q4 | NW00355 | December 20th | 235
NIGHT-WHISPER | **SMELL** 235
Hungry waters **235**
   Song of Solomon 7:6-9 ...... *235*

| Vol 01 | Q4 | NW00356 | December 21st | 237
NIGHT-WHISPER | **PREPARE** 237
Two more twin towers **237**
   Amos 4:11 ...... *237*

| Vol 01 | Q4 | NW00357 | December 22nd | 239
NIGHT-WHISPER | **WISDOM** 239
Satan's claws **239**
   James 4:7 ...... *239*

| Vol 01 | Q4 | NW00358 | December 23rd | 241
NIGHT-WHISPER | **FORGIVE** 241
Hook's 'Pure Poison' or 'Le Jardin Da'Amour?' **241**
   Ephesians 4:31-32 ...... *241*

| Vol 01 | Q4 | NW00359 | December 24th | 243
NIGHT-WHISPER | **STRONG** 243
Libera me **243**

Isaiah 7:14..*243*

| Vol 01 | Q4 | NW00360 | December 25th |.................................**247**
   NIGHT-WHISPER | **HONOUR** 247
Re-gifting ourselves to God **247**
   2 Samuel 24:24a...*247*

| Vol 01 | Q4 | NW00361 | December 26th |.................................**249**
   NIGHT-WHISPER | **COURAGE**..249
Blinded by the light!..**249**
   Isaiah 42:16a-d...*249*

| Vol 01 | Q4 | NW00362 | December 27th |.................................**252**
   NIGHT-WHISPER | **PEACE** 252
Proclamation, provision, peace and power........................**252**
   Esther 6:6-9...*252*

| Vol 01 | Q4 | NW00363 | December 28th |.................................**255**
   NIGHT-WHISPER | **PERSEVERE** 255
Die Hard 48 – applying newness...**255**
   Luke 11:24-26...*255*

| Vol 01 | Q4 | NW00364 | December 29th |.................................**258**
   NIGHT-WHISPER | **PERSEVERE** 258
He's a good! He's a good! He's a good! He's Ebeneezer good!...**258**
   1 Samuel 7:3-5 ....*258*

| Vol 01 | Q4 | NW00365 | December 30th |.................................**261**
   NIGHT-WHISPER | **PASSION** 261
Jewels in the crown **261**
   Malachi 3:17 ....*261*

| Vol 01 | Q4 | NW00366 | December 31st |..................................**263**
   NIGHT-WHISPER | **POWER** 263
The drinking songs of the spirit..**263**
   Psalms 90:12 ....*263*

DID YOU REMEMBER?	269
DON'T FORGET TO ORDER YOUR NEXT QUARTER OF NIGHT WHISPERS	269
THE MISSION STATEMENT OF THE 66 BOOKS MINISTRY	271
MORE ABOUT 'THE 66 BOOKS MINISTRY'	273
AUTHOR BIO | PURPLE ROBERT	275
JOIN THE FELLOWSHIP OF THE BOOK	276
ANOTHER BOOK BY THE AUTHOR, VR	279
Habakkuk A Prophecy For Our Time	279
ANOTHER BOOK BY THE AUTHOR, VR	281
The 66-Minute Bible	281
AN INTRODUCTION TO 'PURPLE ROBERT'	283
Some Dangerously Different Devotionals!	283

Night-Whisper | **SERVE**

The Shades of 'Jesus'

Proverbs 18:10

The name of the LORD is a strong tower; The righteous run to it and are safe. NKJV

A soldier, a peacekeeper, somewhere in a worn torn country, gingerly makes his way through the blackened shell of a now grotesquely, gutted house. The quietness and the too familiar smell of death hits him as he approaches the cracked open door of the inner room. Rifle at the ready, he slips in and beholds the carnage. Before the small child's bludgeoned and burnt remains, his very being crumples like pressed paper in a giant fist and from his angry mouth slips out the words, "Oh Jesus."

The house seemed empty. Her 50th Birthday and no one had remembered. The children had flown the coop years ago, and were now across country, far, far away, taking care of their own families and business. He had taken their red Coupe, all their savings, found a younger model and after 30 years of marriage, was taking care of the other woman's family now. No one, it seemed, cared for her. The Sunday school had helped and the pills, some, but there seemed nothing that could take away the pain of returning to an empty house, an empty bed. She flicked the switched and the roar of the word hit her like warm quick Miami wind, "Surprise!" Leaping up from behind the furniture, underneath balloons and banners and falling streamers, were the happy faces of her children, her grandchildren and her dearest friends. Faces full of care, now filled the aching void of her tired mind. She lifted up her hands and pressed her shaking fingers to her cheeks cupping her astonished jaw and out slipped those wondrous words, "Oh Jesus."

The X rays were not clear. The mass was visible even to the untrained eye. The doctors words echoed in the distance, and seemed to be heard from an unreal and 'other' place. "I'm so sorry, we shall do all we can of course but......." Staring straight ahead, his astonished facial muscles were fixed in unbelief, yet his mouth still moved and out slipped the words again, "Oh Jesus."

Not far away in another building at the same hospital, a brand new father is given a tiny bundle. His wife lays exhausted, sweaty and smiling on the bed before him, but in the blanket wriggles a new life, full of energy. Things will never be the same again. With two fingers he gently pulls back the blanket and reveals the new pink flesh, the damp black hair and the palest, bluest eyes. He shakes his head and tastes the salty tear that has rolled down his own cheek now and slipped into the corner of his smile. With a sigh he says, "Oh Jesus."

> *To His dearly beloved, to His chosen children; God's name said just by itself, is like a prayer poured forth.*

To His dearly beloved, to His chosen children; God's name said just by itself, is like a prayer poured forth. The new man, the hidden heart, moved by the Holy One indwelling us, takes the wonderful name of Jesus, the Son of God, and whether birthed upon our lips in anger, in despair, or in happiness, or thankfulness, takes that same all saving Name, and be it from our mountain tops of exultation, or from the darkest morgues of our mourning, sets it in its many shades of clear and spoken colors; carefully shaping it into pleading petitions, arrows of thankfulness, cries for mercy, calls for help, courage, clarity, or closeness and gently lays them before the Mighty throne of God most High. "Oh Jesus," "Oh Jesus," "Oh Jesus." What a name! What a prayer!

Listen:- *Your name is ointment poured forth; ……..S.O.S. 1:3b*

Pray: - Lord. When words are not enough, let me find Your name alone to be more than enough. Oh Jesus, Oh Jesus, Oh Jesus, amen and let it be so.

Night-Whisper | **RESCUE**

The Breaker

Our text for tonight ascribes to Jesus, a name which we are not overly familiar with, "Jesus the Breaker." This text makes reference to the deliverance of the Jews and their re-gathering to their God. This text is full of hope and that hope and that deliverance, that hope and that reclaiming, that hope and that victory, is built upon nothing less but the arrival of the Messiah within the shrieking mess of a Nation under judgment and His name at that point, the name of Jesus the Messiah, of Jesus the Savior, is called, "The Breaker".

Micah 2:13

"The one who breaks open will come up before them; They will break out, Pass through the gate, And go out by it; Their king will pass before them, With the Lord at their head."
NKJV

Have you ever imagined the styling of the gates of hell, those very gates that are prophesied never to prevail against the church of the living God? Have you ever wondered maybe at their shape? Some imagine them to be linear in their presentation, like some vast movable rampart, sometimes retreating from the advancing Christian army but mostly and menacingly, ever edging themselves, slowly and determinedly towards the defeated sons of His love, whilst demons are screaming insults and firing fiery darts, all falling from their walls upon our retreating blood bought heads. I suggest that we mostly imagine ourselves then, as poor beleaguered Christians, retreating, back, back and ever backwards into some safer areas of our souls and lives.

Unfortunately, my experience has taught me that there is no space for such a safe retreat. You see, the gates of hell are, in fact, circular. In other words, the gates of hell surround me, as if I were the center of some ever decreasing, nasty and all confining, light consuming, ever collapsing circle. There is no retreat to safety here then! When the gates of hell come in upon us like this, they surround us, they constrict us, they limit our movement, they bind us, they break us, they place us into the servitude of a constrictive condemnation. Yes, when the gates of hell advance dear friends, there is no retreat for the Christian, there is only bondage.

This ever tightening manacle of monstrous restraint, whether it is an addiction, whether it is a state of mind or even a state of heart, becomes to us, a surrounding stronghold, a geographical territory even, and like a torturous tyranny it imposes its overlaying, all laboring will upon us! This ever tightening manacle of monstrous restraint, may be a financial sinkhole sucking us dry, or a fear-infested moat of alligators waiting to tear us apart should we ever dare to cross it and friends, we rarely dare to cross it, for as that circle minimizes itself to a most strangling contraction, the bondage and the life-sucking darkness has then become so severe, that we lose all our strength and most importantly, we lose all our hope. As I write, there are millions who are being eaten alive by such a hellish circle of consummate despondency. The circular gates of hell have for now, prevailed against them.

> *Yes, when the gates of hell advance dear friends, there is no retreat for the Christian, there is only bondage*

Those of us in this cannibalizing condition, need nothing short of Christ "The Breaker" to appear among us! We need Him, the Holy Hammer of the Lord God Almighty, to appear within our shrunken circles of death, and burst like a broken Aswan dam upon the gates of the enemy, or to explode like a mighty bomb against his pressing spikes, or throw Himself like some giant battering ram against the hot and horny, metal doors of hell, head butting down the fiery walls and making a broad breach for us to safely travel through, and then, King Harry-like, stand in the gap astride His neighing charger, His silver and glistening sword raised high, with tattooed name upon His thigh, the now golden sky above, raining down angelic troopers, all to make a way, I say again, all to make a way for us, to leave these concentrated and concentric, strangling rings of terror!

Let us then this evening, together invoke this forgotten name of Jesus our Savior, so that as "Christ The Breaker," He would appear among us on the morrow and smash and splinter these gates of hell, that so bear down upon our sorry souls tonight.

Listen: *"'What is the chaff to the wheat?' says the Lord. 'Is not My word like a fire?' says the Lord, 'And like a hammer that breaks the rock in pieces?'"* NKJV

Pray: O Lord of War, Commander of all the Angel Armies, O Captain, O my Captain, please come and rescue me from these all restricting walls. Lord, take Your great Hammer and break in pieces these rocks of evil imposition, that rise before me like mountains of malevolence ready to drive me to distraction, ready to move me to destruction! All my strength has gone, all my courage and all my hope. I have no plans of escape my Lord, no method and no bargaining ransom. My only hope is that You, as Christ the Breaker, appear amongst my mess and make a way of redemption through all this charging host. Father then, send your Son, and with Him, send the Holy Ghost, and let me hear the ring of His crashing hammer within my listening ears, and see the glisten of His spears, protruding from all the bellies of all my now dead and vanquished foes. Christ My Maker, "Christ My Breaker", come an end this encirclement of death today. Amen and let it be so.

Giant monkey business

Of course it is reputed to be the great American huckster, PT Barnum, who is attributed with the quote that, *"There's a sucker born every minute!"* Investigation seems to indicate however, that the observation and phrase is in fact attributed to David Hannum, a banker and wheeler dealer who was the leader in a syndicate backing the exhibition of 'The Cardiff Giant.' Ahh! Now there's a story.

Genesis 6:4a

"There were giants on the earth in those days..." NKJV

In 1866, fraudster George Hull, after studying archaeology and paleontology, found a very large block of gypsum that contained human vein-like striations. He secretly hired carvers to turn this block into a human like figure, who had obviously died in agony whilst being turned to stone. He then artificially aged the stone giant and buried it on an acquaintance's farm in Cardiff, New York. A year later, he had a couple of workmen, who had been hired to dig a new well, "discover" the stone giant buried deep in the ground. Evangelists of the day had been preaching much around the country concerning our text for tonight and so it was quite easy to raise the ruse and ride it! Hull made thousands of dollars from people coming to view his giant fraud, and eventually the giant money-maker was purchased by a financial syndicate headed by Hannum.

The canny showman, PT Barnum, tried to purchase the giant for his own show for some $50,000 dollars but when the syndicate refused to sell, he made his very own, set it up, and then began charging a dollar a head for viewing the *"real giant"* and then had the audacity to call the Hull-Hannum giant a complete fraud! PT Barnum had more people than Hannum who were willing to pay top dollar to see his fraud of the fraud, especially clergymen and scientific folk, and it was at this point that Hannum is reputed to have responded to the incredulity with the words, **"There is a sucker born every minute!"**

This month in 2008, the remains of a "Bigfoot" and associated non-human hybrid DNA samples, found encased in a block of ice in the remote Forests of the Northern State of Georgia were purchased for a similar PT Barnum sum of $50,000. When the purchasers thawed out the costly giant Sasquatch, they found it to be a rubber monkey suit peppered with meat from the deli counter! Yes indeed, ***there is a sucker born every minute.***

I am a Charismatic. I am a man of the Word and of The Spirit and yes I believe in all the gifts of the Holy Spirit and of the gift of discernment in particular. Yet never in all my life, have I seen such a dearth of discernment within the church of the Living God and the associated courage to call a hoax a hoax! Never have I seen so many mislead mugs line up to give away their hard earned cash. I look at my fellow Charismatics, so sucked into the showmanship of many a "Christian" charlatan, that I have to take Hannum's well-used observation and regretfully modify it by saying that,

Never in all my life, have I seen such a dearth of discernment within the church of the Living God and the associated courage to call a hoax a hoax!

"There's a sucker born again every minute and most of them are Charismatic Christians!"

OUCH! Now these are very hard words of mine I know. But there you go. I am sick of picking up the pitiful pieces of the hurt hearts of disappointed disciples. We need to wise up here folks! We need to speak up! Here is an observation of mine tonight that will help some of you to avoid such hurt and such well-fleeced embarrassment.

"Wolves might wear sheep's clothing, yet they are always into fleecing you. So, watch your wallet and look closely at their bank accounts and lifestyle. They're always a teller."

The great apostles of old could rightly say this: *"Silver and Gold have I none!"* How about those slick-faced, smiling, sheep shearing, sharp teethed wolves? Nope, they cannot say that at all! So brother, sister, friend, go check 'em out! And then please God, then GO CHUCK 'EM OUT!

Listen: *"And a certain man lame from his mother's womb was carried, whom they laid daily at the gate of the temple which is called Beautiful, to ask alms from those who entered the temple; who, seeing Peter and John about to go into the temple, asked for alms. And fixing his eyes on him,* *with John, Peter said, 'Look at us.' So he gave them his attention, expecting to receive something from them. Then Peter said, 'Silver and gold I do not have, but what I do have I give you: In the name of Jesus Christ of Nazareth, rise up and walk.'" (Acts 3:2-7 NKJV)*

Pray: Lord! Take us by our hand and strengthen our feet, so that they might not be turned out of the Way, indeed, strengthen our ankle bones, that we might leap with joy, stand before Your holiness and walk in Your temple courts, giving a good testimony to Your true and never ending goodness. Father, help us to have the courage to say " Oh yeah! Right! You've 'gotta' be kidding me mate." In Jesus name we ask it, amen and let it be so!

| Vol 01 | Q4 | NW00278 | October 04th |

Night-Whisper | **COURAGE**

The land of "might's and maybe's"

There is commercial on television at the moment trying to invoke all the simple, exciting, colorful, innocent and happy thoughts of early childhood. Its tag line is, *"When you were a child what did you dream of?"* I like that.

Psalm 23:4

Yea, though I walk through the valley of the shadow of death, I will fear no evil; For You are with me; Your rod and Your staff, they comfort me. NKJV

Apart from the nightmares of course, yes, apart from the black monsters underneath my dark and dusty bed, or those scaly creatures hid inside the tall brown, creaking wardrobe, that coat-hanger clinking den of secret malevolence which stood sentinel like, patiently waiting for my closed eyes, before creaking open its walnut doors and letting the evil slip silently into my room and step with secret stealth, knife outstretched, towards my quaking bed, yes, apart from the nightmares, my own personal little boy dreams were always just sunny delight! Wait a minute, isn't that another commercial?

I wonder what land of delight or land of trouble might, like the dentist's gas, slip you into either Purgatory or Elysium this dream filled night? Who knows? However, one nightmare land I now refuse to enter, both in my waking thoughts and in my sleeping dreams is the land of "might's and maybe's". This land for me and I believe for most folks, is fraught with heart palpitating uncertainty and decked with dripping fear. Fear of judgment, fear of regret, fear of hurt, fear of dishonor, fear of waste and fear of life shattering, unrecoverable loss! It's a nasty land where peace and comfort, where satisfaction and the supposition of eternal wonderment just cannot live, yes, they cannot even begin to grow their gentle roots into that brittle dry ground, whose soil is never bound together by the always wet and always dripping goodness of the God Most High! I tell you tonight, I shall never again enter the gates of the land of "might's and maybe's" and if you might wish to know just how to avoid those bumpy trips and the fearful bends of the winding roads and the blind corners of that sad and sorry place, then rejoice, for I shall now tell you!

Avoiding entrance into the land of "might's and maybe's" is simple really! You must always act, from what you know. What you know in the Word of God and what you know of the goodness of God which echoes clearly in your heart. Now, let me tell you tonight, that you might never be assured of the outcome of your choices, that is you may never possess the assurance of whether the outcome of your choices will move you towards your God desired goal. Life isn't like that anyways! You line up your ducks and you take your best shot! That's really as good as it gets. Only God knows what will happen. There are no guarantees in life, except the eternal fact that God is good. Now friends, be assured that this fact, when acted on in faith, locks the gates to the confederate lands of "what ifs," and of "might's and of maybe's." We need to be thankful for that, for as soon as we enter these dark lands of our doubting dreams, we find them to be full of manmade Adams, all eight feet tall, with yellow, watery eyes, translucent skin, black pupils and hair and lips made from putrefying corpse material, each one striking a paralyzing fear into our fearful eyes. No, this cold land of "might's and maybe's" is not for the Christian.

There are no guarantees in life, except the eternal fact that God is good.

Christian. Victor. Do not make monsters to populate your own land of "might's and maybe's!" Be strong, be a man, and be decisive! Do what you know to be right in the Word of God and do what you know to be right in your heart. Just do it and leave the results with the good hand of your good God. This is pleasing to Him and who knows, it just might put some hairs on your chest, it maybe might increase your faith and thus your victories and therefore the depth of land you could possess.

Oh, and just one final word. If you are going to establish your heart, your intentions, and your desires, in the mouth of two or three witnesses, then make sure you get a prial of stout hearted Christians! Warriors with hair on their chest, scars on their arms and some muscle in their bicep. Don't even go near any momma's boy Christians, those safely still wrapped around their apron strings, 'cause we all know what they will say! "Stay home son, stay warm, stay nice and always wear clean underwear." No, don't even go there! Commit yourself tonight to action and then dream of the good consequence which shall come form in the good hand of our good God. No might's, no maybe's.

Listen: *"Inasmuch then as the children have partaken of flesh and blood, He Himself likewise shared in the same, that through death He might destroy him who had the power of death, that is, the devil, and release those who through fear of death were all their lifetime subject to bondage. For indeed He does not give aid to angels, but He does give aid to the seed of Abraham. Therefore, in all things He had to be made like His brethren, that He might be a merciful and faithful High Priest in things pertaining to God, to make propitiation for the sins of the people. For in that He Himself has suffered, being tempted, He is able to aid those who are tempted." Hebrews 2:14-18 NKJV*

Pray: Lord, please deliver me from these crippling and monstrous fears, these worm like what "if's," these debilitating "might's" and these crippling "maybe's." Allow me to rejoice in Your goodness when even hesitantly doing what I know to be right, in Jesus name I pray, amen and let it be so.

Night-Whisper | **SACRIFICE**

Heavenly abduction

Our text tonight is one of two instances of Heavenly abduction and may I say, "What a way to go!"

Genesis 5:24

"And Enoch walked with God; and he was not, for God took him."
NKJV

First to be abducted by God was Enoch, taken in the cool of a long day whilst walking along with God. Maybe finding himself far from home that one particular evening, God might have turned and said to him, "Enoch, man we've chatted the day away and eaten well into the evening hours, why not stay over at my place tonight?" "Why not?" replies Enoch, "Thank you very much indeed!" After breakfast the next day, no doubt God spilled all the beans about the new job, the necessity of Enoch's skill set, and long story short, Enoch decides to stay. For a long while.

The second case of abduction is regarding the prophet Elijah, where in 2 Kings 2:11 we read, *"Then it happened, as they continued on and talked, that suddenly a chariot of fire appeared with horses of fire, and separated the two of them; and Elijah went up by a whirlwind into heaven."* This was no case of Elijah walking along in the desert whistling a happy tune, when boom! An out-of-control chariot driver, racing his "street cred" wheels whilst drunk on Beulah's grapes, swerves out of his dimension and bumped right into Elijah, accidently knocking him off his feet and scooping him up and over the rim of the fiery chariot, spinning and whirling him up into the clouds, where, along with the out of control chariot, he would shortly crash into heaven's gates and come to a shuddering halt, with all the splinters of chariot wheels, pearl and chunks of mangled gold, now lay strewn all over the place, around the big feet of a "tut, tut, tutting" and head shaking angelic state trooper! No, it wasn't like that, this was Elijah waiting for a bus. He was well aware of his forthcoming departure, yes indeed, he knew along with all the other prophets hooked into the heavenly internet and listening to the eternal chatter, that a ticket had been purchased and that the wheels were on the way!

Now the truth is friends, that neither of these abductions was an accident. No, both were well planned. Indeed, it is my opinion that these two prophets shall plant their earthly feet once more on the top side of this spinning globe, where, at the time of the end, these two walking olive trees, these two fiery lamp stands, Elijah and Enoch, shall fulfil their ministry of turmoil, and shall deliver their ministry of soul tormenting fiery words, shot at an out of control and whoring nation, laid on its back with its open legs in the air and panting for the devil. They both shall in turn be later slaughtered for it, and left for dead and rotting on the streets. Two rotting carcasses, shall cause a whoring planet to rejoice, even to the beginning of brand new Christmas-type celebration for the lost and rebellious peoples of the earth. However, that's another story, for another day.

> *It is my opinion that toward the beginning of the end, these two prophets, these two walking olive trees, these two fiery lamp stand, shall plant their earthly feet once more on the top side of this spinning globe.*

"Any ways," says God to Enoch, *"The reason I asked you to stay over is that I have two future prophetic positions opening up and one of them is reserved for you, so... what do you think? You up for it?" "Yes,"* says God to Elijah, *"Welcome to heaven, now let's get to business. May I introduce you to Enoch? Good. Enough of the shaking of hands already! Now boys, here's the deal..."*

Meanwhile, along this line of space and time, we imagine these two prophets waiting millennia, either partying in heaven, or hanging in a neat little bag, freeze dried in some heavenly pantry, waiting to be breathed upon once more and then released to their future mission in Jerusalem. I wonder though, if Enoch and Elijah's step out of the space time line, was in fact met at a single point of present reality and to them both, no time has passed at all, no time, that is, until they set their feet on earths hoary shores once more and the clock starts clicking once again. I wonder if, after what they both consider to be an exceptionally short stay in heaven, they shall appear long time after, here on earth, endued with special power from on high to complete their ministries? I wonder...

A friend of mine wrote me yesterday, regarding his being made redundant from his long time held position. Rather than being seemingly thrown out with all the other cost cutting garbage, I wonder if it is that

God, like he did with Elijah and with Enoch, has abducted him as well, and has done so, only to carry him somewhere else in the Spirit, to plant his feet some other place on the topside of this earth, to carry out a more important mission? I wonder if my friend was more fully attentive to the heavenly presence, that he would feel the arm of God, slip around his shuddering shoulder and hear Him say, *"You see Dave, the thing is, I've got this opening, and…"*

Maybe you have been abducted today, last week, this month, yes just abducted, for there is no redundancy in God's economy, just relocation, retraining and re-commissioning. Remember that. You are not on the rubbish heap mate. God's got something else for you. Mind you, it might just get you killed!

Listen: *"These are the two olive trees and the two lamp stands standing before the God of the earth. And if anyone wants to harm them, fire proceeds from their mouth and devours their enemies. And if anyone wants to harm them, he must be killed in this manner. These have power to shut heaven, so that no rain falls in the days of their prophecy; and they have power over waters to turn them to blood, and to strike the earth with all plagues, as often as they desire." Revelation 11:4-6 NKJV*

Pray: Lord, time is on my hands and it drips like shed blood into the waiting earth. Lord, time is on my hands, help me to make use of these sands slipping slowly through my fingers. Lord, time is on my hands, help me hear Your voice, know Your new commission, learn quickly from the training You are giving me for Lord, time is on my hands and it drips like precious shed blood into the waiting earth. O help me hear You today. Amen and let it be so.

Night-Whisper | **LIVE**

Laugh, love, live and leave the rest to God

Once upon a time, a long time ago I worked in a fish and chip shop. I worked with varicose veined, permed and hair-dyed, hard and big bosomed ladies who would beat the snot out of you if you put a foot wrong!

Ecclesiastes 7:2

"Better to go to the house of mourning Than to go to the house of feasting, For that is the end of all men; And the living will take it to heart." NKJV

I worked at Boden's fish and chip shop before I joined the Royal Navy and it was these same buxom beauties who increased my colorful language set so considerably that whilst in the service of her Majesty, I did not fail to fall short of any apt or choice word needed for any situation and also was so linguistically enabled by these ladies, that I fully understood what the parade ground instructors were trying to sincerely communicate to me. Many nights in basic training I remember that I was so very pleased to have in my possession, a hard copy of my birth certificate. I read if often just to assure me that what the parade ground instructors were calling me wasn't true! Yes I was little, but contrary to their loud, forceful and your face, spitting suggestions, I was also legitimate. Just. However, that's a story for another day!

Now it was one of these same buxom ladies of Boden's fish and chip shop, over a smoke and a hot greasy cup of tea who opened up to me and shared with me her terrors, her big and bloodshot bulbous eyes almost bursting with fear as she recounted her one haunting nightmare! Talking about it to me seemed to help her, so she recounted to me that she had been to the doctors for help in this matter but it didn't help! In in fact, yes even so, she still insisted that upon her death, she should be placed in a glass coffin, with air holes drilled in the top of it. In addition this, the lid of her coffin should have a latch fixed to it that could be opened from the inside, and also the location her planting, should be far above the soil, even on top of a mountain. Yes, this tough and rough, grouchy and gruff, working class washer woman, had a crippling fear of being buried alive!

Thomas A Kempis, that long deceased Roman Catholic monk is so much respected by Protestants that his book *The Imitation of Christ* is still standard fare in spiritual discipline classes in most modern day seminaries. Yes, Thomas still speaks of Jesus today and his life of quiet contemplation is still envied and pursued by many modern day pilgrims. You would think that such a man would have been by now made a saint by the Roman Church, but no, Thomas failed the test of their applied sainthood as soon as his body was exhumed for their examination, for you see, the folks that recommend old monks for beatification, reckoned that Thomas did not accept his fate too well, certainly not well enough to be made a saint anyhow! You see, when they exhumed his body and took the lid off the coffin, there was more than enough indication both in the coffin wood and on the corpse remains, that this poor man was buried alive! Like many folks at that time, Thomas may have looked dead, but like many folks at that time, he revived when he was in the ground. Maybe my chip shop mentor was right to be concerned about the manner of her being laid to "rest?"

> *Thomas did not accept his fate too well, certainly not well enough to be made a saint anyhow! You see, when they exhumed his body and took the lid off the coffin, there was more than enough indication both in the coffin wood and on the corpse remains, that this poor man was buried alive!*

Most Christians, like most people who are not Christians, do not fear death, but rather fear the manner of their death. We are all dying, we all know this. However, we refuse to face the certain facts of our ever impending demise as well as unknown the manner of our departure. That is, until the long night of all our days draws in and our shadows lengthen on the ground. That is, until the doctor wants us to come into his office for a chat. That is, until someone close to us is snatched away in their prime, out of time, with all their dreams like unopened Christmas presents strewn along the road to the cemetery. So, I remind you tonight Christian friend, that unless the Lord returns in your life time, you too shall die and the coroner shall record the very particular cause of your death, and your watching family and friends shall recount the manner of it to one another after your departure.

Most folks want their death to be dignified, to be swift, to be uncomplicated, 'tween white cotton sheets, with the family looking on. Most want to impart some final words of wisdom and then with a satisfied sigh, shuffle gently off their mortal coil with as much honor and dignity as they and death can muster. However, the business of dying, is rarely that way.

Thomas, that quiet contemplative, after a life of sacrificial service, after a life of being a living signpost, closes his lids in the hope of opening them in heaven, only when he does open them, he finds that his train has not yet arrived and God help us, it has stopped at Gravesend. Nasty! Stephen beholds Christ stood at God's right hand and then gets a few rocks in the head to crush him into heaven. Tradition has it that Isaiah, that visionary extraordinaire, dies in a devilish and maniacal magic trick, as he gets sawn in half. I bet he didn't accept his fate too readily either! Others are eaten alive by flame or festering fungus, hung, drawn, quartered, blown up, gassed, drowned, speared, scalped, frozen, starved, dismembered and even despaired to death!

> *Thomas, that quiet contemplative, after a life of sacrificial service, after a life of being a living signpost, closes his lids in the hope of opening them in heaven, only when he does open them, he finds that his train has not yet arrived and God help us, it has stopped at Gravesend.*

Friends, save for that coming twinkling of an eye moment, there are obviously *no* guarantees regarding the method of our departure. Now I do not think tonight that joining EXIT, or DIGNITAS is an option for anyone, never mind the Christian! No, in this strange fallen world, it is still right for us followers of Jesus to always choose life, both for ourselves and for others. This means that in the vast majority of cases the method of our departure is not our decision. Sure, our manner of death, like our life, is influenced by our choices. For example, if you play on the railroad tracks, or jump into a shark infested pool, you can somewhat guarantee the method of your departure. However, apart from that, from our human perspective, the manner of our death is pretty much a crap shoot.

The truth is that we cannot even guarantee the manner of our life dear friend, and so in the end, how can we continuous choosers of life, begin to guarantee the manner of our death? We can't! No, the only thing we can guarantee is the attitude in which we shall approach the manner of our death. I'm throwing you a bone I know, but it's the only one I've got!

So how then should we die? Well may I say that we should die in the same way in which we live! Be brave, be strong and be as courageous as you possibly can be. Look for angels along the way. Look for Jesus at the end of your road, the end of your bed, the end of your rope. Let go of that which is passing and lay hold on matters eternal. If we live like this then our attitude in the manner of our death might just well reflect some of it! I suppose tonight that I am encouraging you to live like a dying man. In other words, I am calling you to courage, calling you to strength and life, even in death and especially in the manner of your death.

Tomorrow when you get up, laugh, love, live and leave the rest to God. In this fallen world, that's as good as it gets but even that, can be pretty good indeed, especially for the Christian!

Listen: *"The thief does not come except to steal, and to kill, and to destroy. I have come that they may have life, and that they may have it more abundantly." - John 10:10 NKJV*

Pray: O Lord of life, let me not be robbed of it this side of heaven, amen and amen!

| Vol 01 | Q4 | NW00281 | October 07th |

Night-Whisper | **CHOOSE**

Seeing and sailing

Just so as you don't think last night's meditation was a call to simply "eat drink and be merry for tomorrow we die," tonight, I want to unfold to you the incredible power we have over the future!

Numbers 11;29,30

"Then Moses said to him, 'Are you zealous for my sake? Oh, that all the Lord's people were prophets and that the Lord would put His Spirit upon them!'"
NKJV

Yes, we are under the curse of the fall of man, yes we shall die and yes, we shall have little choice in the manner of our departure but maybe, just maybe, we shall have some? I wonder, if in the parameters of life and death, that we do have in fact some choice in our future? Let me unpack this by beginning a long time ago in my own high school years, in fact, in the type of school now long since gone that did my nation good. A grammar school.

I was never a good student. My main problem was in fact twofold. First, I honestly did not have a clue about how to study and secondly, I had no motivation whatsoever to do so! Indeed, one of my school reports remarked something along the lines that **"I was content to let things come"** and that I **"had an overly optimistic viewpoint regarding my future."** Both of these observations were wrong of course. The fact is that I was a slave to the future, the fact is that I had no idea whatsoever, that from a human perspective, I had the power in my own hands to manipulate my future. Do you see that? Yes, I had the capacity to inculcate change into my time line, yes, I had the means to somewhat set the agenda for my life and to become the hero in my own story, but I didn't really understand that! There is no twist here friend! There is no bait and switch in words, nope, what I am telling you is absolutely true. You have power over your future right here in the now. Imagine that!

In 2007, Nicolas Cage starred in a film called '*Next*,' the story of a man who could see two minutes into his own future, whose gifting was then hunted, captured and later utilized to save the world. Same old same old really, yet the tagline and the bookend statement made by the main character at the beginning and at the end of the film really captivated my attention. The tagline for the film called *Next* is **"If you can see the future, you can save it,"** and the film's bookend statement goes like this: **"Here's the thing about the future. Every time you look at it, it changes, because you looked at it! And that changes everything else."**

Some of us are ignorant of this capacity to form our own future. Some of us are fearful of this capacity to form our own future, not wanting to seemingly foil God's plans for us. As if! Conversely, for those aware of this capacity, some of them

"Every time you look at it, it changes, because you looked at it! And that changes everything else."

are fed up in forming their own future because it has been so costly, so exhausting and so disappointing in the trying. So fed up in fact that they are forging and forming their own future, that they allow the winds of time to take them wherever they desire. Lastly, there are those of us who are forgetful regarding this power to form our own future, because we have been locked into someone else's future fur us, have been made passive, made timid, made tame, made lame, never to be the same, again.

Yet, the desire of Moses the man of God was that all of God's people might be prophets, might be seers if you will. Indeed, I want to say this tonight, that God does not wish it but rather demands that you become a seer in your own life! Tonight then, I do not call you to become the master of your own ship or to believe that you Are the ultimate designer of your own fate, but I do call you to become the master of your own ship under the command of the Great First Sea Lord, Christ Jesus Himself! Subject to Him, serving Him and under His sailing orders, yes, but you, you doing the *seeing* and you doing the *sailing*! This is a great mystery. Yet having our hands on the rudder of our own life is no great mystery at all.

Enough of this cowardly, forgetful, fearful and passive approach to the future of your own dear life then friends. Tonight, dream about your tomorrows. Dream big! Then, each day forward, in all righteousness, see the good future you could have and then make some course changes to so reach it! God has given you more power that you ever dared dreamed of, especially in the fulfilling of the Great Commission. Shout down to your own heart's steerage then and shout loudly,

"Bridge to helm! Right full rudder!"

Listen: *"I call heaven and earth as witnesses today against you, that I have set before you life and death, blessing and cursing; therefore choose life, that both you and your descendants may live" Deuteronomy 30:19-20 NKJV*

Pray: Yes Lord, give me strength to lengthen the scope of my looking glass, and strength to man my sails and stay my course. I am under Your sailing orders O Lord and I am sailing. Amen.

Night-Whisper | **BECOME**

Disco balls

I am sure I first saw one of these manmade ballroom satellites hanging in the public halls of my hometown of Staveley. There, the 'Speedwell rooms' could be hired out for a number of functions, including weddings and I was there for one such function, though I cannot remember which, but sure enough, I do remember my first glimpse of this shimmering silver satellite, hanging dead center above the middle of the dance floor.

1 Corinthians 15:41

"There is one glory of the sun, another glory of the moon, and another glory of the stars; for one star differs from another star in glory."
NKJV

I can tell you, I was disappointed at first. You see, it did little but rotate slowly and reflect in some small way, the local wedding singer's surrounding spotlights of reds and greens. It held the center place of all things, it glanced at everyone and everything in its circular rotation but functioned, in my opinion, in a most pitiful way, casting but scant reflections of light, which then seemed to dissipate in power and in effect, just yards from their journey before disappearing into the long hair of short girls and then sliding to the ground, to be quite easily trod into the dark dance floor by recently shined, black leather soled shoes. Pathetic! Yup, in the Speedwell rooms of Staveley, the seemingly thousands of small mirrors, so intricately placed on the spinning sphere of silver, all cut differently, all angled in a particular way, all jig-sawed together by some seeming amateur artist, were a complete and utter waste of time! I was disappointed. I think all my young friends were disappointed as well, as this man made, man centered, silver spinning satellite of a disco ball hung embarrassed in the dark blue ballroom sky.

Then it happened. Behind us, unseen in the upper right hand corner of this small world of working calls joy, hung the strongest light of all, a powerfully pointed spotlight, which fired its focused beam right into the center of the silver spinning sphere disco ball which in turn, exploded with reflected light, I mean, it went *boom*! Filling the enclosed dance hall world with thousands of whirling stars, all now running over tables, running over people, caressing cheeks and sparkling like dying suns in glee filled eyes, making even grey dentures seem lighter, whiter, brighter, than they ever could be before, landing like shimmering wands of magic on the shoulders of wishful men, turning coal miners into knights in shining armor, and strong armed factory girls into fairy tale princesses. Everything was different now for everything was touched with light majestical. It was glorious! It was wondrous and it didn't stop there either, for the spotlight filtered out its strong composite beam through all the colors of the rainbow and filled our world with red foil wrappers, custard yellows, tangerine oranges, royal blues, autumnal browns, and the all the purples of the dancing King of Kings! Yes, I do remember, that as long as the spotlight hit the center of the disco ball, full of jig-sawed wonder, every point of this small world of ours was bathed in dancing magic.

> *Everything was different now for everything was touched with light majestical... for the spotlight filtered out its strong composite beam through all the colors of the rainbow and filled our world with red foil wrappers, custard yellows, tangerine oranges, royal blues, autumnal browns, and the all the purples of the dancing King of Kings!.*

All your jumbled, jig-sawed life tonight, all your cracked and broken mirrors, all your seventy times seven years of bad breath luck, shattered on your moldy, candy cursed life, cracked and glued together with unsure fingers, will mean absolutely nothing to you, nor to anyone else for that matter, if the spotlight of the Son of God does not hit your spinning center. Ah, but when it does, Oh God, but when it does, all the world you walk through will be lit with glittering wonder and so shall you be too.

Do you see the problem friend? Do you see the possibilities?

Listen: *"All nations whom You have made Shall come and worship before You, O Lord, And shall glorify Your name. For You are great, and do wondrous things; You alone are God. Teach me Your way, O Lord; I will walk in Your truth; Unite my heart to fear Your name. I will praise You, O Lord my God, with all my heart, And I will glorify Your name forevermore. For great is Your mercy toward me, And You have delivered my soul from the depths of Sheol." Psalms 86:9-13 NKJV*

Pray: Hit me with Your glory O Lord and may all my fractured mirrors, dazzle even watching angels with Your most merciful display of love, in Jesus name I ask it, amen and shine on Lord, amen and let it be so.

| Vol 01 | Q4 | NW00283 | October 09th |

Night-Whisper | **DIFFERENT**

Some new math & The great equation

In the United Kingdom, the roundabout is a feat of mental and physical engineering, providing both safety and continuous traffic movement along every road. You slow down a little but you keep on moving, saving on the use of petrol, saving on the use of breaks, saving on the use of neck muscles, yup, in the United Kingdom, the roundabout is an economic masterpiece as well as a carbon saving thing of beauty! (I thought I would get PC on you there. Never go full PC mind you. "Never go full retard.")

1 Peter 3:8-10

"Finally, all of you be of one mind, having compassion for one another; love as brothers, be tenderhearted, be courteous; not returning evil for evil or reviling for reviling, but on the contrary blessing, knowing that you were called to this, that you may inherit a blessing."
NKJV

When I lived in small town America, there was but one roundabout and what a dog's breakfast my American friends used to make of it! The old courthouse still stands in the center of this roundabout and therefore the roundabout has four if not five, pedestrian crossings to get to it. Now, these crossings are but two parallel lines painted on the road and without light or sound, pedestrians walk across them with eyes facing straight ahead whilst walking nonchalantly towards the courthouse at the center of the roundabout! In the country where the car is king, you would think this is tantamount to suicide but no, people walk the walk, paying no attention to giant trucks full of bourbon or corn, and the drivers, well the drivers just have to stop in their tracks! Stop on a roundabout! Now to compound matters even further, this single roundabout also has four yield signs! So we have five poor crossings and four yield sings all on the same roundabout! Crazy or what! Yes, my American brethren have absolutely no idea how to run a roundabout. Though to my knowledge, no one has been hurt on it yet, however, I am convinced that it is only a matter of time.

The building of American cities on a grid and block system means that nowhere else in the world is there the conglomeration of millions of intersections and subsequent 4-Way Stop signs. At the end of every block, you have to stop at a four-way intersection! Can you imagine what this does for increased fuel consumption, for break wear, for neck muscle wear and even bowel twist wear! It is just ridiculous and I tell you what, as an Englishman driving in America, I still do not fully understand the polite protocol of who moves first when four cars arrive at exactly the same time at the same intersection! Four-way stops are the most confusing constructions I have ever come across. Oh please God give me always the speed and sensibility of roundabouts!

Now before I give you these tools, let me say that, they are only utilized by sane people! Thus, you will never see them in play in New York, Los Angeles, Houston, or in America's open-air asylum, the whole of South Florida!

Even so, the freaky little Bardstown (KY) roundabout and the millions upon millions of four way stops in America, all seem to work. Yes, they seem to function so well, that people are on the whole, quite, quite safe. Personally, thus far, I have never yet seen an accident at a 4-Way Stop and not even on the freaky Bardstown roundabout, and I believe I know why. You see these American drivers are utilizing three important tools, which the British driver is rarely seen with. Tonight, even though it is the last and most important tool, which is the key to both peace in driving and in peace life, I shall also throw the other two simply for good measure.

Now before I give you these tools, let me say that, they are only utilized by sane people! Thus, you will never see them in play in New York, Los Angeles, Houston, or in America's open-air asylum, the whole of South Florida! With these most obvious exceptions I shall now proceed!

So, the first tool is less haste! I cannot tell you how many old Chevy trucks I have been stuck behind where to the driver; every day seems to be a Sunday afternoon, even if its 8:00 o'clock in the morning! It's as though there is common acknowledgement that, "Hey, it'll still be there when you get there!" These country folks always smile and wave as I over take them at the first unsafe opportunity.

The second tool is a most uncomfortable obedience to traffic laws and speed limits. I know, this is almost unheard of in the UK, yet over in small town America especially, most people obey the traffic laws, even at 2:00am in the morning when no one is around! Crazy people.

However, the third and most powerful tool of all, so fully expressed, seen and tasted at the four-way stop sign, is that most magnificent tool of 'deference.'

Deference is the practice of deferring your practice and even sometimes your rights, to both the practice and action of others. Now stick with me please, for there grows out of deference a most remarkable life equation. However, first let me say, that deference coupled with reluctance leads to bitterness. This is deference with a snarl you see. I have seen this in practice but little however, and I think that is because of the nasty taste it leaves in the mouth of the practitioner! No, deference without reluctance, especially at 4-Way Stop signs, is usually practiced with kindness, and deference plus kindness equals common courtesy. Now, this amazing equation of $d + k = cc$, is most magnificent math, for when worked out with consistency it brings a safe pace to both driving and to life, and a safe pace brings sight! Yes, you begin see things that you might never have been able to see before. You smell the roses a little better, you breathe a little deeper, you work with more ease and completion, good grief, even your bowel movements begin to assume a released regularity! Yes indeed, with this equation of deference plus kindness leading to common courtesy, you literally move to a more seated, unstrained, relaxed enjoyed approach to people, jobs, life, relationships and problems of every kind and sort! Common courtesy is brotherly kindness on legs and that, dear friends, is the beginning of selflessness, the beginning of the humbling of pride, which in turn is the preparation of the heart for the poured in, poured out, poured through goodness of God! Imagine that.

> *Deference is the practice of deferring your practice and even sometimes your rights, to both the practice and action of others.*

So tomorrow, especially if today you have been a miserable old trout, why not amaze your colleagues, your family and your friends, yes, why not even trick the rest of humanity into thinking you're mentally ill, by practicing some deference, kindness and common courtesy. Go on; amaze people with your new math, by adding deference with kindness. I tell you what, it will change your world.

Maybe, in the United Kingdom for the sole purpose of promoting common courtesy, we should get rid of all our roundabouts! Yeah right!

Listen: *"For 'He who would love life And see good days, Let him refrain his tongue from evil, And his lips from speaking deceit. Let him turn away from evil and do good; Let him seek peace and pursue it. For the eyes of the Lord are on the righteous, And His ears are open to their prayers; But the face of the Lord is against those who do evil.'" 1 Peter 3:10-12 NKJV*

Pray: Lord, help me practice the good selflessness of deferent kindness. So may You be glorified, so may I be granted peace, so may my prayers be granted favor in Your ears, in Jesus name I pray, amen!

| Vol 01 | Q4 | NW00284 | October 10th |

Night-Whisper | **WISDOM**

Flying Rowans and The Whispering Word

Outside my window, tall and solid, sentinel like in standing and spreading its rich red, fruit laden branches, is a "whispering tree." Warding off witches and wafting its knowledge in the warm autumn wind. Through the slight crack of my ajar'd window pane, its ancient words land with feather like gentleness upon my listening ears. They say, *"Be ready. Look up. For your salvation draweth nigh."* Yes, Rowan, the ancient and scarlet clad woman of the autumn, is now ready to speak her secrets to all who shall take the time to listen.

Luke 21:25-28

"And there shall be signs in the sun, and in the moon, and in the stars; and upon the earth distress of nations, with perplexity; the sea and the waves roaring; Men's hearts failing them for fear, and for looking after those things which are coming on the earth: for the powers of heaven shall be shaken. And then shall they see the Son of man coming in a cloud with power and great glory. And when these things begin to come to pass, then look up, and lift up your heads; for your redemption draweth nigh." KJV.

As I write this whisper on this autumn day of 2008, the current of many global financial crashes is already beginning to bite. The world shall never be the same again and soon, the tsunamious repercussions of all our gaudy greed shall wet the lowland waiting fields, though they shall never wipe their face again. Yet still, amidst the shocking turmoil, talked up on all our 24-hour, astonished and fear-filled news channels, there is not one head that is turned to God. There is not one eye that looketh up. There is not one mouth that cries to God for help. My God! Even the church sits stupefyingly quiet, saucer-eyed and gormless, twitching toddler-like in its dung-filled nappy, sucking on a yellow plastic hammer. It has nothing to say either! For what can it say? It regressed into an imbecilic infancy long, long time ago, when in its worldly wisdom, it took on an "inoffensive safety" stance whilst acting as an old age care giver to a dying world as it hooked up with the virgin of "acceptant spirituality" to lie between the sheets of the crumbling world and keep warm its old and cold, most impotent of feet. The church may have lost its ministerial pension funds in this crash, but its keeping schtum! The church may be tussling out free food and advice against poverty but it's still investing in British Airways shares.

The banquet of the Rowan tree, the bird catcher, filled the bellies of those feather ideas of the heavens, with orange flesh and rich seedlings in small coal black jackets. These same full birds, then on their travels of speaking testimony to the goodness of God, fertilizingly deposit those seeds in the waiting arches of other trees, high crags, weather split rocks, and all the hard to reach and impossible places of the earth with all the possibilities of a growing rich red goodness. Taking root, these small fresh trees, these so called "flying Rowans" then become even more mythical and valuable in their prowess and their power. Revealed secrets you see. Implanted words, when they produce a crop in the most unlikeliest of places, take on miraculous power of their own. The ancients knew this.

Revealed secrets you see. Implanted words, when they produce a crop in the most unlikeliest of places, take on miraculous power of their own. The ancients knew this.

The Bible is a Rowan tree which whispers its secrets to all who hungrily sit beneath its rich and hanging, red fruit bending boughs. The Word of God is a seed to be planted, a red fruit to be sought after full of orange sun, and its squeezed juices, when mingled with our daily wine, shall make us glad indeed. To all who love the Lord then and also long for His appearing, I say that now, yes now more than any other, is the time to sit beneath His Rowan tree Word and listen to His whispers for there are things you need to know. In the coming disasters, God still has His flying Rowans. He who has ears to hear, let him hear.

Listen: *"A word came to me in secret — a mere whisper of a word, but I heard it clearly. It came in a scary dream one night, after I had fallen into a deep, deep sleep. Dread stared me in the face, and Terror. I was scared to death — I shook from head to foot. A spirit glided right in front of me — the hair on my head stood on end. I couldn't tell what it was that appeared there — a blur . . . and then I heard a muffled voice: 'How can mere mortals be more righteous than God? How can humans be purer than their Creator? Why, God doesn't even trust his own servants, doesn't even cheer his angels, So how much less these bodies composed of* *mud,fragile as moths? These bodies of ours are here today and gone tomorrow, and no one even notices — gone without a trace. When the tent stakes are ripped up, the tent collapses — we die and are never the wiser for having lived.'" (Job 4:12-21 THE MESSAGE)*

Pray: Teach me, O Lord, the way of Your statutes, and I shall keep it to the end. Give me understanding, and I shall keep Your law; Indeed, I shall observe it with my whole heart. Make me walk in the path of Your commandments, for I delight in it. Incline my heart to Your testimonies, and not to covetousness. Turn away my eyes from looking at worthless things, and revive me in Your way. Establish Your word to Your servant, who is devoted to fearing You. Turn away my reproach which I dread, for Your judgments are good. Behold, I long for Your precepts; Revive me in Your righteousness. Amen, and let it be so. (Psalms 119:33-40 NKJV)

| Vol 01 | Q4 | NW00285 | October 11th |

Night-Whisper | **COURAGE**

"Hurry now for today..."

I once heard of a man who divorced his wife because of her infidelity. It was nearly two years later, having got his head and his heart back together, that he had forgiven her, found her, and asked to remarry her. Though she still loved him, she was now married to another man and was also with child. Timing, you see, its everything.

1 Samuel 9:12,13

"And they answered them and said, 'Yes, there he is, just ahead of you. Hurry now; for today he came to this city, because there is a sacrifice of the people today on the high place.'" NKJV

I once knew a group of people looking for a church home in a particular area, who having found the property and the land and had their verbal offer accepted, waited a few days to make sure the whole group were on board with the decision. Twenty-four hours later, someone else had made a cash offer for the property. It was gone. The difference that property would have made to the course, direction and dedication of that small church planting core group of people would have been substantial. Timing, you see, its everything.

The man left the doctor's office, his wife in tears, the words of his physician ringing in his ears: "Just six months earlier and we would have been able to do something but now, I am afraid..." Timing, you see, its everything.

The Church pastoral selection committee had spent fifteen months deliberating over the initial three hundred applications they received for the widely advertised position of Senior Pastor. They weeded out the rest, kept the best, interviewed and tested them, exhausted and examined them, eventually presenting some of them, to the rest of the congregation. After much prayer and deliberation, they called the man that God had most obviously chosen. He however, had a family to take care of and though fifteen months ago, maybe even three, he would have wanted to have come and served there, he took a comparatively more speedy offer, and has been settled in his new pastorate now for two months and is loving it! Timing, you see, its everything.

I spoke with a good friend even yesterday, who it seems is being presented with a tremendous opportunity for the future. His response to that offer will have to be quick if he is to take full opportunity of what is being presented and such an acceptance, will bring mighty and profound changes on his and his family's life. If he rejects it, other offers may eventually come along in his life, maybe even better offers, maybe. However, this offer will not pass his way again. Timing, you see, its everything.

I have observed in life that many wrong choices are recoverable but that many missed opportunities, may never manifest themselves again. Timing, you see, its everything.

Brutus: "There is a tide in the affairs of men. Which, taken at the flood, leads on to fortune; Omitted, all the voyage of their life is bound in shallows and in miseries. On such a full sea are we now afloat, and we must take the current when it serves, or lose our ventures.

Julius Caesar Act 4, scene 3, 218–224

Listen: *"Come now, you who say, 'Today or tomorrow we will go to such and such a city, spend a year there, buy and sell, and make a profit'; whereas you do not know what will happen tomorrow. For what is your life? It is even a vapor that appears for a little time and then vanishes away." James 4:13-15 NKJV*

Pray: Lord, grant me great courage to make scary decisions and hard choices. Help me not to procrastinate to eternal loss, when heaven sent opportunities are before me. Lord give me the faith to gamble on Your goodness and the grace and humility to confess my faults before You in all my cowardly failings. Deliver me from fear O Lord and grant me a spirit of adventure with You, in Jesus name I pray, amen and let it be so!

Night-Whisper | **HOPE**

Dream insurance

Our text for tonight shows Joseph, bless his little heart, in all his rambunctious stupidity, jumping all over the feet of this sorry set of scoundrels! Read on in the story dear friends and you shall see that it was after the sharing of this particular dream, that Joseph's brothers decided to do him in!

Genesis 37:9-11

"Then he dreamed still another dream and told it to his brothers, and said, 'Look, I have dreamed another dream. And this time, the sun, the moon, and the eleven stars bowed down to me.' So he told it to his father and his brothers; and his father rebuked him and said to him, 'What is this dream that you have dreamed? Shall your mother and I and your brothers indeed come to bow down to the earth before you?' And his brothers envied him, but his father kept the matter in mind. NKJV

These two connected dreams, both indicating that Joseph would be the head of the clan, that Joseph would be the pre-eminent one, that Joseph would be the head and not the tail, that Joseph would be indeed be blessed above them all! How wonderful for Joseph, but then on the sharing these dreams with his brothers, they go ahead and beat him up, throw him in a pit, sell him into slavery and then lie about his supposed and most dreadful demise to their most fearful and fretful father.

Meanwhile, Joseph is alive but very alone, lonely, surviving first and prospering next, only then to be falsely accused of rape and flung into a dungeon, while the key is decidedly dumped in the nasty river Nile. Even when Joseph would eventually be catapulted to second in command in Egypt, it would be an additional seven-plus years before those dreams of his were ere fulfilled. Yes, from the first arrival of those pictures in Joseph's spoilt little head, those same dreams would take many torturous years to reach their birth and their fulfilment. Isn't life just like that! Oh yes it is!

Their once was an insurance commercial running on TV with the tagline that said, "It's not just a matter of where your dreams will take you but where you will take your dreams." How Biblical is that? I like it! You see friend, I do believe that God gives us dreams to be fulfilled. However, it is obvious as well, that God, in His Divine sovereignty, allows life, that terrible trickster and rubbisher of our visions, that putrefier of the damson jam of our dreams, to make their initial fragrance turn to a sometimes sorry stench in our nostrils and their start out sweetness into a terrible taste in our once proclaiming mouths of faith. Yes, in the form of bad choices, the intervention of envious idiots, forced slavery, seducing and slandering spirits, lying dogs, dark dungeons of every kind and forgetful benefactors in many shapes and sizes, our delightful dreams, so often, yes, so very often, turn moldy, blue and bad.

> *...life, that terrible trickster and rubbisher of our visions, that putrefier of the damson jam of our dreams, to make their initial fragrance turn to a sometimes sorry stench in our nostrils and their start out sweetness into a terrible taste in our once proclaiming mouths of faith.*

When this happens, as it so surely will, we need to get to our insurance policy out and then picnic well upon the telling tag line, repeating often to our soul the truth of those fine words that, "It's not just a matter of where your dreams will take you but where you will take your dreams."

Don't let your present and continuing distress, destroy the dreams that God has given you in times past, but rather, take those dreams with you into every single and solitary situation. Cosset them, caress them, muse on them, wonder over them, pray over them and plan again, for I tell you the truth tonight, that if those dreams are from God, then they shall surely come to pass and nothing even in hell or in a hell manifest on top side of this earth shall stop them being fulfilled! The tagline of your God given insurance policy tonight is absolutely true. Remember, "It's not just a matter of where your dreams will take you but where you will take your dreams."

Believe it!

Listen: *"And when Gideon had come, there was a man telling a dream to his companion. He said, 'I have had a dream: To my surprise, a loaf of barley bread tumbled into the camp of Midian; it came to a tent and struck it so that it fell and overturned, and the tent collapsed.' Then his companion answered and said, 'This is nothing else but the sword of Gideon the son of Joash, a man of Israel! Into his hand God has delivered Midian and the whole camp.'" Judges 7:13-14 NKJV*

Pray: Lord, I give you my dreams tonight, unfulfilled, thwarted, unbirthed and waiting. Lord, tonight I give you my dreams, and in watching faithfulness I wait for their fulfilment, in Jesus name I pray amen, and let them be so.

| Vol 01 | Q4 | NW00287 | October 13th |

Night-Whisper | **MERRY**

The pessimist mug

Proverbs 15:15

"All the days of the afflicted are evil, But he who is of a merry heart has a continual feast."
NKJV

One of my favorite websites is dedicated to the practice of Socratic irony to expose the silly failings of the corporate encouragement machine and tries to replace it with caring reality. Despair.com makes its money by selling its ironic products and my current favorite is the pessimist mug where the glass is always half empty and consequently it makes everything taste bitter. My wife tells me that she is going to buy me a dozen, so as I have one for every month of the year. I am a Celt! I am not happy unless I have something to worry or be cynical about! What does the woman expect for goodness sake? Sheesh!

Consequently then, when I am asked that old worn out adage of, "Is this cup half empty or half full?" My reply is always, "Well it depends." It depends on if I am full or if I am thirsty. It depends on if I have to share it with others or if it is for my own consumption. It depends on if it's my cup because if it's not my cup then I don't have to make that judgement call. It depends on…and on and on I go. Never a straight answer!

The truth is that whether I perceive the standing cup to be either half empty or half full depends upon my attitude. For me dear friends, without even trying at all, the cup is always half empty. For me dear friends, the light at the end of the tunnel is always on the front of a very large train coming to run me down. My naturally melancholic disposition is quite damaging you know, and unfortunately attitudes are contagious, mine, you see, just might kill you!

Here's my point for tonight. We need to have a much more positive attitude. I am not talking about not facing reality (Despair.com will help you do that with a smile) but rather acknowledging that we can have a much better attitude and that this will bring us life and you never know, others might just catch some life from us as well!

If everything is tasting bitter in your life at the moment then maybe the way you view that standing cup, just might have something to do with it? So you see, our text for tonight is saying something both profound and practical. "Get a merry heart, maintain it and feed on it. If you don't, then you are in great danger of becoming an old misery guts." So, what should you do tomorrow or more importantly, tomorrow, how should you be tomorrow?

> *all the people who glibly look at the church of the present day and speak positively. They are idiot dealers in death.*

I must close tonight by pointing you to my purposeful little adjective of 'standing' as in, the 'standing' cup. In other words, where a cup is being drunk or its contents are being poured out of, or leaking out of the bottom, that is not a 'standing' cup and you would be a fool to say that the cup is half full! NO! Its half empty and getting emptier still. To say otherwise is not being positive giving life, it is being an idiot and allowing for death. So are all the people who glibly look at the church of the present day and speak positively. They are idiot dealers in death.

Listen: *"Seize life! Eat bread with gusto, Drink wine with a robust heart. Oh yes — God takes pleasure in your pleasure! Dress festively every morning. Don't skimp on colours and scarves." Ecclesiastes 9:7-8 THE MESSAGE*

Pray: Lord, give me rest tonight, and clothe my soul with lightness and lift my heart with a chosen happiness, in Jesus name I pray, amen and let it be. However Lord, don't let me deal in lies, don't' let me sully faith by clothing the dead honest truth in bright Sunday school clothes, don't let me dress up a corpse in the clothes of so called faith! Truly O Lord, our nations cups are at the dregs and we are almost empty. Have mercy O Lord upon us and give us hope and a fill our cup. Amen and let it be so.

| Vol 01 | Q4 | NW00288 | October 14th |

Night-Whisper | **RETURN**

Two little tomcats

As is my usual routine, I got up early this morning, acquiesced to the instant ablutions of a man in his late forties, put the kitchen light on, put some heavily caffeinated, rich, dark Columbian in the percolator in preparation for some later laxitivity, and sat down to write tonight's Whisper. The light from the kitchen shone in the surrounding darkness of this Kentucky hillside and drew the boys from afar. "The boys" as we call them are Itsy and Bitsy, two little gifts from God, found meowing on the side of the road by my wife on her birthday some 18 months ago. Two dumped and orphaned ginger little tomcats. Two twitching faced Davy Crocket hats, two foul wind machines, two sources of pest control, two mouse deliverers, two purring, warm and cozy sources of comfort and caressing. Two little creatures curled at the bottom of the bed, two sets of bright eyes in the long night, two little sources of God's comfort that turn up each morning, greet you with a smile, bite your feet to let you know you live today and wrap their warm and fuzzy tails around your cold morning calves, to let you know your loved today! Yes, the boys, those two little ginger toms, those two little gifts from God, come banging at my early morning door, most each and every day.

Jonah 4:6

"And the Lord God prepared a plant and made it come up over Jonah, that it might be shade for his head to deliver him from his misery. So Jonah was very grateful for the plant." NKJV

It is interesting how attached you get to little things. In our text for tonight, for that peculiar and pugnacious prophet called Jonah, it was a plant and a simple day plant at that upon which his cold heart got caught upon! For me and for my wife, it is our current cats, our furry substitutes for our missed children and two warm little distractions from the cold loneliness that such a missing generates. In a few days we shall return to our homeland, and leave these two little creatures behind. As the little ginger duet, crouching side by side, eats in unison from their full blue bowls, I think how much I will miss this furry morning routine. Then I thought to myself, "Man! If we ever have to leave them for good, that's gonna' be a hard one, especially for my wife."

It's amazing how misery can so easily leap upon a Celt. That last thought of mine allowed the cat of melancholia to come and curl up in my lap, look me in my eye and remind me that in this life, everything and everyone shall be said goodbye to. *"The longer you live,"* it said, *"the more you shall say goodbye. Until at last they shall say goodbye to you."* It then relaxed and in the relaxing, it broke some very smelly and unwanted wind.

> *Al things pass and eventually pass way. All that is, except Jesus, and in Jesus, all that has passed and all who have passed, shall be seen together with Him and in Him at the last.*

By now the coffee was beginning to take effect so I quickly grabbed that mangy little melancholic visitor by its scabby little neck and threw it out the window! It had said nothing new. No, I am aware of all that. I am a pilgrim for goodness sake! En route to His Holy City, to my Hometown in my Homeland and in being a pilgrim then, I am therefore already preparing my goodbyes well in advance but more than that, oh mangy and smelly little kitten, I am preparing my "Hellos" and practicing my "How yer doings!"

How about you tonight? What hellos are you looking forward to after your final goodbye is said?

It was Alfred Lord Tennyson that wrote, "The Crossing of the Bar". It is a majestic piece and the last two lines read:

"I hope to see my Pilot face to face
When I have crost the bar."

The Poem below is called "Bar One." The term 'bar one,' means , 'except one.' This points to the terrible fact that all things pass and eventually pass way. All that is, except Jesus, and in Jesus, all that has passed and all who have passed, shall be seen together with Him and in Him at the last. This is my great hope.

----------O----------

Over all crowns of glory
There drips a crown of thorns
And in each seasonal cup
Bubbles a groaning joy
And with every loving , bar one
There is a leaving

The morning brings a cloud of blue
At lunch a fluff of cotton white
And then to end each goodly day
A blue sky full of grey
And with every loving , bar one
There is a leaving

The pink of brand new flesh
The happiness and the joy
May yet become a memory
In the rebellion of the boy
And with every loving , bar one
There is a leaving

With every providence
There seems to be a persecution
No gain without a loss
No advance without a cost
And with every loving, bar one
There is a leaving

A life of growing
Of one flesh knowing
Of hope and dreams and prayerful sowing
Will leave one of us alone a while
Standing, looking down the clay walls on bright pine
For with every loving , bar one
There is a leaving

----------O----------

Listen: *Cor 15:50-52 "Behold, I tell you a mystery: We shall not all sleep, but we shall all be changed-- in a moment, in the twinkling of an* *eye, at the last trumpet. For the trumpet will sound, and the dead will be raised incorruptible, and we shall be changed." NKJV*

Pray: Goodnight dear Lord, good night and goodbye my friends, goodbye, for tomorrow might I wake in the comfort of His sky. So, goodnight dear Lord, good night my King and goodbye my friends, goodbye, for tomorrow might I wake, in the comfort of His sky. (Anon.)

| Vol 01 | Q4 | NW00289 | October 15th |

Night-Whisper | **CHANGE**

Divine dental floss and its present need

Amos 4:6

"'Also I gave you cleanness of teeth in all your cities. And lack of bread in all your places; Yet you have not returned to Me,' Says the Lord."
NKJV

The little term "cleanness of teeth" has always seemed to me to be a most humorous way to describe the utterly disgusting ravages of famine! Yet I think a most descriptive way as well, for after a fine Sunday lunch with friends, even after brushing my teeth, there is always an afternoon of tongue discovery and subsequent meal remembrance. Ah yes, there is always evidence of the previous meal hiding amongst the molars and refusing to be swallowed. Cleanness of teeth means the complete and continued absence of food.

Since not so long after WW11, we in the West have eaten very well indeed, over-eaten even. Indeed, the visual rise of obesity is a swelling testimony to that fat fact seen daily waddling through all our burgeoning cities. "Avast behind!" is no longer a quaint old naval term.

I have never gone hungry. Oh, I've missed a meal or two maybe, but never gone hungry. I have used the word starving, but have never starved, no, nowhere near. I do not know either the chilling chase of a hunting hunger or the forever-ness feeling of a finger sucking famine. In these full times, maybe that lack of a hungry experience, is a big problem for us all, rather than a blessing?

Our text for tonight in all its terrible stunningness, nevertheless offers hope to a cared for covenant people. God at least is saying, "Hey, you have broken our contract and these are the consequences and they are now in effect solely to cause you to come back to me and to gain the promised blessings of the other end of the deal!" We have none of this verbal intervention in our Western world today, but rather, we are struck on all sides by the stunning indifference of God! It is as though God is saying by His lack of action, "Go ahead, eat yourself stupid and sin yourself silly. See if I care!" And so we sail on, super-sized and sick, settled on simply satisfying a cesspit of selfishness, that has quietly sold us into a seething self-serving slavery, leaving both us and our societies, foolish, foul and fat, in all our festering forms, then no wonder that God doesn't seem to care one bit.

On the contrary however, God is not indifferent. If anything, God has sent a worrying wind, scooping up in its angry path, ten billion quail, filling our waiting nets, whilst saying, "You want it? OK here it is! Eat it until you are sick of it. Consume it with such a vicious voraciousness until you vomit it out of your growling and grunting, green snot dripping, piggy like snouts. I'm past caring." It's a nasty and nauseating picture isn't it? I wonder then, if famine would be better than this foul fatness? I wonder if famine would be better than this overwhelming and blinding fullness? For, it seems to me, that being sick of fullness, is always the long way round to seeking God.

For, it seems to me, that being sick of fullness, is always the long way round to seeking God.

I think we need Elijah. I think we need men and women anointed with the spirit of Elijah. I think we need people of great power who can command the heavens to withhold their watery goodness, for years if needs be, so that our crops would fail, so that our bones would become familiar with our skin once more, and so that we would seek out the Divine dental floss, that we might eat what is left between our historical little canines. Maybe such a famine will foster a seeking that such fatness never will?

Where shall we get such people to call for a famine in the land, for they shall not come from the church. Not from the church fearful. Not from the church pandering. Not from the church flat on its back before the masses, her legs laid open wide to all the world and its mass marketing methodology. No, the last Elijahs shall not come from the church but rather from the desert places, the secret places, the waste places of God's wilderness. And when they come, they shall suddenly appear on the scene like Elijah of old, seemingly without father and without mother, but with a message from on High nevertheless, lit with fire and formed in thunder! My heart looks out daily for such prophets, for they will prepare the final coming of our Lord.

I fear this fat generation of ours shall miss this fast coming and mighty message. Ah, but our children, maybe they shall hear it? Maybe a famine of a terrible kind shall come upon them and turn them to the Lord.

Listen: *"But the angel said to him, 'Do not be afraid, Zacharias, for your prayer is heard; and your wife Elizabeth will bear you a son, and you shall call his name John. And you will have joy and gladness, and many will rejoice at his birth. For he will be great in the sight of the Lord, and shall drink neither wine nor strong drink. He will also be filled with the Holy Spirit, even from his mother's womb. And he will turn many of the children of Israel to the Lord their God. He will also go before Him in the spirit and power of Elijah, "to turn the hearts of the fathers to the children," and the disobedient to the wisdom of the just, to make ready a people prepared for the Lord.'" Luke 1:13-17 NKJV*

Pray: Lord, tonight we pray that You would anoint Your wilderness warriors with the spirit and power of Elijah and that you would bring them to Your fold with this mighty message of preparation. Lord, please cease Your fattening indifference to us and send the Holy Spirit, to convict our societies of sin, righteousness and coming judgement, in Jesus name we pray, amen and let it be so!

Night-Whisper | **PREPARE**

The evocations of Bagpipe music and other weird skirling!

Today, I was again reading one of the best devotionals ever written, Nicholas Albery's *Poem for the Day*. I came across a piece by British poet, Louis MacNeice, called "Bagpipe Music." The poem is most certainly a crashing and crusading, inviting and indicting, cacophony of skirling and moving music! I loved it, I enjoyed it, I was moved by it and read it several times whilst wondering what on earth it meant?

Jeremiah 18:15a

"Because My people have forgotten Me, They have burned incense to worthless idols. And they have caused themselves to stumble in their ways, From the ancient paths..." NKJV

One of the wonderful aspects about poetry is its evocative nature. The poem itself might present itself to be so complex and full of color that even a third and fourth reading may still leave you with the sense that you didn't get it, or you missed the point. Nevertheless, the poem stirred something in you, it revived that something which was almost a remembrance of something else and for a few moments, it hooked you, it took you somewhere into your past, into a memory, into a sound maybe, a smell, a sight, a circumstance and it reminded you, it warned you, it warmed you, it caressed you and maybe even comforted you. Yes, one of the wonderful aspects of poetry, even if you don't fully understand the totality of the piece itself, is its evocative nature.

Sermons too have an evocative aspect to them. Many times folks have left me in confusion, when coming up to me after a sermon they say, "I really was blessed by that point you made....", or, "It was so helpful when you said...," or, "God really spoke to me when you made reference to..." Yes, it has been confusing because often I wasn't making that point, or wasn't speaking on that matter and certainly had made no reference to the thing they thought I had! Yes, though not half as much fun, listening to a sermon should be like listening to poetry, in that though the point may be missed, some other new spiritual synaptic pathway is nevertheless being burrowed into the brain, or more often than not, an old way of remembrance, like an old mine shaft, is being surprisingly opened up again! The new spiritual synaptic pathway will bring all the connectivity of light and life and joy whilst when the latter happens, that is, when old mine shafts are opened up by words, ghosts are released, sometimes weeping, sometimes screaming, sometimes laughing but always, yes always bringing the haunting to a close. This is good, for when a haunting's over, then the rubbish can be removed, the wells can be unclogged and fresh air allowed to circulate once more in the inner recesses of our being.

> *This is good, for when a haunting's over, then the rubbish can be removed, the wells can be unclogged and fresh air allowed to circulate once more in the inner recesses of our being.*

Sometimes, often times, in both poetry and in sermons, it's OK to miss the point as long as you let the words do their most wonderful of evocative works. It is only with the poet-prophet that God can do His evocative burrowing, and His sealed mineshaft revealing.

Listen: *"Your words were found, and I ate them, And Your word was to me the joy and rejoicing of my heart" Jeremiah 15:16 NKJV*

Pray: I am called by Your name, O Lord God of hosts. I did not sit in the assembly of the mockers, nor did I rejoice; No, I sat alone because of Your hand, for You have filled me with indignation. So, why is my pain perpetual and my wound incurable, why does it refuse to be healed? Will You surely be to me like an unreliable stream, like failing waters? No, I know that if I return, then You will bring me back; So Lord, in all Your words, come and stand before me and reveal the hidden shaft and help me take out the precious from the vile, yes, with all your evocative drilling come burrow in my brain right through to my knower, in Jesus name I pray, amen and let it be so.

Night-Whisper | **DESIRE**

Replacing your dry wall dust with the vigor of Rhino!

I was in a large food supplement store recently looking for some powerful vitamins and was once again overwhelmed by the choice before me. "Can I help you today?" says the assistant. So, I explain my need and requirement of information to make the right decision and he looks at me with piercing eyes and says, "Well, let me guess, I am pretty sure you are in your fifties so I would recommend…" Astonished I replied, "In my fifties! I might soon be knocking on the mid-century door mate but I'm not there yet!" I was not well pleased.

I became a Christian when I was in my nineteenth year and being nearly in my fifties now, I have been walking with God for nearly thirty years and tonight, being such an expert on walking with God, I have been invited to speak at a Presbyterian church about the need for a strong devotional life. I shall of course, be talking about the need for some real spiritual Viagra.

Our text for tonight makes reference to Mandrakes. These are part of the potato family and are also linked to Belladonna or Deadly Nightshade. They are referred to as "The Devil's fruit" or "love apples" and the reason for this, that they are in effect, an aphrodisiac! It is not just for their mild narcotic, aromatic and therapeutic properties that mandrakes were sought after but in heavy doses, the mandrake can also act as an anesthetic

Genesis 30:14-16

"Now Reuben went in the days of wheat harvest and found mandrakes in the field, and brought them to his mother Leah. Then Rachel said to Leah, 'Please give me some of your son's mandrakes.' But she said to her, 'Is it a small matter that you have taken away my husband? Would you take away my son's mandrakes also?' And Rachel said, 'Therefore he will lie with you tonight for your son's mandrakes.' When Jacob came out of the field in the evening, Leah went out to meet him and said, 'You must come in to me, for I have surely hired you with my son's mandrakes.' And he lay with her that night."
NKJV

whilst in mild doses, they can, as one old commentator put it, "excite the nerves to act as a stimulant and have power to excite voluptuousness!" Sounds good to me!

So, in our text tonight, Leah, the loser in love to Rachel for the heart attention and associated passion of their husband Jacob, is very simply, trying to get the sexual edge. Leah is trying to use artificial means to no doubt excite both her and Jacob into a such a passionate love making session, that it will in turn, result in babies. You see, Rachel and Leah, through the means of child production, are locked into a competition of love. Believe me when I tell you, that this still goes on today.

Old Testament stories present us in the 21st Century with such a foreign cultural context that the stories we read seem so very strange to us. Yet, what an equally strange world we live in! A world where have murdered unwanted children in their tens of millions and yet a world in which conception control coupled with erections out of control, magnifies and increases sexual activity to such an extent, that all the associated terrible transmissions of sexually acquired diseases are multiplied in a mad voluptuous viciousness. Yes, it is a mad, mad, mad, mad world!

A world where have murdered unwanted children in their tens of millions and yet a world in which conception control coupled with erections out of control, magnifies and increases sexual activity to such an extent, that all the associated terrible transmissions of sexually acquired diseases are multiplied in a mad voluptuous viciousness.

Viagra of course is the brand name of one of the latest 21st century chemical mandrakes. It's not uber cheap though, and so many folks are buying the drug online and/or from cheaper places of production like South America or China. One of the latest drug manufacturing scams of course involves the production of Viagra, so that the "knock off" of the drug, whilst presenting itself in identical packaging, coloring, shape and sizing, is not in fact anywhere near the real deal. Pharmacists have been examining the cheaper product coming into the country to find that not only is not of the same potency and consistency as the more expensive local product, but millions of pills are in fact very simply, nothing but compressed dry wall dust! That's right, what many men thought were mandrakes, were in fact just dry white plasterboard dust and the only thing the consumption of that material will make solid, is your stools! Hilarious!

The truth is that just about all Christians believe that the only way to maintain a strong devotional life, a close and passionate, long–lasting, life-producing love affair with Jesus kind of life, is to get hold of some spiritual Viagra. Therefore, with this rising demand of desperate and unsatisfied Christians, our Christian bookshop selves are bending under the weight of all the spiritual motivational potency you could ever imagine and most of our sermons and seminars are really selling the same kind of spiritual Viagra as well. " Do this for a solid Christian life!" Unfortunately though friends, I have to tell you tonight, that it's all mostly plain old dry wall dust. It might all be presented in shiny packaging and brightly colored covers, it might give the promises of the fulfilment of all your wildest dreams as well, but in the end, it's mostly a load of old dry wall dust. Expensive, ineffectual dry wall dust. Difficult to digest, difficult to pass and very difficult to flush.

> *I tell my lovely wife that she is all the Viagra I need. I can think of no greater compliment. I tell Jesus the same. "Show me Your glory," I ask Him, "in all Your glorious nakedness my Lord, please reveal Yourself to me for I know that You are all I need."*

I tell my lovely wife that she is all the Viagra I need. I can think of no greater compliment. I tell Jesus the same. "Show me Your glory," I ask Him, "in all Your glorious nakedness my Lord, please reveal Yourself to me for I know that You are all I need." I tell you, all the religious dry wall dust in all the long wide world cannot compete with that! The satisfaction of such a desire is the only thing that will maintain the vibrant circle of relationship with God. If you see Him, you will want Him! If you get Him, you will be satisfied.

Do you want to have a strong devotional life even an ever increasing inspirational life? Do you want some potency and power, some strength and solidness put back into your spiritual wick? In other words, do you want a more passionate life in Jesus? Then be a Rhino with Him! Pursue desire, pursue satisfaction, yes, pursue real holiness in naked openness, all the time! Real Holiness In Naked Openness - RHINO! Clear your shelves of all your old dry wall dust folks and get passionate about your pursuance of Jesus. Got it? Be a RHINO – charge!

Listen: *"Come, my beloved, Let us go forth to the field; Let us lodge in the villages. Let us get up early to the vineyards; Let us see if the vine has budded, Whether the grape blossoms are open, And the pomegranates are in bloom. There I will give you my love. The mandrakes give off a fragrance, And at our gates are pleasant fruits, All manner, new and old, Which I have laid up for you, my beloved." Song of Solomon 7:11-13 NKJV*

Pray: O God, You are my God; Early will I seek You; My soul thirsts for You; My flesh longs for You In a dry and thirsty land Where there is no water. So I have looked for You in the sanctuary, To see Your power and Your glory. Because Your loving kindness is better than life, My lips shall praise You. Thus I will bless You while I live; I will lift up my hands in Your name. My soul shall be satisfied as with marrow and fatness, And my mouth shall praise You with joyful lips. When I remember You on my bed, I meditate on You in the night watches. Because You have been my help, Therefore in the shadow of Your wings I will rejoice. My soul follows close behind You; Your right hand upholds me. (Psalms 63:1-8 NKJV)

Night-Whisper | **ACTION**

Two agendas but only one game. Be prepared. Preach The Gospel.

In a very small way I understand what it is to be a legal alien. I entered the United States twice on two student Visas. Twice I changed to religious workers Visa's and while on them I applied for a green card. The cost of doing this was in the thousands of dollars. Of course, whilst the application was in process, my wife and I could not leave the country. The cost of not being able to visit our kids for a number of years was a very high one to pay. Suffice to say, despite thousands of dollars spent, we could not get a Green card and so had to leave the country. If I was to summarize why we never got a green card, I would have to say that it is because we were white, we were British, we were Christians, and we were ministers. Oh, and we could no longer afford the legal costs. In any event, after a total of over 6 years in our new home country, we had to leave. Compared to what is going on today, in a very small way, I do understand what it is to be unwanted and ejected. I suppose the big question is, just what IS going on with all this mass migration?

The stage of the world is but the place to play out two big agendas within only one game. Yes, there is only one game. The first agenda of Jesus is the gathering in of 'the found' by the proclamation of the Gospel of the Lord

2 Kings 18:28-32

... "Hear the word of the great king, the king of Assyria! ... 'Do not let Hezekiah deceive you, for he shall not be able to deliver you from his hand; nor let Hezekiah make you trust in the Lord, saying, "The Lord will surely deliver us; this city shall not be given into the hand of the king of Assyria." 'Do not listen to Hezekiah; for thus says the king of Assyria: 'Make peace with me by a present and come out to me; and every one of you eat from his own vine and every one from his own fig tree, and every one of you drink the waters of his own cistern; until I come and take you away to a land like your own land......NKJV

Jesus Christ, and the making of disciples before the return of the King of Kings. The second outworked agenda is the preparation, pre-programming and shaping of the world, society, technology and culture, to receive the coming of the Anti-Christ, that terrible man of sin. This is the one and only game of the gaining of eternal life, either with the one agenda or the other.

> *Remember, since the fall of Lucifer, there has only ever been one game.*

National identity produces a cohesive distinctiveness in a people and religion plays a massive part of this national identity. Therefore remove or replace religion and a great part of national identity is destroyed. Mix religions and the foaming cup that follows, like sulfuric acid, also eats away at a cohesive national identity. This is far more deadly. Following this mix of religions, the distinct cultural and social expressions of national identity are also eventually destroyed. The dominant religion then has comparatively free range to express itself spiritually, politically, culturally, sociologically and to such an extent, that languages, skylines, and even times and seasons are changed beyond previous recognition to the desire of those who have now conquered. And yes, it is a conquering. Eternal life through the plan of God or a mock and manufactured eternal life without God, this one 'game,' is being played out in the world and the outworking of these two agendas is the massive clash of spiritual powers which we see since the fall of Lucifer to this very day.

In times past, earthly Empires in this same game, employed forced migration to destroy national cohesiveness, for Nationalism, you see, will always stand against an homogenized whole. A one world, new world order of one religion and state, over which Anti-Christ shall rule, cannot have any form of resistive national patriotism. If Christian heritage cannot be adapted and assimilated then it must be destroyed. Remember, since the fall of Lucifer, there has only ever been one game. Therefore note that Islam is THE self-stated Anti-Christ religion, and with the massive and overwhelming influx of mostly Muslim migrants, the former Christian culture of Western Europe is being eaten away. Within this one game, this old strategy of forced migration is being employed once again. If this mass migration were to be stopped now, today, even immediately, it would make little difference, for the damage to Christian Culture has already been done, the acid has been poured, the cup is foaming. Remember, there is one game. Islam will not dwell peaceably in the nations it now occupies. It will remain separate, and it will purposefully consume. When it is dominant, all things bow to Islam. They are bowing already.

I was born in 1960 and daily mourn and grieve over the passing of my own culture and nation. What once was, is now gone and can never be revived. This, I believe, is the judgement of God upon us. It's passing and my grieving for it is, however, and on a number of important levels, of no real consequence whatsoever! It is of no real consequence firstly because this world is not my home and I look for a city whose builder and maker is God, even Jerusalem above, the eternal city of the Lamb, the dwelling place of all blood bought men. So then, forgetting my own instinctive and earthly national response to the destruction of my own culture, what should be my more important heavenly response the global migration moves now occurring in the outworking of these two agendas in the one big game? Here are a handful of thoughts for your consideration.

Muslim migrants shall not adapt, they shall not adapt, they shall simply multiply quickly and propagate Islam.

First of all, we Christians need to wise up! Many migrants already have connections in the West, and those that do not, shall be quickly embraced and welcomed to currently established Islam. Muslim migrants shall not adapt, they shall not adapt, they shall multiply quickly and propagate Islam. Make no mistake, the fall in German birthrates has been the great pushing factor in filling it's cities and factories with new quick breeding stock. Germany wants to remain at the powerful center of Europe and it needs a well taxed economy to do so, and that means people. Germany, however, like the rest of Europe, is riding a tiger. Wise up! Massive cultural change is here and the mushrooming of the same, needs planning and preparing for. We far too late for that. Wise up Christian.

Secondly, heavenly Christianity must not glibly abandon its current majority indigenous cultures. It has done so. Churches are seen to be more involved with migrants, refugees and asylum seekers than with those it has previously flowered amongst. The sane nationalistic remnant of majority culture will not forget this, for the church seems almost complicit in its own nation's Christian cultural destruction. It is. The heavenly church therefore needs to learn how to re-evangelize its own current majority culture. Quickly! Preach the Gospel to your own nation! It won't be the majority culture for too much longer.

Thirdly, the church as individuals, and that includes its currently self and happily gagged and silent leaders, must engage politically. We must learn to embrace political disagreements within ourselves and to fight with our tongues and with our votes. If we do not do this, then not only are we politically complicit in the current cultural destruction, but we may be forced into physical fighting in the future. Political correctness must be faced down now and we need to get our hands dirty in the political arena. Live the Gospel. Argue, disagree, debate. This is democracy. Use it whilst you have it.

Political correctness must be faced down now and we need to get our hands dirty in the political arena. Live the Gospel. Argue, disagree, debate. This is democracy. Use it whilst you have it.

Fourthly, we must pray. The judgement of God is upon us. All our walls are broken down, God's sword of Islam shall soon replace His sword of secular humanism. Yes Christian, the problem is not Islam, or our own secular Government, the problem is Almighty God! God is holy and righteous, and in our rebellion and sin, in our going over to the enemy, He has also given us over to judgement. Our prayers then must be one of sincere repentance. Our preaching must be a call to sincere repentance. Listen. Our prayers; are they? Our preaching; is it?

Fifthly, for those migrants in whom the Spirit of God is moving, let us tell them the Gospel. Let us see them converted and welcomed into the Kingdom of God. For many of them, Islam being what it is, it will mean the loss of their families and the even the loss of their lives. Let us embrace, provide and protect our new brethren.

In the mass migrations we currently see, remember that this is the outworking of two agendas in but one game. The clash of these two agendas is changing the shape of the world once more. Whilst we are here in the body, let us be aware of what is going on, prepare for what is to come and the preach the Gospel of peace with God, through the death burial and resurrection of Jesus the Son of God, to one and to all.

Wise up Christian. Maranatha!

Listen: *Then Hezekiah prayed before the Lord, and said: "O Lord God of Israel, the One who dwells between the cherubim, You are God, You alone, of all the kingdoms of the earth. You have made heaven and earth. Incline Your ear, O Lord, and hear; open Your eyes, O Lord, and see; and hear the words of Sennacherib, which he has sent to reproach the living God. Truly, Lord, the kings of Assyria have laid waste the nations and their lands, and have cast their gods into the fire; for they were not gods, but the work of men's hands — wood and stone. Therefore they destroyed them. Now therefore, O Lord our God, I pray, save us from his hand, that all the kingdoms of the earth may know that You are the Lord God, You alone." 2 Kings 19:15-19 NKJV*

Pray: Father, forgive us in being in complicit ignorance in the casting away of our current Christian culture. Has the shed blood of the past been all for nothing? It would appear so. Oh God, how much can be lost so quickly. Even so, now O Lord, the nations which barred the message of Your Son are now come into us. O God, whilst the window of opportunity is still open, help us proclaim Your Gospel to them and to our earthly brethren for oh my God, the night comes, when no man can work. Help us see this and help us live and fight whilst it is yet day. Amen and let it be so.

Night-Whisper | **PRAISE**

Building chantries

Ephesians 5:19

"...speaking to one another in psalms and hymns and spiritual songs, singing and making melody in your heart to the Lord..."
NKJV

Many evenings, my wife and I take an hour's walk together in the Kentucky countryside, past all the entrances to the hollers where the black top ends and amongst the brush and on the green hillsides. These are sometimes speckled with light blue cornflowers, or sometimes freckled with the rich red leaves of disrobing hardwood trees getting ready to go to sleep for winter, whilst the ground itself smiles with the plump pumpkin orange of the earth's chubby, child like little cheeks, all full of falls fatness at winters beckoning bedtime.

Amidst the colors of this Kentucky beauty, you can see the old cold, angle ironed markers, still stuck upright in the dark and bloody ground. These property markers might be in the right legal place but they are completely out of place amongst such singing beauty. Standing there like old tramps, rusty and un-camouflaged amongst the foliage, sometimes even flagged with pink fluorescent plastic ribbons and all of them asking for a cigarette, whilst shouting out the various property lines of a people proud to own a Southern piece of all-American pecan pie. Yup, personal real estate is especially important in settled Kentucky. The rusted poles of old angle iron might be more permanent than the old wooden staves previously used but still, they are very, very unsightly.

My hometown, over a thousand years ago, was once an Anglo-Saxon settlement in the center of a meadow called a lea. Records show that some sixty acres of this lea land had already been marked off by wooden staves and designated for a new town area. After the battle of Hastings in 1066, William the Conqueror gave this same area of Stave-Lea, or Staveley as it is known now, as a victory present to one his warriors. The Normans had finally arrived in my hometown.

The family of that warrior, Ascuit Musard, held Staveley for generations until the death of Nicholas Musard, a Roman Catholic priest, who, because he could not legally leave his land to his bastard children, had his property dispersed among his sisters, one of whom married Anker De Frechville, Baron of Crich. The Frechvilles left their mark on Staveley in the form of the old and well-haunted Hagge farm, manor house, Rectory and of course, a chantry, some parts of which date back to the thirteenth century, well before the ownership and sponsorship of the Frechville family.

A chantry is a private chapel, where a priest sang or chanted psalms for the soul of the founder. The religious rich have always had their spiritual insurance policies, paying those they believed to have the ear of God to intercede on their behalf whilst they got on producing more bastards. A chantry was such a place, a place of paid private prayer, praise and supplication for the person who had enough in his wallet to make it so. It sounds so crass doesn't it, yet I tell you tonight, that I like the idea of a chantry. I like the idea of a private place of singing psalms, a private place to go into and sing to God some choice songs of the spirit.

> *The religious rich have always had their spiritual insurance policies, paying those they believed to have the ear of God to intercede on their behalf whilst they got on producing more bastards.*

Today in his devotional "My Utmost for His Highest," Oswald Chambers from a speech to theological students says, "It is not the practical activities that are the strength of this Bible training College – its entire strength lies in the fact that here you are immersed in the truths of God to soak in them before Him. You have no idea of where or how God is going to engineer your future circumstances, and no knowledge of what stress and strain is going to be placed on you either at home or abroad. And if you waste your time in over activity, instead of being immersed in the great fundamental truths of God's redemption, then you will snap when the stress and strain do come." How true and friends and I am afraid, how descriptive of the modern day Christian.

I have seen many Christians snap and I do not want to be one of them. So tomorrow, I am going to build a room for singing psalms. Tomorrow I am going to pay the price to hear some happy hymns sung in my heart. Tomorrow I am going to set some spiritual songs to some merry music and sing them with my Father. Yes tomorrow, this priest of the most High God is going to build a chantry in a chamber of his heart and take some time each day thereafter to retreat into it and sing some songs of glory, sing some songs of my redemption, sing some psalms of praise, sing some songs of happy hope!

Tonight then, let us rest underneath His lullaby of love in Jesus and tomorrow let us each build ourselves a chantry of constant praise to God Most High.

Listen: *"O My God, I cry in the daytime, but You do not hear; And in the night season, and am not silent. But You are holy, Enthroned in the praises of Israel. Our fathers trusted in You; They trusted, and You delivered them. They cried to You, and were delivered; They trusted in You, and were not ashamed." Psalms 22:2-5 NKJV*

Pray: I will sing unto the Lord for He has triumphed gloriously the horse and rider thrown into the sea. The Lord is God and I will praise Him, my Father's God and I will extol Him!

Night-Whisper | **CONSIDER**

Angel delight

Ever and always, the Scriptures present the angelic creation as occupying higher realms, as higher beings possessing higher powers, in every respect their capacities in each and every way, being more awesome and richer than humanity could ever appear to be! CS Lewis, whilst acknowledging our confused and glass darkened senses, gives thanks for such present befuddlement, such witchery of our smoke covered senses, and then most majestically lays out for us a golden thought for tonight. Will you listen:

Psalms 8:3-4

"When I consider Your heavens, the work of Your fingers, the moon and the stars, which You have ordained, what is man that You are mindful of him, and the son of man that You visit him?" NKJV.

Far richer they! I know senses' witchery
Guards us, like air, from heavens too big to see;
Imminant death to man that barb'd sublimity
And dazzling edge of beauty unsheathed would be
Yet here. Within this tiny, charm'd interior,
This parlour of the brain, their Maker shares
With living men some secrets in a privacy
Forever ours, not theirs.

(from the Poem – "On Being Human" - CS Lewis)

The angels know of both our design and our direction. Yes, they are well aware of both our fall and of our coming exaltation and among them all, I wonder if this chatter of the ages, spread to some like cancerous jealousy and caused them to fall and plummet, down to the depths beneath, in all consuming and envious desperation? Even so, what we the redeemed are now, and what we shall become quite soon, so very soon indeed, are for the good angels of the good God, things which they ever and always both desire and delight to look into, for they understand that the secrets of redemption which have been planted by the Holy Spirit, like loving seeds in the dead ground of a poor man's soul, and shall at the adoption, even the redemption of our bodies, lead to another Genesis, the like of which is only told of in the longing cries of a groaning creation, presently, all gone wrong.

Concerning the jealousy of the foul and fallen host and concerning the delight of the Lord's 'looking into' angels, I wonder if we each have a personal and private inner sanctuary, even in our hearts the very dwelling place of the Most High, which is a secret place of private audiences with our Father, where we laugh at wondrous love and together with Him, sing away our cares, and unwrap His silver secrets in a privacy that is forever ours, that can be never theirs?

I have no doubt that many of you think the secret place of the Most High is out there somewhere? I tell you, like the kingdom of God, it is within you. Have you built that chantry yet?

> *Angels understand that the secrets of redemption which have been planted by the Holy Spirit, like loving seeds in the dead ground of a poor man's soul, and shall at the adoption, even the redemption of our bodies, lead to another Genesis, the like of which is only told of in the longing cries of a groaning creation, presently, all gone wrong.*

Listen: *"Of this salvation the prophets have inquired and searched carefully, who prophesied of the grace that would come to you, searching what, or what manner of time, the Spirit of Christ who was in them was indicating when He testified beforehand the sufferings of Christ and the glories that would follow. To them it was revealed that, not to themselves, but to us they were ministering the things which now have been reported to you through those who have preached the Gospel to you by the Holy Spirit sent from heaven --- things which angels desire to look into." (1 Peter 1:10-12)*

Pray: Dad, do please deliver me from distraction, just for a little bit even, that we together may look deep into Your magnificent midnight, whilst you help me take the wrapping of all the singing and silver secrets of the skies, which tell of the glories yet to come, the glories of that other Genesis. Amen.

Night-Whisper | WORRY

Nasal drips

This time of year, this time of leaf changing, this time of chemical release from dying vegetation, always leaves me allergically congested. Subsequently, my nose runs a lot! I mean sometimes like a waterfall, my sinuses draining down the back of my throat, trickling tickliness into an annoying cough and a constant clearing of the throat. It is annoying and all the throat clearing makes it sound like I am about to say something very, very important! However all I say is, "Excuse me," to those living on the receiving edge of such expectorant expectancy, which as we all know, can be so very tiring.

Ezekiel 8:17,18

"And He said to me, 'Have you seen this, O son of man? Is it a trivial thing to the house of Judah to commit the abominations which they commit here? For they have filled the land with violence; then they have returned to provoke Me to anger. Indeed they put the branch to their nose. Therefore I also will act in fury. My eye will not spare nor will I have pity; and though they cry in My ears with a loud voice, I will not hear them.'" NKJV

Our text for tonight is about to say something very important but the exact meaning of that little phrase, "put the branch to their nose" is widely misunderstood amongst the Biblical commentators. In any event friends, whatever it means is an irrelevance really, for the focus of the text is not so much on the heinous practice itself but rather the response from God to it. Whatever this nasal insult was, it became such a grievous and gross insult, such a putrid and offensive stench to His bitter and outraged heart that it perniciously provoked Him to both an astonishing and outraged anger! Yup, this secret sinning, this putting the branch to the nose, this indulgence in idolatrous and outrageous obscenity, caused such a "Divine nasal drip" that God coughed Himself to such a fuming fury that He phlegmed out Israel from His Holy and congested lungs!

Make no mistake about it, the outcome of such coughing fury did result in dire and dreadful decimation and dissolution and desolation of Israel. Indeed, if God Himself had not chosen to save for Himself a remnant of those who both sighed and cried at the loathsome state that their nation had gotten itself into, then the apple of God's eye would surely have lain forever rotting upon the sodden soil.

> *Look! God sees it! Look at the land! See the famine of the Word, see the disease of man and beast, see the fear, see the war, see the tear.*

Tonight I have to tell you that I have seen the secret sin of His leaders and His so-called prophets of today. I have seen the secret sins of God's people today. I have seen the present indifference of God in their lives, in our lives, in the life of the church at large; which lead us to wrongly conclude that God is not watching, indeed that even maybe, there is no God!

I have seen the secret sin.

Look! God sees it! Look at the land! See the famine of the Word, see the disease of man and beast, see the fear, see the war, see the tear. Hear the vines now long dead, crackle in the fire. Hear the other nations and the foreign cultures, now at home within us, suck the marrow from the dry bones left, see the violation of His law look at the rape of His love, be astonished at the idols now moved from the secret chambers of the heart and paraded high on haughty shoulders! Look! God sees! Look at the land!

I tell you tonight that whatever you, or your nation so consistently now have put to your nose in the very face of the Lord Christ, shall cause such a fit of righteous coughing in Him, that the very lungs you breathe with shall fill your gasping mouth with death.

Unless the idols are dealt with, the earth in all its fullness and God in all His fury shall turn against us completely. Maybe the Muslims have come to do what we refuse to do. Pull down all our idols.

Listen: *"Therefore, whore, listen to God's Message: I, God, the Master, say, Because you've been unrestrained in your promiscuity, stripped down for every lover, flaunting your sex, and because of your pornographic idols and all the slaughtered children you offered to them, therefore, because of all this, I'm going to get all your lovers together, all those* *you've used for your own pleasure, the ones you loved and the ones you loathed. I'll assemble them as a courtroom of spectators around you. In broad daylight I'll strip you naked before them — they'll see what you really look like. Then I'll sentence you to the punishment for an adulterous woman and a murderous woman. I'll give you a taste of my wrath! "'I'll gather all your lovers around you and turn you over to them. They'll tear down your bold brothels and sex shrines. They'll rip off your clothes, take your jewels, and leave you naked and exposed. Then they'll call for a mass meeting. The mob will stone you and hack you to pieces with their swords. They'll burn down your houses. A massive judgment — with all the women watching! "'I'll have put a full stop to your whoring life — no more paying lovers to come to your bed! By then my anger will be played out. My jealousy will subside. "'Because you didn't remember what happened when you were young but made me angry with all this behavior, I'll make you pay for your waywardness. Didn't you just exponentially compound your outrageous obscenities with all your sluttish ways? Ezekiel 16:35-43 from THE MESSAGE*

Pray: Lord tonight we remember our sins. We beg forgiveness for the sins of our nation, its people and its leaders. We ask for mercy regarding the secret sins of Your church in both its leaders and its people. We ask for forgiveness and cleansing for our secret sins, our bad love idols, our kept grievances, festering angers, and unforgiving hearts. Oh, Lord tonight we cast down our idols. Have mercy upon us and restore us we pray, in the mighty name of Jesus, amen.

Night-Whisper | **CONFIDENCE**

Of blow holes in the barley corn

I love the Old Testament book of Ruth and the verses in our text for tonight, are probably my favorites from the whole of the book. Of course, being a lover of God's deeps, I like these verses in particular, because of the two great whales that break the surface of the crashing waves and spout their presence abroad for all the world to see. Do you see them?

Ruth 2:2-4

"Naomi said to her, 'Go ahead, my daughter.' So she went out and began to glean in the fields behind the harvesters. As it turned out, she found herself working in a field belonging to Boaz, who was from the clan of Elimelech. Just then Boaz arrived from Bethlehem and greeted the harvesters, 'The Lord be with you!'" NIV

The scene is set for us in the book when the pleasant Naomi has returned in marred bitterness to her former country, clan and city. Naomi left with her husband and two sons for Moab, just ten years previously. She did so because there was no bread in Bethlehem, yes, there was no bread in "the house of bread," the singing has ceased in Judah, former the land of praise!

In those ten years away from her homeland, she lost her husband and two sons to tragic deaths and gained two lovely but very needy daughters-in-law, one of whom, despite her best efforts, she could not shake from her apron strings and so had to drag her back to Bethlehem to endure, along with her, the want, the ridicule, the gossip and the incessant questioning.

It has been rightly said that God planted a garden, that man created the cities but the devil made the small town! Here, in the goldfish bowl of Bethlehem, all Naomi's poverty and despondency, all of her bitter declarations of the hand of the Lord going out against her, could be seen and heard by everyone and oh the gossip my friends, oh the looks, oh the condemnation, oh the accusation, oh the intense intrigue and the consistent observation of this beautiful foreigner called Ruth. My

goodness friends, if it wasn't for the whales of God's presence, if it wasn't for the warm mammals of Gods providence, if it wasn't for these two giants of His goodness breaking the surface of these deep and troubled waters, then all in the story would be nothing but bleak despondency. Thank God for the whales!
Do you see them yet?

This story has a good ending though. Ruth the Moabites, shall be loved by Boaz, in whom is great strength, courage, and cash! Yes, Naomi shall at last be blessed, she shall be well taken care of and children shall bounce upon her knee and from this foreign exchange, shall eventually come David the King and Christ the Savior! At this point in the story, a testimony to God's greatness and overwhelming and coming goodness, are the whales. Do you see them yet?

Those two whales are called "As it turned out" and "Just then." An even bigger one of these buggers, seen mostly spouting amongst the covers of the New Testament, is called "But God!" That's a special one though, because it can only be seen with the eyes of faith. This particular pair however, "As it turned out" and 'Just then," can be seen quite clearly on the horizon of our lives almost each and every day. Do you see them yet?

Do you know that whale watching is akin to hearing the voice of God? Oh yes, when God speaks from the sky, some will recognize it and be both blessed and warmed, others will say it was merely thunder. In similar manner, when folks see this pair of whales break the surface of their lives, some will cry mere coincidence, but those who shall be truly blessed by whales, shall praise the Lord! Yes, they shall raise their sail of faith, they shall prepare their nets for a great catch of fish and hope shall feed their hunger, until the real catch comes in.

Whales, don't you love them? Do you see them yet?

Listen: *"So Boaz took Ruth and she became his wife. Then he went to her, and the Lord enabled her to conceive, and she gave birth to a son. The women said to Naomi: 'Praise be to the Lord, who this day has not left* *you without a kinsman-redeemer. May he become famous throughout Israel! He will renew your life and sustain you in your old age. For your daughter-in-law, who loves you and who is better to you than seven sons, has given him birth.' Then Naomi took the child, laid him in her lap and cared for him. The women living there said, 'Naomi has a son.' And they named him Obed. He was the father of Jesse, the father of David. This, then, is the family line of Perez: Perez was the father of Hezron, Hezron the father of Ram, Ram the father of Amminadab, Amminadab the father of Nahshon, Nahshon the father of Salmon, Salmon the father of Boaz, Boaz the father of Obed, Obed the father of Jesse, and Jesse the father of David. Ruth 4:13-22 NIV*

Pray: Lord tomorrow and always on the horizon of my life, may I see the whales of Your goodness, Your care, Your provision and Your presence, break the surface of all my waiting seas, in Jesus name I pray, amen!

Night-Whisper | GOODNESS

Non loquimur sed vivimus

Acts 9:36-37

"At Joppa there was a certain disciple named Tabitha, which is translated Dorcas. This woman was full of good works and charitable deeds which she did." NKJV.

And she died. The death of Dorcas, the old Christian gazelle, had a profound impact upon the community in which she lived. So much so, that the saints decided that they would go and fetch an apostle to see what could be done! Peter and his entourage later turn up to the room of the deathbed scene, to find it packed with people all a-weeping and a-wailing, each one clutching their garment and saying, "Look! She made this for me. Sat up all night she did, God bless 'er." And another person with one hand on Peter's shoulder and the other holding on to the cloak, now neatly folded and well cared for which she holds in her shaking grip, "Look! She went without food for a week to buy me this, then tailored the cloth to fit my old round shoulders." And another, then another, all clothed and warm, all pointing and praising, all weeping and watching just what Peter might do for them. So, Peter raises Dorcas from the dead and presents her to them alive! Just like that. Her most necessary of serving and sewing days apparently still not over. Now I don't know if Dorcas was happy about this turn of events, (I doubt she was) but all who loved her and had benefited from her full life of good deeds toward them for the glory of God, well, they were ecstatic!

My mother died two years before I became a Christian. Whilst serving in HMS Collingwood down in Portsmouth I was given the number of a Brigadier of the Salvation army, a retired old woman who I had never met. I rang the number, introduced myself and was immediately told, "Ah yes, I met your mum before she died and led her to the Lord. Don't worry, she's with Jesus now." I was happy but very stunned! How did this happen, how had I not known about it?

The old woman that had given me the number to call was my next-door neighbor. A grand old gal she was called Olive Hinchcliffe, a former tambourine basher herself, Captain in the militant wing of the Salvation Army. I think? My old mum was a hard worker, but bless her heart, she couldn't sew for toffee, so it was this lady who lived next door to us, who, had for years, sewn up the holes in my trousers, altered the leg length on my school uniforms, bought me white shirts to wear for school and the most amazing text books at the beginning of each term. For years she had prayed for us and for me especially, and for years by her good works, had slowly drip, drip, drip watered the parched and hard heart of my old mum's soul. When my mother was dying, the hardness had been so softened over the years that it was easy for Captain Olive to introduce her Brigadier friend to my mother's own deathbed scene. Olive Hinchcliffe had never shared the Gospel with me or my mother, but her good works and prayers brought us both into the Kingdom of the Savior she loved most dearly and honored most profoundly.

> *For years she had prayed for us and for me especially, and for years by her good works, had slowly drip, drip, drip watered the parched and hard heart of my old mum's soul.*

In Joppa, another old woman, *full* of good works had drip, drip, drip watered the hearts of many people in the city. When Peter arrived and raised her from the dead and shared the source of such power with parched hearts now most thoroughly moistened, the rain of God was absorbed and life sprang anew, the tale of which, was carried far and wide from this great sea port of Joppa by a wide range of gossiping sailors and merchants.

Two old ladies, Dorcas and Olive. Their motto was "Non liquimur sed vivimus" – "We do not speak great things but *we live them!*" Tell me friend, what's your motto tonight?

Listen: *"...and turning to the body he said, 'Tabitha, arise.' And she opened her eyes, and when she saw Peter she sat up. Then he gave her his hand and lifted her up; and when he had called the saints and widows, he presented her alive. And it became known throughout all Joppa, and many believed on the Lord." (Acts 9:40-43NKJV)*

Pray: Father, bring such women into our lives and make them honored in our churches. Father, turn us into such old women we pray, that we might follow their hard working example and not only talk the talk, but more importantly, walk the talk as well. In Jesus name I ask it, amen, and let it be so.

Night-Whisper | **CONTINUE**

A kicker with a gun 'til heaven doth come

Like it, or not, intended or not, released in 1967, the Paul Newman film classic, *Cool Hand Luke* is a veritable mine of Christian metaphor.

Luke 3:7,8

Then he said to the multitudes that came out to be baptised by him, "Brood of vipers! Who warned you to flee from the wrath to come? NKJV

In 2007, Don Pearce the writer of both the novel and the majestic screenplay for this film, was still living and writing in Fort Lauderdale Florida. Leaving home aged only fifteen, the author's personal life is a rich source of story for the film.

Pearce lied about his age when joining the army in 1944, went absent without leave because he was a rebel against what he saw as unnecessary rules, and spent time in the stockade before the intervention of his mother, who finally informed the army of his true age! Then, thrown out of the army, Pearce joined the merchant navy, travelling the world, only to be imprisoned in France for the black market counterfeiting of money! Escaping from the outside prison detail, he fraudulently makes his way back to America where he takes up a new career in burglary. Being imprisoned aged twenty for safe cracking he had to serve two years in the Florida State Department of correction chain gangs. At the very least, this young man experienced more of life in those eight years than many would dare to do in 800 years! Having previously given up writing, as a much older man he had now taken up his pen once more. In those intervening years he had an office where I used to live in Dania Beech, from which he arrested run away killers from the Carolinas, and Store Front Preachers who moonlighted in the drug trade. I often wonder if some of the latter are still operating in that same trade in Broward county even today!

I tell you all this because Don Pearce is not a financially successful author. At the time of my writing, he was struggling to take care of his ailing wife, and to find extra money for medical bills. He most certainly feels like Sysiphus, bound to an eternity of frustration in forever rolling a rock uphill and never reaching the top. Ben Alsup, writing in *Esquire* magazine from an interview with Pearce in 2005, records Don Pearce telling him one very particular story:

"A man, beaten and bleeding, is crawling after a gun. Every time he comes near to laying hands on the gun, another man kicks it up the road a little farther, keeping it always just out of reach. The kicker holds a gun of his own. And the crawler knows, should he ever succeed in reaching the gun he's after, that the kicker will shoot him dead. The kicker knows this as well. Still they travel up the road. The crawler crawls, and the kicker kicks, and the road, it never ends."

Friends, under this present sun, there is a seeming futility in the circle of life, there is seeming pointlessness to all our journeying. If that outrages some of you, then you are either too young, or too insulated to know the truth of it. The former condition of youth is excusable and will pass with time, the latter one insulation however, is a chosen state of lunacy and the church is full of such lunatics.

Tonight I say to you three things.

First enjoy our journey, enjoy the day, enjoy the night, the peace the fight, the hot still days and the wind borne kite. Enjoy life!

> *Tonight I say to you three things. First enjoy our journey, enjoy the day, enjoy the night, the peace the fight, the hot still days and the wind borne kite. Enjoy life! Enjoy life! Enjoy life!*

Second, enjoy your own story! See yourself as a character within the pages of a book where you have a start a middle and an end, and with it a development. Enjoy being who you are and enjoy becoming who you can become. Enjoy life!

Thirdly and above all though, know that this story, under this present sun, is terribly tainted. It is marked with a curse and a futility, it is stained with loss, it is full of open crosses, upon which you might climb or be forced upon. In the middle of a groaning creation, creaking and falling apart, happy endings are rare and frankly, so they should be. So, whenever you can, enjoy life!

You see, "what we've got here, is a failure to communicate." The church under this present sun, is guilty today. Absolutely and totally guilty of selling snake oil to the masses. Guilty of promising heaven on earth. Guilty of promising better days ahead for a small weekly tithing. "Yessiree, just turn up, sit up, shut up and above all, pay up, and all shall be well this side of heaven!" I tell you now, this snake oil selling of better days under the sun for a small fee, is not Christianity and it is a damnable lie!

For you to find hope at the beginning, middle and end of your story, for you to find true hope at the end of each hard day of yours under this present sun, you must turn your mind to thoughts fantastical! Yes tonight and every night, you must steer your heart to the deepest of dreamy wonders. Tonight you must pass beyond the outer and much restrictive boundaries of human possibilities and step through the portal of childlike fancy, into gross and startling human impossibility! Tonight, you must fly, Peter Pan like, into unknown worlds, even worlds to come, worlds that one day, as in the long, so long ago, will once more shatter the space time dimensional boundaries and shine again in our forever changed and star lit skies. For friends, amidst the frustrations of the long journey which we find ourselves upon, true Christianity will be a dream yet to be realized, even an unclothed mystery yet to sprout its breasts of fullness. Do not forget tonight, that in our Christian story, the best is always yet to come, yes the best is ever and is always, "Milk and honey on the morrow, with skipping lambs and jam tomorrow." Tomorrow, as much as you can, enjoy your life under this present sun but expect frustration until heaven doth come.

> *Tonight, you must fly, Peter Pan like, into unknown worlds, even worlds to come, worlds that one day, as in the long, so long ago, will once more shatter the space time dimensional boundaries and shine again in our forever changed and star lit skies.*

Listen: *"Now I saw a new heaven and a new earth, for the first heaven and the first earth had passed away. Also there was no more sea. Then I, John, saw the holy city, New Jerusalem, coming down out of heaven from God, prepared as a bride adorned for her husband. And I heard a loud voice from heaven saying, 'Behold, the tabernacle of God is with men, and He will dwell with them, and they shall be His people. God Himself will be with them and be their God. And God will wipe away every tear from their eyes; there shall be no more death, nor sorrow, nor crying. There shall be no more pain, for the former things have passed away.' Then He who sat on the throne said, 'Behold, I make all things new.' And He said to me, 'Write, for these words are true and faithful.' And He said* to me, 'It is done! I am the Alpha and the Omega, the Beginning and the End. I will give of the fountain of the water of life freely to him who thirsts. He who overcomes shall inherit all things, and I will be his God and he shall be My son. But the cowardly, unbelieving, abominable, murderers, sexually immoral, sorcerers, idolaters, and all liars shall have their part in the lake which burns with fire and brimstone, which is the second death.'" NKJV*

Pray: Lord, help me tonight to see beyond the boundary, in Jesus name I pray, amen and let it be so!

Night-Whisper | **CHARACTER**

The deal of death

I might have said this before but like it or not, intended or not, the Paul Newman film classic, *Cool Hand Luke* is a veritable mine of Christian metaphor.

Luke 3:7

"Then he said to the multitudes that came out to be baptised by him, 'Brood of vipers! Who warned you to flee from the wrath to come?'"

NKJV

Taking note of the crucifixion like posturing of the character Luke following his eating of fifty eggs, to all the crosses at the end of the film, I nevertheless especially like the fact that the character of Luke is assigned the prison number of 37. Of course Luke 3:7 is our text for tonight and speaks to hypocrites regarding "fleeing the wrath to come!" And what are hypocrites, except those folk who are not true to themselves?

In any event, the film of *Cool Hand Luke* is, on the positive side, the story of a misfit and a rebellious one at that. It is the story of man who will not give up being who is, and in being who he is, brings hope, inspiration and happiness to the rest of the motley chain gang he is in prison with. These, in turn begin to feed on both him and his exploits. Like Luke Jackson, Jesus, in simply being who He was, most certainly clashed with those in authority and in the same way, that clash also most certainly brought life to others! There are many Christ like comparisons to that fact in the film, but for tonight, I have found three things in the movie and in my own life that prove being your authentic self, often can bring life and light and hope to others.

First, please note that God has put certain people on this planet, that no matter how hard you or they try, just will not fit the standard mold of things, in any shape or form! These circus folk, these rebels who are too often without a cause, need to be celebrated for who they are and guided in the planning for what they shall become. Unfortunately and very often, all of society's social misfits, are kept hidden in the attic, or way back in the research and development area of businesses that benefit from their exploits but are embarrassed by their seeming eccentricities. Yes, in one way or another, this circus crowd is always hidden away because of their seemingly weird and wacky ways. Yet given the right kind of encouragement and direction, these shooting stars can shine brighter and longer than anyone ever imagined, across the sky of which they long to streak. Embrace such circus folk with happiness and laughter, for even though they might be firecrackers, they will light up your life and light up your world! God made them and their individuality needs to be seen as a gift and not a curse.

> *Embrace such circus folk with happiness and laughter, for even though they might be firecrackers, they will light up your life and light up your world! God made them and their individuality needs to be seen as a gift and not a curse.*

Secondly, know that all of us are cramped in some way by our sin-sick societies. All of us are crippled by unnecessary rules and may I say, most of the sick, restricted, stunted, stayed and stifled people I have ever met are those which have been brought up in, or brought into the present expression of the Kingdom of God on earth, the church of the living God! Like it or not, that is the truth. The church of the Lord of life, is often more guilty of the control of and perpetuation of death. The church needs to learn to release the uniqueness of the individual within its walls and outside to the world. Oh my, imagine when people are finally served into their destinies! Imagine what an uncontrolled explosion of life and light, might just envelope our communities of boring darkness. Yes boring! For darkness, death and Hell are above all things, boring. Think about that.

Thirdly and most importantly, please recognize the "deal of death" which is often presented to firecrackers. I personally have had this deal presented to me so many times now, that I am astonished that the devil continues with the presentation! Yet he does and throughout the ages of the time and the seasons of our life still persists in his coming to us with the same sad deal.

This deal of death and with it, the destruction of destiny, is seen in the Scriptures passing across the lips of the best friend which Jesus ever had on this planet, Peter the rock. Here the devil tries to use this best of friendships to scupper the eternal destiny of the Son of God and all who should be found in Him!

"From that time Jesus began to show to His disciples that He must go to Jerusalem, and suffer many things from the elders and chief priests and scribes, and be killed, and be raised the third day. Then Peter took Him aside and began to rebuke Him, saying, 'Far be it from You, Lord; this shall not happen to You!'" Matthew 16:21-22 NKJV.

This deal of death often comes from the best of places, the best of intentions and the best of friends, yet if you listen you can hear the serpents hissin.' In the film *Cool Hand Luke*, it is Luke's best friend, Dragline, played by George Kennedy, who comes to him after his passion in the church and amidst all the sirens, police and the crazy correctional officers waiting to tear Luke apart, says to him with a nice big hopeful smile, "You've got to listen to me, all you've got to do is give up, nice and quiet. Just play it cool."

For death of both the individual and the team will always follow such cowardly compliance to play it cool and draw back from our own uniqueness. Life will no longer be communicated when the draw back from who we are.

There you have it! Do you see it? If life, if change, revival, love and light and world shaking can only come through the release of authentic Christians into destinies which are designed uniquely for them, then the devil will always, and I mean always, come to them, come to you and say, "Draw back, be quiet, be cool," and my dear brother and my brave sister, when that happens, then "what we've got here, is a failure to communicate!" For death of both the individual and the team will always follow such cowardly compliance to play it cool and draw back from our own uniqueness. Life will no longer be communicated when the draw back from who we are.

If you want to shake that tree your hiding behind, if you want to shake the earth for Jesus, then you must be all you are in Jesus and do all He wants you to do! Do not let anyone stop you being otherwise. Do not enter any deals of death! Do not comply. Do not go into that good night! No, go on being who you are, for despite the embarrassment of the populace, true and lovely life will always follow hard on the heels of any release of your spirit.

Listen: *"For You formed my inward parts; You covered me in my mother's womb. I will praise You, for I am fearfully and wonderfully made; Marvelous are Your works, And that my soul knows very well. My* *frame was not hidden from You, When I was made in secret, And skillfully wrought in the lowest parts of the earth. Your eyes saw my substance, being yet unformed. And in Your book they all were written, The days fashioned for me, When as yet there were none of them." Psalms 139:13-16 NKJV*

Pray: Lord, help us all tonight, to see beyond any restrictive boundaries set for us by others simply wanting us to play it cool, in Jesus name we pray, amen!

Night-Whisper | **GIVE**

The real road show

An examination of the Old Testament use of the received Tithe, that New Testament fictitious 10% the church is always so focused upon, reveals that it was used essentially in three major areas, that is, for the support of personnel, the purchase and upkeep of premises and the financing of various people keeping, money spinning programs. Local churches of today, and I suppose every Christian para-church organization as well, uses the larger percentage of its collected finances for exactly the same three Ps in the same old pod. Premises, people and programs.

2 Samuel 24:24,25

"Then the king said to Araunah, 'No, but I will surely buy it from you for a price; nor will I offer burnt offerings to the Lord my God with that which costs me nothing.' So David bought the threshing floor and the oxen for fifty shekels of silver." NKJV

Now do not get wrong here! The workman is worthy of his hire, though often some Pastors just are not as worthy as much as we pay them and more often than not, some Pastors are worthy of so much more. Yes, the workman is worthy of his hire, and premises should be warm inviting and attractive, though not necessarily plushy, lushy and cushy, and correctly funded programs are not only justifiers of our existence but they sometimes actually do some good. Sometimes.

OK, so now we are clear on that, let me say six things tonight in closing.

First, that 10% of giving is far too much for some people. Giving 10%bof nothing, when you have less than nothing coming in and more than nothing going out, is just stupidity. Either that, or faith. I hope it is faith, because that alone will please God, and that alone will unite your family in the cost of such sacrificial giving.

Secondly, that 10% is just not enough for some people. Ten percent of "loadsamoney" is an accounting line item that your accountant needs to use to ensure tax relief at the end of the fiscal year. There is no sacrifice here. No really, there is no sacrifice here.

Thirdly, that tithing though a Biblical principle is not a New Testament practice. The practice of the New Testament is the hilariously happy and regular giving of that which we have decided in our hearts. New Testament giving might be a whole lot less than 10% and then again it might be a whole lot more. It may vary from gift to gift and giver to giver and that's OK.

> *Tithing though a Biblical principle is not a New Testament practice. The practice of the New Testament is the hilariously happy and regular giving of that which we have decided in our hearts.*

Fourthly, that if you have committed to regular giving to the three P's in that oh so pesky pod, then give and give regularly! Other people are relying on your regular committed giving.

Fifthly, that there is another principle to be applied to giving that precedes the hilarity of the task. Giving that honors God, giving that incites belief, giving that is astonishing, and giving that will be utilized by the receiver in the most holiest and astute of ways, is giving that is sacrificial. Giving that can most easily have the largess of hilarity affixed to it is giving that has cost you something.

Lastly a confession. It's a double edged confession really, in that while living on the cutting edge of Gospel ministry I tell you that I have given my all to God. Many times I have regretted it and often I have wanted to take it back and much of the time it has not been done with hilarious abandon. I am sorry to God for this sometimes, very reluctant kind of giving. On the back edge of such giving I have to tell you as well that regarding the basic material stuff of life, in the form of food, clothing, transport and tools, it has cost me nothing to give myself away as a bond servant of Jesus Christ. That's a little scary eh? The feeling, that it has cost me nothing to give myself away. So far, I have been able to do it with joy. The real test is yet to come. And I know it.

I do not know what kind of accounting software package the Lord has but I do know that He has got one and that it is open access, there for all to see. One day, we shall all know the true cost of our sacrificial works in terms of the gold, silver, precious stones, wood, hay and stubble in the right hand column of God's great balance sheet. I must tell you, that this is one of the great things that I am most looking forward to finding out about at the great *Antiques Road Show* in the sky. That is, finding out what is the real value of all our goofy looking investments! Imagine all those disappoint faces at the sad evaluations of treasures both touted and shouted about, and all the other wide eyed intakes of breath that shall be seen and heard, when a gift that some considered to be a piece of old junk, unknown to everyone, actually released untold treasure to millions! And that now,

> *those that gave the sacrificial gift, shall now receive rewards that might be later spent at their leisure, in every angelic outlet shop, spread across the universe anew.-*

those that gave the sacrificial gift, shall now receive rewards that might be later spent at their leisure, in every angelic outlet shop, spread across the universe anew. Oh yes, even angels engage in trading and therefore obviously engage in manufacturer. However, that's another story.

Tonight, I dare not and I will not set myself up as anything but a reluctant disciple and a reluctant giver to boot, but I do find it interesting when considering these things, that on some counts I feel the cost of giving, yet on many counts I simply feel both the need to give and the pull of greed not to give. What about you tonight? In all your giving of self and stuff, what do you think shall be the real price tag placed upon all your giving to Jesus? Invest in eternals dear friends and invest well.

Listen: *"If anyone serves Me, him My Father will honour." John 12:26b NKJV*

Pray: Thank you Lord for the great cost you paid for me. Thank you Lord for others that count the cost for me, of me, with me. I am willing Lord to pay the price of pleasing You right now! Help the hilarity of the gift become then that much more insane to my head and helplessly funny to my heart, to my soul and spirit and my body. Yes, help me laugh like a lion, in Jesus name I pray amen.

| Vol 01 | Q4 | NW00301 | October 27th |

Night-Whisper | **POWER**

What to do with this old house

Britain still has the abysmal record of currently the worst serial killer ever the stalk the earth. The Doctor of Death, Harold Shipman, was convicted for the murder of hundreds of his patients. No one really knows that actual number.

James 3:11,12

"Does a spring send forth fresh water and bitter from the same opening? Can a fig tree, my brethren, bear olives, or a grapevine bear figs? Thus no spring yields both salt water and fresh." NKJV

Before the horror of Harold, it was the ferocity of the serial killer Fred West that haunted people's dreams. Fred West and his wife Rose confessed to killing thirty people, many of whom were found to be an integral part of the structure of 25 Cromwell Street. This house has since been demolished and every brick has been crushed and every piece of timber has been burnt.

Tonight, it is not 25 Cromwell Street that bothers me, but rather 27 Cromwell street, the building next door, which was and still is a Seventh Day Adventist Church, still offering Sunday School and Divine worship on a Saturday. These services both are, and were then, held right next door to this house of death, I mean just feet from these grotesque happenings! Twice on a Saturday and no doubt mid-week as well, the Adventists would lift their faces to God Most High in prayer, for themselves, for their missionaries, for their communities and for their neighbors, even the people who lived next door to them.

As God looked down from heaven, He saw in the same screen shot, both the hands of these worshippers lifted high in praise and supplication and no doubt the pleading hands of women being brutally murdered, mistreated, and begging for their life, before being hacked to death and hidden just feet away from the all the prayers and praise. God saw the living and the loving wanting to be anointed for service and sacrifice whilst next door, He saw the blood in the basement and the bodies in the walled up chimney, their screams settled silent in concrete. One, a community of life and light pleading for mercy and another a community of darkness and death, screaming for justice and both just feet from one another. All this happened down a simple street in England, down our street, down my street, down your street. Now tell me, how haunting is that.

I have observed how darkness can hide itself in plain view. The powerful preaching Pastor who is having it away with the women's Pastor. The charismatic conservative Christian leader who visits rent boys late at night. The Christian psychologist who sleeps with his patient, the grandfather who fiddles with his grandkids, the smiler who murders in his heart, the day sweet talker who curses at night….and so it goes on. Darkness, hides itself in plain view and we that love and hope for the best, get devastated when our failing discernment fails to reveal the deception.

> *One, a community of life and light pleading for mercy and another a community of darkness and death, screaming for justice and both just feet from one another. All this happened down a simple street in England, down our street, down my street, down your street. Now tell me, how haunting is that.*

In the same way, God looks at every happening on our planet. In the same screen shot, God takes in every happening on our planet that has happened, is happening and will happen, in both space and time, all at the same time. He sees the darkness growing alongside the light shining, He sees all the double dealing deceptions of the heart. Imagine that! What holds Him back in judging this great evil? Such knowledge is too much for me.

So, in a smaller but same way, we Christians all, draw near to God in a sometimes light and shade kind of way. Our might be lips full of praise whilst our hearts are like the sinking Titanic. Some chambers might be playing "Nearer my God to thee," whilst other chambers might be full of laughing and hope. Other, behind the water tight doors, already being full of death and drowned bodies, even gossip and murder. Still other chambers of our hearts are sealed with unforgiveness, vengeance, bitterness, greed, foul and pestilent thoughts and all this in the same body, next to each other, drawing near to God at the same time, whilst trying to offer praise and worship. Imagine that. This is not right. It can never be right.

The growth of the new man, the expansion of the new heart, does not reclaim old death, neither does it live next door to it! Rather it demolishes it, crushing every brick and burning every timber in open and continual consistent confession, letting the wind of God's freshness blow the ashes of its demise across His own great deeps where they are dissolved forever in the blood of The Lamb. No, the growth of the new man, the expansion of the new heart does not reclaim old death, cannot live with it and refuses to countenance it! Rather, it builds something new and grows something better than there ever was there before. Then, at such a new life prospect, God the Holy Spirit says, "Come on in! Let me show you around a little. Come and discover all the newness that is mine, all the newness that is thine even and let me teach you how to live in its freshness, how to live in its fullness, how to decorate it according to your eternal future and not according to your piddly little past. Christ cam to give you life and righteous living NOW!"

> *Let me encourage you tonight then, to stop revisiting the old house of death, and stop visiting with the Father whilst you are still at the same inhabiting the old house of death! That will never do.*

Let me encourage you tonight then, to stop revisiting the old house of death, and stop visiting with the Father whilst you are still at the same inhabiting the old house of death! That will never do. Rather friend, move houses, move into the new and living, ever growing, ever renewing, ever fresh and flowering new man of the heart. Let it be so! There are too many torture chambers, too many screams, too many Ghosts in the old man's house. MOVE!

Listen: *"But now you yourselves are to put off all these: anger, wrath, malice, blasphemy, filthy language out of your mouth. Do not lie to one another, since you have put off the old man with his deeds, 10 and have put on the new man who is renewed in knowledge according to the image of Him who created him" Colossians 3:8-11 NKJV*

Pray: Lord, do not allow me to decorate the new with the language of the old. Lord, do not allow me to put my old furniture on the rooms of the new. Lord, do not allow me to invite old smelly guests into my new home. Lord, do not allow, do not allow, do not allow. In Jesus name I pray, Amen.

| Vol 01 | Q4 | NW00302 | October 28th |

Night-Whisper | **CLEAN**

Remembering the hidden rock piles of redemption

There is little that is more enduring than rock. In my homeland, the famous Stonehenge and many dancing rock circles are even now intriguing testimonies to ancient communities long since wiped from the face of the planet. Yet, still the testimony of speaking rocks remain for there is little that is more enduring than a rock.

Joshua 4:4-7

"Then Joshua called the twelve men whom he had appointed from the children of Israel, one man from every tribe; and Joshua said to them: 'Cross over before the ark of the Lord your God into the midst of the Jordan, and each one of you take up a stone on his shoulder, according to the number of the tribes of the children of Israel, that this may be a sign among you when your children ask in time to come, saying, "What do these stones mean to you?" Then you shall answer them that the waters of the Jordan were cut off before the ark of the covenant of the Lord; when it crossed over the Jordan, the waters of the Jordan were cut off. And these stones shall be for a memorial to the children of Israel forever.'" NKJV

My suspicion is, that God delights in rock more than He delights in any other non-sentient part of His creation. The fixed, protective immovability of rock is at the very least, that which He desires most for us. Yet I think there may be also a secret and metaphysical side to rocks yet to be fully comprehended, for what other singing sentinels stand so firm in the bearing of their living water spewing testimonials? There is little more enduring than a rock. Yes, water gushed from the rock and yes Christ said they would sing praises to God if the Jews refused to do so.

So, God wants us to remember important things, and like so much of the Old Testament, begins to bookend the chapters of His redemptive story with rock altars and rock piles! In our text for tonight, it is from the middle of a presently dried up Jordan river, that twelve burly tribal representatives obey the command of God and remove the smooth stone rocks to dry Canaan land, to stand as a generational testimony to what God has done for the Israelites. Yet tonight, it is not this rock pile which I am focused upon, but rather the Joshua rock pile that is listed in verse nine:

"And the children of Israel did so, just as Joshua commanded, and took up twelve stones from the midst of the Jordan, as the Lord had spoken to Joshua, according to the number of the tribes of the children of Israel, and carried them over with them to the place where they lodged, and laid them down there. Then Joshua set up twelve stones in the midst of the Jordan, in the place where the feet of the priests who bore the ark of the covenant stood; and they are there to this day." Joshua 4:8-9 NKJV

Maybe Joshua was following some other unrecorded explicit command of God right here in verse nine, or maybe, Joshua did this off his own bat? Who knows? Still, tonight, even today, underneath the rolling Jordan lay twelve, now very smooth stones, all huddled together in the wet and fishy darkness! Here is a hidden rock pile, an unseen testimony, yet known by one and all who have been redeemed. Yes, the visible pile, brought up from the center of Jordan, speaks of another pile of large and ragged old rocks laid down in the center of the river, brought from the wilderness maybe, but now long since hidden, covered and all smoothed out by flowing water, a long, long time ago.

For every one of us tonight, for all the true Israel of God, I say that every past life sinful stone is hidden, is covered and is long, long smoothed out beneath the rolling waters of redemption that once piled up high at a city called Adam far, now so very far away.

Our present life of victory, should be full of present and permanent testimonies to a salvation once wrought upon us, rock like testimonies to a redemption from a dreadful slavery to sin and lost-ness in a wandering and dried up wilderness, even though our old life, our past life, like Joshua's rock pile is covered and long lost in the way once parted for us.

For every one of us tonight, for all the true Israel of God, I say that every past life sinful stone is hidden, is covered and is long, long smoothed out beneath the rolling waters of redemption that once piled up high at a city called Adam far, now so very far away. Look to your own Salvation's seen rock piles, brought up from your own river of death and ask yourself tonight, "What do these stones mean to me?" They shall mean something special for you and especially, that everything else, everything my dear friend concerning your old life on the other side of Jordan, is gone and lost forever in the middle of God's redemptive pathway. It is gone. The past now smoothed over and covered in the depths of His river rolling love.

There is nothing more enduring than a rock. Let your seen rock piles, remind you of the smoothed over and now hidden sins of your old past life. They are covered forever.

Listen: *"......and as those who bore the ark came to the Jordan, and the feet of the priests who bore the ark dipped in the edge of the water (for the Jordan overflows all its banks during the whole time of harvest), that the waters which came down from upstream stood still, and rose in a heap very far away at Adam, the city that is beside Zaretan. So the waters that went down into the Sea of the Arabah, the Salt Sea, failed, and were cut off; and the people crossed over opposite Jericho. Then the priests who bore the ark of the covenant of the LORD stood firm on dry ground in the midst of the Jordan; and all Israel crossed over on dry ground, until all the people had crossed completely over the Jordan." Josh 3:15-17 NKJV*

Pray: Jesus, when Your feet stepped into Jordan's floods, t'wean heaven's desire and the Father's will, the waters rose up O Lord, rose up in a heap so very far away, at the base feet of Adam, hoping still and in the pathway of redemption every testimony to my sin, is now covered by the waters of Your love. Thank you. Thank you. Thank you. Amen.

Night-Whisper | **BECOME**

God's Russian dolls are always opened in reverse

True Karmic destiny is to be content with your position and calling in life, even if you're gifted as a doctor but still cleaning out the elephant cages! Breaking Karmic destiny, creating bad Karma by ceasing to be an elephant keeper and actually becoming a doctor can have grave consequences for both you and your family both now and in all future life cycles. So is the understanding on one world view held by countless millions in other parts of this weird and weary world. Most people in the West do not understand that which is called true Karma!

Psalm 47:1-4

"Oh, clap your hands, all you peoples! Shout to God with the voice of triumph! For the Lord Most High is awesome; He is a great King over all the earth. He will subdue the peoples under us, And the nations under our feet. He will choose our inheritance for us, The excellence of Jacob whom He loves." NKJV

Tonight I do want to talk about receiving an inheritance but in cosmic proportions and not in Karmic propensity. In other words, when God gives us an inheritance, though it has location with respect to boundaries, both materially and metaphysically, it also has within it, infinite room for eternal growth which can only be gained through a continuing conquest of personal faith. Yes, spiritual acquisition always takes faith, strength and courage! When this trident of pursuance is stabbed into the rear end of all our resistant enemies, they will eventually fall back screaming or be destroyed in the possession! Faith and the need to walk and act by faith is an eternal necessity to receive the felt pleasure of God most High. Friends, get this now…..You are not as limited to where and who you think you are or for that matter, even what you do.

When God divides to us our inheritance, we still have the possibility, the need, the desire, even I believe, the expectation of God to also say to Him, "Give me this mountain!" Or, "Give me also springs of water!" Or "Give me also this better gift which I seek", Or,..well you get the picture.

God never tires of us asking for more of ourselves and our inheritance to possess. Oh that we would bless Him by doing so!

That possession God has divided to you is an unfolding, never ending, expanding universe of conquest and discovery. I speak mostly metaphysically when I say that there is no need to envy another person's inheritance, when whole continents, planets, star systems and universes, lay waiting for the discovery in that particular inheritance which is yours. God's gifts, you see, are like Russian dolls, the opening of which goes on forever and forever, amen. So, stop whining about your seeming inadequacies and instead start discovering the unfolding of all God's good gifts to you. There is more in you and more to come out of you than you ever imagined! Gods gifts to you, you see, are like Russian Dolls, except when you open them up and take out the next gift and shining possibility, the one inside is always bigger than the one it came from. Believe this and begin to enjoy your discoveries, for at His right hand are pleasures for ever more.

Listen: *"For the gifts and the calling of God are irrevocable." Romans 11:29-30 NKJV*

Pray: Lord, what wonders lay waiting, all wrapped in sparkling paper, within Your purposeful and never ending gifts to me? Give me O Lord, a spirit of adventure to seek these out and help me take full possession of all Your inheritance divided in love to me, in Jesus name I pray, amen!

Night-Whisper | **ACTION**

Decisive of Tunbridge Wells

Once upon a time, I resided in Tunbridge Wells, which has often been referred to as the spiritual home of Middle England, that is, the home of the presumed right-wing views of middle class, mainstream, non-urban white folks. In light of this, it was the satirical magazine *Private Eye*, who in its playfully constructed, obsessively and excessively complaining 'letters to the editor,' always signed them off with mock outrage as "Yours, Disgusted of Tunbridge Wells." Mock social outrage is of course hilarious! Mock religious outrage born out of a lifetime of fat slumber is, however, absolutely anything but funny, for it is both in and of itself a mockery.

Matthew 9:11-13a

"And when the Pharisees saw it, they said to His disciples, 'Why does your Teacher eat with tax collectors and sinners?' When Jesus heard that, He said to them, 'Those who are well have no need of a physician, but those who are sick. But go and learn what this means'" NKJV.

In this mad world in which we presently live, in this end of the age relationship freak show, this silicon sideshow of drug induced enhancement and totally spiritually disenfranchised and demonized societies, I am afraid we need to lay aside any semblance of an attitude which lifts its nose, and shakes its head while writing letters to the *Evangelical Times* signed by Yours Faithfully, Disgusted of Tunbridge Wells. For many years far too many folk have done nothing to remedy our societies worsening situation and so really, just how can we act so disgusted? What right do we have? Oh and by the way, political intervention and social action is good, but it is no remedy for society's ills.

I wonder if it is at all possible for us to be shocked anymore. No, I didn't think so. Therefore, do not act shocked sister? Therefore, do not feign religious disgust brother? It will do no good anyhow. Rather, guard yourself and become an exemplary point of moral reference. Rather, gird yourself with grace and stoop to conquer. Rather, go into this entire mad and messy world and preach the Gospel to every crazy creature you will come across. Don't be disgusted by society but be decisive about doing something about our society for it is most certainly sick and in great need of the Great Physician. Oh and by the way, He shall do those house calls through you! So, are you ready for the sacrifice? Yes, are you ready to call sinners to repentance? Are you learning what this means? Look, feed the poor, but preach the Gospel to them. Look, clothe the naked, but preach the Gospel to them. Sing your heart out down at the Grey Lady pub, but preach the Gospel to them. Get local council to clean up the dog dirt, but preach the Gospel to them. (The council or the dogs on the council, the choice is yours.) Brethren, don't just be disgusted, preach the Gospel and do something about it!

Listen: *"'I desire mercy and not sacrifice.' For I did not come to call the righteous, but sinners, to repentance." (Matthew 9:13b NKJV)*

Pray: Lord, help us not to feign disgust anymore, but rather, to fight so compassionately that we would become the beacons of moral direction, the spiritual samples of redemption that this old world most desperately needs. I decide to wake up tonight then! Yes, I decide to take action tonight then, and so on the morrow, become the medic with the medicine even the carer with the call to full Gospel repentance, sacrificing myself for the salvation of others, seeking Your mercy, sowing in hope and striving for goodness sake in the preaching of Your Gospel.

Yours forever, 'Decisive' of Tunbridge Wells.

| Vol 01 | Q4 | NW00305 | October 31ˢᵗ |

Night-Whisper | **CHANGE**

The dark billions and the baptism at Bellarmine

I am sat in Detroit Airport as I write this Night Whisper. Already I have been the recipient of free candy distributed by personnel dressed as thieves and one-eyed pirates. Cutesie little Japanese girls dressed as witches holding their daddy's hand have just walked past me as maniacal laughter echoed over the intercom. It's 2007 and Halloween here in America and this week, depending on which statistics you read, anywhere from 2.5 to 6.5 billion dollars will be spent on all things, gruesome. I tell you this because tonight's whisper is a Halloween humdinger. Be afraid, be very afraid.

Romans 1:21,23

"..because, although they knew God, they did not glorify Him as God, nor were thankful, but became futile in their thoughts, and their foolish hearts were darkened. Professing to be wise, they became fools," NKJV

I set the scene at Bellarmine Roman Catholic University, even the repository of the writings of the world renowned, spiritual giant, Thomas Merton. Here this Halloween week, late one night in the decked and darkened halls, a young mother, who for months had been hiding her pregnancy from others, went to the bathroom and whilst all alone, gave birth to a beautiful baby girl. The child was plopped directly from the watery womb, right into the watery U-bend of the lavatory, where it drowned. Hidden in a garbage bag, the dead child was eventually found by the police. The mother, as I write, is being charged with murder.

The most shocking thing about this harrowing Halloween story is, however, not so much the dreadful event, but the cries of "My God! How can such a terrible thing be happening in our country and at one of our prized universities!" Since the dark drowning, I have heard this cry on all media sources and I tell you that on this not so happy Halloween, it is this cry which is the most astonishingly shocking thing I have heard, in its bared faced stupidity and unforgiving ignorance.

Friends, we have sown to the wind and now we are reaping the whirlwind.

Ten percent of the nearly one million women getting an abortion in America in 2007, would have cited "an inability to successfully complete their chosen education" as a reason for killing the kid not yet born. It's an Halloween haunting to consider that if this young mother, just six months previously or even less maybe, had gone to a licensed practitioner, citing her education and golfing career as a reason for the need for help with murder, then she could have had her baby ripped from her womb, soaked in salt, or vacuumed out in little pieces and all done free of charge. This acceptable and legalized murder would have been followed by all the care and counselling she could ever need of, delivered hard on heels of the dastardly deed, yes indeed, she could have even gotten on with her golfing, whilst the murderers themselves would have received their fee as usual and all the surrounding industry of death been able to further and statistically justify their existence whilst applying for even more government funding to continue the silent genocide, and make a few more bucks on the side selling baby body parts retrieved form the fleshy mess. If she had only acted six months previously, then all would be have been well with the law. Now, you just think about that!

It is estimated that by 2015, America alone murdered nearly 58 MILLION babies since 1973 Roe V Wade!

As I edit this Whisper, it is estimated that by 2015, America alone murdered nearly 58 MILLION babies since 1973 Roe V Wade! With such genocidal figures just whose family I wonder, has not been touched by tragedy such as this. I tell you, that I pity this one solitary, sad and silly girl, who out of above 40 million murdered babies in 2007, from all the other murderers and countless millions more in complicit genocide, stands as the only one at present counted guilty today. At present, I say, for judgement is still to come. Still, let's not think too much for after all, it's Halloween and the orange sugared candy corn abounds, and laughing witches invite me to smile. Judgement is coming against the Western Nation's for the genocide of generations.

In this "One Nation Under God," with websites hosting billions of pornographic pages, with billions of dollars being spent on Halloween, billions being spent on treating sexually transmitted diseases, billions being spent on armaments and war, billions being spent on an entertainment and communications industry that glorifies supernatural darkness as sexy and all the accompanying violence, selfishness, pride, witchcraft, rebellion, atrocity and atrociousness in all its meanest forms as what we should all aspire to, then the real shocker which remains for me this Halloween, is the startling stupidity of that media cry, that shakes it head in wonder, and asks the reason, "Why?"

This Halloween, despite all the sugarcoated laughter around the shocker of a murderer mum, are all your sins forgiven, are you prepared to flee the wrath to come? Get ready. It is coming.

Listen: *"They sow the wind, And reap the whirlwind." Hosea 8:7 NKJV*

Pray: Lord, come carve the word accounting, into the temples of our thick old pumpkin head, that no more little babies would be murdered, left for dead. In Jesus name I pray, amen and let it be so.

PAUSE FOR PRAYER | 66CITIES

Well, I do pray that the first month of this quarter of NightWhispers written with you in mind, have prospered you spiritually and pushed you on a little farther down the road in knowing, obeying and immediately following the commands of the God of the whole Bible. This is my desire.

I am Victor Robert Farrell and I am the author of Night-Whispers. I also have the privilege of being the President of The 66 Books Ministry and I want to tell you a little bit about our major project which is: 66Cities. I believe one of the problems with the rapid moral decline of the West coupled with the influx of other religions, has been the compromise of the local church. It is as though we leaders have watered down the wine of the Gospel with the methods and culture of the world and have done so to such an extent that all we are left with is an anemic and slightly rose colored, fluoride-filled cup of poor tepid mouth wash. It is good for nothing except to be poured down the drain. This compromise I speak of, was to stop speaking about the God of the whole Bible and to such an extent that Christians were left in a strange kind of idolatry, worshiping the God of a cultural constructed Christianity, and so much so, that when these same Christians came into contact with the real God of the Bible, He troubled them and offended them. Indeed, they were embarrassed by Him and wanted Him excluded from their parties. The world of course, found more substance in the other gods, especially that kind of unbiblical Trinitarian spirituality which allowed science and hedonism to mate with the X factor of their own particular choosing.

We at The 66 Books Ministry intend to preach the Gospel of Jesus Christ and the God of the whole Bible, from each of the 66 Books of the Bible in the 66 most influential cities of the nations of the world. That's 16,500 cities in an annual and ongoing basis. To make this happen we are prayerfully raising up teams of proclaimers and 'prayer rangers' to go into these cities. We see this is a true prophetic witness to the glory of God. Indeed. This is the main reason why we are doing this: that God the Father and God the Son may be seen and Glorified in the power of God The Holy Spirit. We hope and pray, that many will see the Father, trust in the Son and be saved by the power of the Holy Spirit as well. Brethren, **we covet your prayers as we do this.** Check out WWW.66Books.TV

| Vol 01 | Q4 | NW00306 | November 01ˢᵗ |

Night-Whisper | **COURAGE**

Beware this flower's power

Numbers 14:31

"But your little ones, whom you said would be victims, I will bring in, and they shall know the land which you have despised." NKJV

Fear is a most fantastic flower, unfolding itself into the most colorful of forms and fragrances. From concerned and seemingly mild musings, to loud and strong, fist shuddering rebellion, fear flowers and shakes its leafy bough even in the most mild of summer breezes, casting forth the very seeds of its own ultimate and most deserved destruction. Yes, from sweet to sour, fear perfumes its own perverted way with the most justifying of scents. "Well after all," it says, "what about the kids? We have to think about them. If anything happens to us, well, what about them? I mean, how can we provide for them if...well, they shall never forgive us if...and if we ever did do what You ignorantly intimate, what you wildly and most seemingly suggest, then how could we ever provide. I mean, if we went there, how would they survive? I mean, this is fanatical...I mean, this is totally irresponsible...I mean, this is not a command to respond to with a 'yes sir' salute and a fast return to the seams of the pants with a quick to obey like snap. No! This is a bear baited trap! A deception that will lead to our destruction, a madness that if followed will surely only lead to misery!" Yes, fear is a most fantastic flower, its roots finding their abundant sustenance in even the scantest of soils, which is nevertheless, so rich in unbelief and that's your problem friend. Unbelief. Fear justifies its own sensibilities as it clothes itself in unbelief

So these same flowers of fear now find themselves within the tent doors of the whole camp of Israel, whose many open blooms, all together sucked out of the blue and sunlit skies of the waiting to be possessed, giant filled promised land, such a gross and debilitating deformity, that God their Savior could not fail to find it both offensive and disgusting to His soul. So offensive in fact, that He would now kill them for it. Yes, He would scour them from the smelly pan of baked on unbelief and start again with a new and fear pollen free people. It was only Moses who stopped Him from killing the self-convicted and self-condemned nation in an instant as one man.

Restrained by the prayers of Moses then, God limits His most terrible tirade and goes to His fear flower powered people saying, "There is no reason for this soul of unbelief. For if you had taken the salt of My signs and wonders performed among you, and sprinkled it upon those places of death in your hearts, then fear would have found no sustenance to spread its roots. Now, not only have you have failed to deal rightly with the soul of your souls, but you have fertilized your own hearts with the mad manure of your most consistent and complacent disdain. Concerning those whom you deceitfully feigned to fear for the most, even your children, well they shall possess that which you now most scurrilously are rejecting and you shall never see their joy, nor settle in the places I had prepared for you along with them."

> ...you have fertilized your own hearts with the mad manure of your most consistent and complacent disdain.

Granted, this is a stark message, yet there it is. So, let us daily take the salt of His greatness and sow it with great extravagance upon the surface of our own unbelieving souls, that we might be kept from the flowering of those most pernicious of fear filled blooms.

Look now. God can take care of your kids far better than you can. So go ahead and obey Him! Do what He has told you to do.

Listen: *"How long shall I bear with this evil congregation who complain against Me? I have heard the complaints which the children of Israel make against Me." (Numbers 14:27-28 NKJV)*

Pray: Help us daily then Lord, each night to salt our souls with the remembrance of Your so great and daily, power and goodness that faith would flower in the night and so make our mornings ever fresh. Deliver us from fear that and all the self-righteous justifiers of our sinful unbelief. In Jesus name I pray, amen and let it be so.

Night-Whisper | **CHOOSE**

The undertone of the overtone, or the rat in the scat

Overtone singing is practiced by many peoples of the world and is the ability to produce two or even four voices from but one human being!

Psalms 29:3

"The voice of the Lord is over the waters; The God of glory thunders; The Lord is over many waters." NKJV.

The ethereal quality of such voice production has led many to believe that this kind of throat singing is indeed a metaphysical event! Some proponents go further, even suggesting that it taps into what Jung referred to as the collective unconscious, or, the collective human and racial metaphysical memory. In other words, some would have it that human beings are somehow endowed with a common ancestral memory, which can be accessed through over tonal singing. Interesting.

The nearest we come to overtone singing in the west I think, would be scat singing, the chief and most famous proponent of this being the great Ella Fitzgerald, whose use of non-lexical vocables in music, or rather, nonsense syllables, made her the most famous of scat singers! It was musician and lecturer Roberto Laneri, who suggested that even scat, was a metaphysical event and that this kind of vocal of improvisation could be rooted in different states of consciousness, which in turn would draw on the Jungian model of being able to access the collective unconscious. Again, interesting!

I also find that it is of note that the association of such vocal overtone techniques have long been and continue to be associated with, not only performance art, but also ancient Shamanistic practices. Well so what?

Friends, I do believe that there are three things here for us tonight.

Whether we carry a particular cultural or ancestral consciousness, I do not know. However, the first thing to note this evening is that I believe we carry a humanity wide collective unconsciousness! It is however not Jungian but rather 'Jehoviam,' in that God has put eternity in all of our hearts and a sighing God shaped hole that only He might fill.

The second is that in many of our charismatic churches, the practice of having open and singing prayer encouraged by so many young worship leaders, means that the congregation often erupts (and is encouraged to do so) into a cacophony of sound. This may sound metaphysical in connection but is rarely as good as scat and hardly ever as evocative as true overtone throat singing! Its rubbish. If you are a worship leader tonight, then please remember that people want to sing! They want to sing corporately, and most of all, they want to sing sensible syllables of meaningful praise and practical prayer. Look you now, if you want to scat in the Spirit go and do it by yourself somewhere.

> *All kinds of overtone are usually carrying an undertone, that is, they are usually singing another not so nice tune.*

The third and final thought is that all kinds of overtone are usually carrying an undertone, that is, they are usually singing another not so nice tune. When we as individuals or as collective bodies even, begin to communicate with more than one voice, on more than one frequency, then let us beware of the undertone of malevolence that can so easily be carried on such dancing and deceitful waves of sound.

How's your tone tonight? How's your timbre? How's the color of your words? The voice of the Lord is as sharp as a pin. Don't you forget that.

Listen: *"Therefore do not be unwise, but understand what the will of the Lord is. And do not be drunk with wine, in which is dissipation; but be filled with the Spirit, speaking to one another in psalms and hymns and spiritual songs, singing and making melody in your heart to the Lord, giving thanks always for all things to God the Father in the name of our Lord Jesus Christ, 21 submitting to one another in the fear of God." (Ephesians 5:17-21 NKJV)*

Pray: Lord, help us not to be too scatty in both our joint and public praise of You and in our public prayer, in Jesus name we sing it, amen and let it be so!

Night-Whisper | **TRUST**

Of jennels, jiggers, snickleways and twittens

Having lived on the border of East Sussex and the county of Kent, many of the towns are riddled with well-established and beautiful cut-throughs and short cuts between all the walls and hedges, fences and houses. In my home county of Derbyshire we call these short cuts, these new ways, "jennels," and in other parts of the country they are referred to as "jiggers" or "snickleways" (isn't that cute!) Down in that part of the "soft and sunny" South, however, these cut-throughs are delightfully referred to as "twittens."

Isaiah 35:4-6

"Say to them that are of a fearful heart, Be strong, fear not: behold, your God will come with vengeance, even God with a recompence; he will come and save you. Then the eyes of the blind shall be opened, and the ears of the deaf shall be unstopped. Then shall the lame man leap as an hart, and the tongue of the dumb sing: for in the wilderness shall waters break out, and streams in the desert." KJV.

A synapse is a highly specialized junction between either two neurons (nerve cells) or a neuron and a protein cell, which in turn allows the transmission of chemical and electrical signals, resulting in a quick cascade of a physical response. These established synaptic pathways are of course especially important in brain function, and can be easily destroyed by anything from drugs to disease, thus limiting the capacity of brain functionality. The brain however is quite remarkable, especially in younger people, in that even with the destruction of existing synaptic pathways, other cut throughs, other new ways, other twittens, other synaptic pathways can be established as time goes on.

Now, I have neither the knowledge or understanding to correctly communicate how the brain works, but then again, who does! The investigation and understanding of brain function and the defining of intelligence and consciousness seems almost as accurate as describing a single star on the Eagle Nebula whilst using a bottle top for a telescope! Yup, I reckon we understand about that much! Nevertheless, this phenomenon of the damaged brain's capacity to establish new cut-throughs and short cuts, or if you will, new jennels, snickleways and twittens is quite remarkable.

My point tonight is this: In the establishment and growth of towns and cities, human beings have always been in the business of establishing twittens, those quicker and often prettier cut-throughs, so as to arrive speedier and more refreshed at their desired destination. In the same way, even nature, from rivers to streams and from the establishment or reestablishment of broken brain synaptic pathways, has also been in the business of making new ways were there are none and quicker ways where there needs to be some. Do you not think tonight then, that our God can make for ways for where at the moment there are none? Of course He can! So, to some of you tonight, I need to tell you that God can make a way for you! A new way. A quick way. A more safe and beautiful way. A quiet way. A provided way. Whatever it is. God can make a way for you. Trust Him in this.

> *God can make a way for you! A new way. A quick way. A more safe and beautiful way. A quiet way. A provided way. Whatever it is. God can make a way for you.*
>
> *Trust Him in this.*

Listen: *"No temptation has overtaken you except such as is common to man; but God is faithful, who will not allow you to be tempted beyond what you are able, but with the temptation will also make the way of escape, that you may be able to bear it." (1 Corinthians 10:13 NKJV.)*

Pray: It is a very simple prayer of mine tonight dear Jesus, please make a way, open up a new way, a hidden way, a forgotten way, where at the moment there appears to be none. In Jesus name I pray, amen.

| Vol 01 | Q4 | NW00309 | November 04th |

Night-Whisper | **TRUST**

The antidote to Christian cannibalism

Barren Hannah was desperate for a child and in her desperate prayer she promises to give the gift she has received right on back to God. Samuel is born and Hannah does indeed follow through on her vow.

1 Samuel 1:9-11

"So Hannah arose after they had finished eating and drinking in Shiloh. Now Eli the priest was sitting on the seat by the doorpost of the tabernacle of the Lord. And she was in bitterness of soul, and prayed to the Lord and wept in anguish. Then she made a vow and said, 'O Lord of hosts, if You will indeed look on the affliction of Your maidservant and remember me, and not forget Your maidservant, but will give Your maidservant a male child, then I will give him to the Lord all the days of his life, and no razor shall come upon his head.'" NKJV

All children are of course gifts from God and it does a person good to both realize this and act on it, for these good gifts are always kept longer and remain far fresher to us when they are dedicated right on back to Him. Please note tonight that any gift selfishly consumed by us will in the end corrupt us and I tell you, this is especially true if we eat our own children, you know, consume them in our own desires and make them the cherished idols of our hearts. If you are doing this, you had best watch out, for cannibalized children always give the very worst of stomachaches! So, following the blessed example of the Holy Family, give back your gift to God! Dedicate them to the Lord. This dedication means a letting go of and a laying hold of.

As to letting go, you must remember that this child is not yours. It shall grow and shall become and in the all of its becoming the child shall decide on so many things for itself, including whether or not they shall follow the Lord. You must have faith in letting the child of your care be found by the God that you love.

As to laying hold, well, you must lay hold of Your God and of yourself. It is imperative that you grow in grace and in the knowledge of the Lord Jesus Christ. As the child becomes and as the child decides, You must lay hold of God on its behalf. You must also lay hold of yourself, for you must become a model of godliness before them, a mentor of graciousness and hope, a mother of love prayer and care, a father of manly courage, wisdom, perseverance and provision. The child will become and will make its own decisions, you are not responsible for this. However, you are greatly responsible for laying hold of both God Himself and of you yourself.

> *You must have faith in letting the child of your care be found by the God that you love..*

Whatever you do tonight, do not eat your children.

Listen: *"Hear, O Israel: The Lord our God, the Lord is one! You shall love the Lord your God with all your heart, with all your soul, and with all your strength. And these words which I command you today shall be in your heart. You shall teach them diligently to your children, and shall talk of them when you sit in your house, when you walk by the way, when you lie down, and when you rise up. You shall bind them as a sign on your hand, and they shall be as frontlets between your eyes. You shall write them on the doorposts of your house and on your gates." (Deuteronomy 6:4-9 NKJV)*

Pray: O Lord we cast down our idols, even if they are our most dearly beloved children. So help us to leave them with Your good discipline and Your love and Your care, yes, this we do tonight with both hope and faith in Your goodness. Now O Lord, we lay hold of Your goodness and lay hold of ourselves to walk with You, as models and mentors of the Christ like life before the gifts You have so graciously granted us. Amen and let it be so.

Night-Whisper | **LOVE**

Spontaneity and the sizzle of the Spirit of God

Stale and boring, safe and same. This is what he said. "I'm not having an affair, she's not having an affair, it's just that we've lost our 'zing,' and frankly, it's killing our relationship. You see, everything is scripted. We do the same as everyone else. We have gotten into a rut, a common rut I know, but a rut nevertheless. We get up at this time. Go there at that time. Buy this because. We use the same language, day in, day out. There is nothing new to talk about! Nothing unique to us to get excited about. To go 'WOW' about! It's the same old song, week after week. I try to bring some sparkle into our life and say 'Hey! Let's go to such and such, let's try this, let's just do that!' You know, try to bring some spontaneity back into our relationship. However, the response all too often I get is, 'I'm too tired. We've arranged to meet so and so. We can't really afford it. What if it rains. What if there is nowhere to stay when we get there,' and so on and so forth and on and on. It's all so negative. It's all so boring. It's all so deadly. I married an exciting woman for goodness sake! Now all I've got is a 'Stepford' wife.' No, we are not sinning Pastor, we are just boring, and you know, I am sick of it."

Acts 8:26-40

Now an angel of the Lord spoke to Philip, saying, "Arise and go toward the south along the road which goes down from Jerusalem to Gaza." ... So he arose and went. And behold, a man of Ethiopia, ... Then the Spirit said to Philip, "Go near and overtake this chariot." So Philip ran to him....... ... Now when they came up out of the water, the Spirit of the Lord caught Philip away, so that the eunuch saw him no more; and he went on his way rejoicing. But Philip was found at Azotus. till he came to Caesarea. NKJV

Two opposing deficiencies of action can slowly kill a relationship. Lack of being sensible and lack of spontaneity. We as individuals and we as one local church body are in relationship with God the Father, through Jesus Christ, via the ministry of the Holy

Spirit. May I be outrageous tonight and say this; "I wonder if God the Holy Spirit is become a frustrated lover when it comes to His local church? I wonder if Jesus is bored out of His skull with it all? I wonder if the Father is tired and indifferent toward us?"

Now, before you stone me for blasphemy, I say before you close these pages, let me say that I am purposely casting God here as the bored husband of a sensible wife. I am highlighting, and possibly quite badly, but highlighting nevertheless, some of the 'possible' feelings of God toward parts of His global militant church. God, after all, is a person. God, after all, has feelings. God, after all, is in a deep relationship with His church and the only construct of understanding given to us whereby we might understand this relationship is one of earthly 'marriage.' Isn't it? Therefore, please allow me this transference of emotion on my part so that I might communicate a possible sense of staleness to you today on God's part! Yes, so that I might agitate you to a deeper and more abandoned loving, please allow me to continue on a little while before flushing this Whisper down the toilet.

Now look you. My own personal failings are vast. I mean, ridiculously large. Therefore, I have no approved ground to stand upon and cast stones.

In reaching out to the United Kingdom with the Gospel and trying to include existing churches in that outreach, I have had hundreds of points of communication with Pastors and church leaders. After asking each of them what they are doing to reach out to their communities with the Gospel of Jesus Christ, I find that they are all doing the same little handful of very good things. Yes, from 'Lands End' to 'John O'Groats' local churches are doing the same handful of great things. They are copying one another. They are clones of one another. In their actions of Evangelism, they are all the same. So much so, that on the odd occasion I have even prefixed the conversation with Pastors by saying 'Brother, let me tell me about your church. You have so many people attending your main gathering, the percentage male female split is such and such, your Sunday service begins at this time, lasts for this long, and you speak for this length of time. Your congregations favorite songs are, you are involved in W X and Y and are preparing to do Z, and your hope for the future is this and your fear for the future is that.' I am usually quite spot on, and the response to such a word of knowledge (ha!) is 'My goodness, how did you know that?' I am usually kind in my response, but the truth I feel like communicating is this, 'Because you are the same as everybody else mate! Because you are a copycat. Because You lack local innovation. Because you are quite boring brother.' There. I've said it. Look now though, for the real question I now come to ask myself, and I will leave it hanging for now, is this, "Is God so unifyingly the same in taste touch and outreach throughout this land? Is God simply a McDonald's franchise of service? Is God a chain store replicating model? Is the Lord Jesus Christ just so unimaginative and just so blinkin' boring?"

Like I say, in reaching out to the United Kingdom with the Gospel and trying to include existing churches in that outreach, I have had hundreds of points of communication with Pastors and church leaders and find that for any possible 'event' to take place, you have to book in advance. I mean way in advance! Indeed, I have often wondered if God the Holy Spirit were to turn up Himself with an idea that He too might have to get in line and wait for a year for a date to become clear in the collective calendar of the cloned church? It seems to me that we have lost the ability for spontaneity in the local church. I wonder if any Pastor opens his eyes in a morning and says out loud "Good morning Jesus! I wonder what we are going to do today! I am so excited." Nope. I don't think that ever happens. "BORING!"

"The local church has become boring and that we have lost our ability for spontaneity. We are a Stepford wife. Robotic. Programmed and relationally quite stayed and dead and this lack of spontaneity is killing the personal passion of our leaders, it's killing the vital energy of our church, it's killing our communities, and more importantly, I say much more importantly, it's boring God into a vomit gagging indifference!"

Now look you. My own personal failings are vast. I mean, ridiculously large. Therefore, I have no approved ground to stand upon and cast stones. So, please be assured that I am not criticizing the good works of local churches, and neither am I criticizing their service to their communities for the Glory of God, nor am not deriding their sense of sensibility. However, I am clearly saying this, that "The local church has become boring and that we have lost our ability for spontaneity. We are a Stepford wife. Robotic. Programmed and relationally quite stayed and dead and this lack of spontaneity is killing the personal passion of our leaders, it's killing the vital energy of our church, it's killing our communities, and more importantly, I say much more importantly, it's boring God into a vomit gagging indifference!"

Yes, as I make so many calls to so many 'samey' churches I have to ask just "Where is the innovation and spontaneity of the Spirit of God? Where is the uniqueness of the local churches individual relationship with Jesus? Where is that flower and fragrance of expression which is ours and ours alone?" Where's the excitement? Where's the desire? Where's the love and passion with God!" Let me get personal with some of you tonight then, for I want to suggest to some of you that if you are feeling bored with church tonight, then maybe God is even more so?

Sensibility and spontaneity must bow to one another, they must, at times, be overcome by one another. This being true, I know two other things for sure as well. First, that spontaneity needs space. I wonder then if in all the clearance and closures that I see happening around the land that God might be making just that very space? I say this because of the second thing I know; we have lost our ability to accept, and our desire for the spontaneity of the Holy Spirit. We have become 'Stepford,' we are become stale and we have lost our spiritual sizzle. Indeed, we have committed the second greatest sin of all, in that we have lost our first love of the Lord. How about you? Is it time to spice things up with Your Lord!

> *Sensibility and spontaneity must bow to one another, they must, at times, be overcome by one another.*

Listen: *"I know your works, your labor, your patience, and that you cannot bear those who are evil. And you have tested those who say they are apostles and are not, and have found them liars; and you have persevered and have patience, and have labored for My name's sake and have not become weary. Nevertheless I have this against you, that you have left your first love. Remember therefore from where you have fallen; repent and do the first works, or else I will come to you quickly and remove your lampstand from its place — unless you repent." (Revelation 2:2-5) NKJV*

Pray: Father, my own sins of silliness and stupidity and sometimes unsoundness, are evident and clear for all the world to see. Of these I do repent. For these I am so sorry. Please forgive me. But O my Lord, I would not bore You! Lord Jesus, Great Commander, I know there is time for duty and consistent marching, even one boot upon another on the unrelenting ground, I know that Father God. But O My Lord, I would not bore You! For this lack of first love, for that is what it is, I do repent. I am so sorry, please forgive me. In the coming day of duties and responsibilities I do also commit myself also to cancellations, to wonders, to diversions, and to unexpected dates. Yes Lord, I commit myself to that never-ending love tumble between the sheets of sensibility and spontaneity. Love demands courage, I know this Lord. Therefore, asking for this courage, I now do lay me down this night to sleep upon the bed of morning expectancy. My day and my diary I give to Thee O God, and not only do I long for what You might do tomorrow, but I would have You also long My Lord, to see what I might do for You! Let therefore the moon this night, O Lord, tingle with anticipation, and let the morning sun, prepare to rise with expectant smile. Amen and let it be so.

Night-Whisper | ACTION

Are you a 'Faith Leader' and are you on a 'little list?'

In the United Kingdom I was ordained in the late 1990's. Legally I am a 'Reverend,' even a revered man. What a bunch of Baloney! In the USA and the UK, I have also been involved in setting up two charities of the Christian Religion, which allow those charities to ordain men to the ministry and bestow upon them the title of Pastor and Reverend. Again, what a bunch of Baloney. The fact that the title of 'Reverend' rarely appears on title designations within the capture of contact details of most current software programs is not only a derisory backhanded slap from the secular world, but is maybe a good thing. Let me tell you why.

Luke 2:3-5

So all went to be registered, everyone to his own city. Joseph also went up from Galilee, out of the city of Nazareth, into Judea, to the city of David, which is called Bethlehem, because he was of the house and lineage of David, to be registered with Mary, his betrothed wife, who was with child. NKJV

The term 'Reverend' became recognition of completed training and of rank within the clerical classes. It is not and neither is there any hint of this title within the Scriptures. Neither is there any ordination to priesthood or to the church. Every believer is a priest and we are all part of the church. Neither is there any ordination into the church or to leadership. You are either one of God's gifts to the church or you are not, you are either acknowledged by a local congregation as an elder, or are not, Holy Spirit and local body prompted elders either lay hands on you for entrance into the 'Stores and Supply' team or they do not. (Remember Elders and Deacons and are simply the spiritual and temporal purveyors of stores and supply into the local church body of believers.)

All the title Reverend has ever done for me is allow me into hospitals to spiritually attend the sick and the dying when other people might not be allowed, and accorded me some respect from the spiritually ignorant both within and outside Christendom. Baloney! The only validation of any ministry, is the seen Divine stamp, which is measured only in the blessing of God. Or 'certain death' if you are a prophet.

It is time to ditch these titles. It is time to be seen as a servant, even a purveyor of stores and supply, that the whole body of Christ might be equipped for works of service. I say this, because very soon these 'Officers of Religion,' these recognized 'Faith Leaders' will be made part of a secular registry, even a roundup of Rabbis, Vicars, Imams, Bishops and Baptist Reverends which will all put on a monitoring list for the protection of society from rogue terrorists. Once on the 'little list,' they will no doubt give you another title, a badge and a big hat of some kind, together with Govt. approval to receive appropriate funding. They might even recruit you to help with gathering information and keeping the congregation calm in times of national crisis (self-created or otherwise) and if you are very lucky, a small financial stipend on the side, or benefits 'in kind,' for your service to the good of the wider society.

YOU MUST NOT GO ON THIS LIST AND YOU MUST TELL THEM TO STICK IT WHERE THE SUN DOES NOT SHINE!

There shall, no doubt, be placed before you a number of reason to be part of such a list, least of which will be your ability to 'operate' with recognition as an approved minister in the eyes of the state. The present need for system trained Cultural Respectability will make most ministers comply. Indeed, their own denominations will require it, especially when the continued supply of their salaries, pension plans and housing will be sued as a beating stick. However, there are three reasons why YOU MUST NOT GO ON THIS LIST AND YOU MUST TELL THEM TO STICK IT WHERE THE SUN DOES NOT SHINE!

First of all, my dear servant of Christ, adopted son of the living God, when did you fall so far as to allow yourself to be grouped with heretics, apostates, compromisers and purveyors of false gods? When did you ditch your one and only saving faith for the filth of the lowest common denominator that is leading billions to hell? When did you become just a 'faith leader' instead of a Servant of the Living God? Any national government faith leader list is for cowards and compromisers. Do not stoop so low.

Secondly, when did you sell out Jesus as your Lord? When did these secular authorities become your master and your king? When did you bow your knees to the devil's Muppets instead of to Christ your king? When did you sell out brother? This list is for cowards and compromisers. Do not bend the knee to Caesar.

Thirdly, when did you take the big fat stupid pill? Being on any national register of faith leaders will let the anti-Christ authorities know where you live, what you do, what you believe, how far you will go for them, as well as who you are currently 'taking care of,' in your congregations, together with and any other information you may be required to pass on to them. This list is for idiots.

I am afraid we need now to be prepared to lose our charitable status. I am afraid we need to be prepared to lose our well-loved titles and positions and all the accouterments of pay, pensions, premises and prestige that goes along with them. A time of choosing has now come to the true SAS of God. It is time to separate and begin again. It is time for the sheep to leave the goats. It is time.

DO NOT GO ON THIS LIST and my friends, do not truck with, or trust anyone else who is on it. Remember, as Ko-Ko (or Cuckoo) the Executioner once said, "As someday it may happen that a victim must be found, I've got a little list — I've got a little list of society offenders who might well be underground. I've got a little list, I've got a little list."

Listen: *Then Herod, when he saw that he was deceived by the wise men, was exceedingly angry; and he sent forth and put to death all the male children who were in Bethlehem and in all its districts, from two years old and under, according to the time which he had determined from the wise men. Then was fulfilled what was spoken by Jeremiah the prophet, saying: "A voice was heard in Ramah, Lamentation, weeping, and great mourning, Rachel weeping for her children, Refusing to be comforted, Because they are no more." (Matthew 2:16-18 NKJV)*

Pray: Awake, awake, put on strength, O arm of the Lord! Awake as in the ancient days, in the generations of old. Are You not the arm that cut Rahab apart, and wounded the serpent? Are You not the One who dried up the sea, the waters of the great deep; that made the depths of the sea a road For the redeemed to cross over? So the ransomed of the Lord shall return, And come to Zion with singing, With everlasting joy on their heads. They shall obtain joy and gladness; Sorrow and sighing shall flee away. (Isaiah 51:9-11 NKJV)

Night-Whisper | **TRUST**

How to get high by not believing a lie!

Standing on the warm beach and looking at the deep blue ocean lapping against the distant horizon and splashing up against the far stretched clouds sinking with the setting sun, the sea looks beautiful and inviting, even an all enfolding loveliness. On the land, looking out at that immeasurable coldness, you still feel warm, secure, steady, rock like, safe. Now climb aboard a small yacht and set sail for a day or two into that vast deep blue and its enormity becomes seemingly infinite, seemingly never ending, eternal, dangerous, deep, sucking, scary, and I tell you, when you are there, as a small bobbing speck in the middle of that desert of blue water, you feel anything but safe.

When a storm comes up across the bay of Biscay and stirs the deep beneath into a leaping hunter, a force nine howler even, the insignificance of your little self against the roaring of so great a watery and all-consuming lion makes you feel less than nothing, an angry voice maybe, but never less, simply a small dot of dust, trodden on by gigantic watery actors who are fighting hot, living violently, and screaming their way into a fiery death upon a vast eternal stage, each one playing out a story of cosmic and multidimensional

Psalms 107:25-32

"For He commands and raises the stormy wind, Which lifts up the waves of the sea. They mount up to the heavens, They go down again to the depths; Their soul melts because of trouble. They reel to and fro, and stagger like a drunken man, And are at their wits' end. Then they cry out to the Lord in their trouble, And He brings them out of their distresses. He calms the storm, So that its waves are still. Then they are glad because they are quiet; So He guides them to their desired haven. Oh, that men would give thanks to the Lord for His goodness, And for His wonderful works to the children of men! Let them exalt Him also in the assembly of the people, And praise Him in the company of the elders."
(Psalms 107:25-32 NKJV)

proportions, to which you seem to be as less an insignificant worm who is in their way. In the same way, I tell you that the more I read the Bible, the more days I set out to sea upon this deep and never ending story of God, this narrative, this poetry, this journey, this revelation of the Most High, these players, these decisions, the whole kit and caboodle of it all become to me nothing short of terrifying! For the Bible, the very Word of God is the most troubling book that has ever been written. If you disagree with me here, then friend, I do not think you have even begun to read it.

> *The Bible, the very Word of God, is the most troubling book that has ever been written. If you disagree with me here, then friend, I do not think you have even begun to read it.*

It was writer Frank Cottrell Boyce who wrote the screenplay for the BBC's television Drama, **God on Trial.** May I say that it is a quite brilliant and terrifying performance piece, for the screen play wrestles with the deep question we all have on our hearts, which is "Why do bad things happen to good people?" Or better still, "How can a good God allow so much suffering in the world?" The 90-minute play has the unpacking of these questions take place amongst a group of inmates in Auschwitz, just hours before half of them shall be murdered. Cottrell himself confesses that his seemingly invulnerable Catholic faith was beaten black and blue as he wrote the screenplay. The fact of prisoners in Auschwitz concentration camp actually putting God on trial is rooted in an apocryphal story from WWII to which the Auswitch survivor and writer, Elie Weisel, gives some credence to when he made his statement that "God was hanged on the gallows in Auschwitz." In the play **God On Trial** the closing statement made by the prosecutor is that,

"God is not good, He is just powerful. Once upon a time He was on our side and now He is on the side of the Nazis. God is not good, He is simply all powerful. God is guilty of breaking His covenant with us."

God is then pronounced guilty of the charge.

The narrative and supposition of Cottrell's screenplay can be Biblically contested at every God-damning point but that is not the point. The point is that on this great sea of History which we find ourselves floating upon, the storms of our own life stir up the dregs of our days and from that sin matted mud, the festering odor of the foul stench of that constant and unremitting theme exudes daily from it, always runs gangrene-like along the ground proclaiming to one and all and to the delight of the devil himself especially, when it always proclaims that "God is not good!" The truth is that as individuals and communities, as nations and now even as continents and soon, maybe sooner than we dare to think, the whole world will have put God on trial and found Him guilty as charged, and so much so is this a possibility, because that we all together now, today, in our own black hearts, sing in condemning proclamation like some great accusing choir, of both God's seeming failings and His dreadful lack of goodness toward us. The old lie, you see, never dies. Not really. The old lie that God is not good, is alive and well today.

Let me say that I have no doubt that if I had been in Auschwitz I would have put God on trial and found Him guilty. Good grief, I have done it often enough in comparative kind kindergarten picnics when compared to that most terrible place. How about you? Even so, whether in the terrors of Auschwitz or the comforts of Ipswich, this most sinful of singing, just has to stop. Why? Because it is a big fat lie! God is good!

> *Let me say that I have no doubt that if I had been in Auschwitz I would have put God on trial and found Him guilty. Good grief, I have done it often enough in comparative kind kindergarten picnics when compared to that most terrible place.*

My friends, if we dare, we need to truly get to grips with the meta-narrative of this great redemptive story of the Bible and more so, we need to see the true state of our own God condemning heart. We need to wake up to the old lie whispered by the devil since Eden's paradise was lost which is even today embedded in our very genes. We need to grow up regarding this natural tendency to curse God and bear false witness to His character. Let's be honest with ourselves, let's get real. For the old lie has robbed us of so much hope and faith and joy. Yes, we need to set our bow of faith toward the great horizon of His all-consuming love and with the courage of belief, set sail across the turbulent deeps of all life's waiting blues. For sure, this is a terrifying journey across wild seas of temptations and the deepest oceans of doubt, but I tell you that it is a journey into a God that we shall indeed find not only to be so very powerful but also to be so very wonderfully good. Stop believing the old lie. Stop singing the sinning song, by both inwardly condemning the lie and outwardly proclaiming His goodness through living in expectant joy.

I mean Have a blast today! Laugh wildly whenever you can! Enjoy life to the full for God is good!

Listen: *"Those who go down to the sea in ships, who do business on great waters, They see the works of the Lord, and His wonders in the deep." (Psalms 107:23-24 NKJV)*

Pray:

Lord, let Your glory fall, as on an ancient day.
Songs of enduring love, and then Your glory came.
And as a sign to You, that we will love the same,
Our hearts will sing that song, as we pray!
God, let Your glory come!

You are good, You are good, and Your love endures.
You are good, You are good, and Your love endures.
You are good, You are good, and Your love endures today.

Voices in unison, giving You thanks and praise,
Joined by the instruments, and then Your glory came.
Your presence like a cloud, upon that ancient day,
The priests were overwhelmed, all because, because Your glory came!

You are good, You are good, and Your love endures.
You are good, You are good, and Your love endures.
You are good! You are good, and Your love endures today.

A sacrifice was made, and then Your fire came.
They knelt upon the ground, and with one voice they prayed,
And they sang as we sing today, That,
You are good, You are good, and Your love endures.
You are good, You are good, and Your love endures.
You are good, You are good, and Your love endures today.

(Lord Let Your Glory Fall – by Matt Redman)

| Vol 01 | Q4 | NW00313 | November 08th |

Night-Whisper | **TRUST**

Scattered, covered and smothered

I have said it before but I'll say it again. I love Waffle House! Started in 1955 in Georgia, those low-rent, yellow restaurants at the side of the road not only serve well over half a million eggs per day but their daily offering of sausage patties alone, if stacked on top of one another would be higher than the Empire State building!

Acts 8:1b-5

"At that time a great persecution arose against the church which was at Jerusalem; and they were all scattered throughout the regions of Judea and Samaria, except the apostles. And devout men carried Stephen to his burial, and made great lamentation over him. As for Saul, he made havoc of the church, entering every house, and

You will have heard the old joke, "What's got 8 legs and 4 black teeth?" Answer, "The 3rd shift at Waffle House." Even so, Waffle house waitresses are a wonderful breed apart, they are to be experienced rather than to be described, God bless their hearts! The fun part of their food order delivery to the ever-frying short order cook, is in turn a never to be forgotten short order diner dictation service! Hashed brown potatoes for example, are called in as "scattered" (spread on the grill,) "smothered" (with onions,) or "covered" (with cheese,) and oh, by the way, everything is covered in cheese in America! Now there's a three-point Waffle House sermon if ever there was one! "The Church, scattered, smothered and covered!"

Our text for tonight us informs us that God allowed a rabid religious Rottweiler to be let loose within the gentle flock of His the church and his name was Saul of Tarsus. As Saul ripped the flock apart like a mad Mastiff, (I know, you though he was a Rottweiler!) not only were body parts and blood scattered all over the place, but the very people of God themselves were also scattered like speaking seeds across the face of the then known world, smothering it with the Good News about Jesus. Yes, even in the face of such terrible persecution, these early followers of The

Way smothered the demographic landscape with the savory knowledge of God's goodness toward us in Jesus and covered the land with the spicy practice of the all-gracious and all forgiving love of God. Indeed, it is obvious to me, that God even used this religious dog called Saul to harry his sheep into obeying His command to take the Gospel into the entire world.

So tonight then dear friends, if you are being "chunked," "diced," "peppered," "capped," and "topped," all along your tired way, then I tell you that God maybe also have a purpose for all the religious Rottweilers that are in your life at the moment, for though they may be destroying some stuff, they are also pushing you somewhere. Tell me, where are they driving you tonight? Maybe that's where you should be going? After all, maybe you are part of the church, which is scattered, smothered and covered? Think about that and rejoice that you suffer for the name of Christ!

Listen: *"Then Philip went down to the city of Samaria and preached Christ to them. And the multitudes with one accord heeded the things spoken by Philip, hearing and seeing the miracles which he did. For unclean spirits, crying with a loud voice, came out of many who were possessed; and many who were paralyzed and lame were healed. And there was great joy in that city." (Acts 8:5-8 NKJV.)*

Pray: Lord, use these religious Rottweilers in my life to make me a city cleaner, a sidewalk healer and a certain joy giver. Please put me where You want me, in Your great name I ask it, amen and let it be so.

Night-Whisper | **COURAGE**

Loving on Len

Proverbs 20:29

"The glory of young men is their strength, And the splendour of old men is their grey head." NKJV

Len was 87 when I met him. He had been a Christian for 77 years! He was old school, you know? Grey hair parted to the right, pinstripe Sunday suit, black Bible and had been part of a Brethren Assembly for years. You've maybe seen the breed; you've maybe known the type. From another age, old, irrelevant, out of touch, useless. The leader of the service that morning had given way to him though, as Len, apparently, wanted to make an announcement.

Len stood up. Len stood to attention, yet he was still smaller in stature than even me, time and gravity had compressed his backbone you see. Yet, it was still straight, as straight as the old creases in his well-kept trousers; his steely eyes without blinking, staring into mine, searching out my soul.

Len was a former Regimental Sergeant Major in the Gordon Highlanders, the second wave to hit Gold beach and fight his way into Nazi Germany. He later told me that whilst out of ammunition, he and a friend had been captured by the SS outside of a prison camp. It was when moving in and out of consciousness whilst his fingernails were being ripped out, that he had, in pain and desperation, simply cried out, *"Jesus! It's Len!"* Amidst the blood, the agony and the shouting, he says that a great peace came over him and as he heard the voice, *"Len! It's Jesus!"* The door was then kicked open by rescuing Gurkha soldiers, who, after dealing with his captors, fell on Len, embracing him, crying, *"Master my master."* One of these fierce Nepalese warriors put him on his back, and carried him four miles to a field hospital and stayed with him until his recovery. Len never forgot that.

The leader of the service that morning had given way to Len, as he wanted to make an announcement. In a broad Northern accent Len began, *"Let us praise God together!"* The story went on that he had been woken that morning by the Padre of Lincoln prison who reported that the man Len had visited the previous week and spoken with until 1:30 in the morning had committed his life to Jesus! The prison governor was now apparently very happy that his worse inmate, once permanently handcuffed, was now out of shackles and praising God.

Len was 87 when I met him. He had been a Christian for 77 years! He was old school, you know? Grey hair parted to the right, pinstripe Sunday suit, black Bible and had been part of a Brethren Assembly for years. You've maybe seen the breed; you've maybe known the type. From another age, old, irrelevant, out of touch, useless.

Listen:

"Rather proclaim it, Westmoreland, through my host, That he which hath no stomach to this fight, Let him depart; his passport shall be made, And crowns for convoy put into his purse; We would not die in that man's company That fears his fellowship to die with us. This day is call'd the feast of Crispian. He that outlives this day, and comes safe home, Will stand a tip-toe when this day is nam'd, And rouse him at the name of Crispian. He that shall live this day, and see old age, Will yearly on the vigil feast his neighbours, And say 'To-morrow is Saint Crispian.' Then will he strip his sleeve and show his scars, And say 'These wounds I had on Crispian's day.' Old men forget; yet all shall be forgot, But he'll remember, with advantages, What feats he did that day. Then shall our names, Familiar in his mouth as household words - Harry the King, Bedford and Exeter, Warwick and Talbot, Salisbury and Gloucester - Be in their flowing cups freshly rememb'red. This story shall the good man teach his son; And Crispin Crispian shall ne'er go by, From this day to the ending of the world, But we in it shall be remembered - We few, we happy few, we band of brothers; For he to-day that sheds his blood with me Shall be my brother; be he ne'er so vile, This day shall gentle his condition; And gentlemen in England now-a-bed Shall think themselves accurs'd they were not here, And hold their manhoods cheap whiles any speaks That fought with us upon Saint Crispin's day. (----from Henry V)

Pray: Lord, come gentle my condition and allow me some battle scars to brag about in heaven in Your great name I pray, amen and let it be so!

Night-Whisper | **FIGHT**

Of Gurkhas and gherkins

A gherkin is a sweet little vegetable suitable for the hamburger generation. Last night at the boxing club, a local councilor in his seventies popped in to lend his support to the new endeavor. This one-legged veteran was in his seventies and had been up and working for the last 12 hours of the day getting a petition together for an old Gurkha colleague who was sick, infirm, destitute and deserted by the Government of the country he had fought for, and in urgent need of a pension. The old soldier still had a four-mile journey home in his electric invalid carriage, in the dark and in the rain. It was parked near the door, in the light, just in case the local teenagers vandalized it, trashed it or stole from it.

2 Samuel 21:15-17a

"War broke out again between the Philistines and Israel. David and his men went down to fight. David became exhausted. Ishbi-Benob, a warrior descended from Rapha, with a spear weighing nearly eight pounds and outfitted in brand-new armour, announced that he'd kill David. But Abishai son of Zeruiah came to the rescue, struck the Philistine, and killed him." (from THE MESSAGE:.)

I am preparing for a sermon series entitled: "War! What is it good for?" My answer shall be a Biblical one and so the answer shall not be, "Absolutely nothing!" Doing some background research on the subject then, I am reading the ***WWII War narrative of Major General Sir John Kennedy, entitled, 'The Business of War.'*** This man served in the war ministry for the length of WWII, being responsible to the Chief of the Imperial General Staff for all plans and operations. It's a fascinating read concerning the background state, preparations and ambitions of the British Empire around that particular period of just 60 odd years ago, or if you will, just two or three generations ago. I was chatting about those times with a woman in her early seventies just this morning and commented that this England in which we now live bore virtually no resemblance whatsoever to the one I was reading about and that I suspected that the folk who sacrificed so much during those dreadful times, even their very lives for the defense and continuance of our freedom, our culture and our country, might not have lain it all on the line so willingly for such a state as this. She agreed. Whichever way we cut this so sad a state of affairs, that we have to say that the freedom so valiantly fought for by that most recent of warring generations, has been in the peaceful aftermath, thrown away, frittered and lost. The oh so sad evidence of this is clearly seen in a poll taken of the present younger generation, who think that Winston Churchill is either a myth or a nodding dog that sells insurance! How did we come to this most paupered position? Well, it seems to me that although we won the war, we most dreadfully and most definitely lost the peace. And there we have it!

> *The present younger generation, who think that Winston Churchill is either a myth or a nodding dog that sells insurance!*

What we thought was the end of the war, was merely the end of an expression of the war, for it did in fact continue at more vicious a pace than ever, and the V3 rocket targets of utter destruction and total annihilation were our Christian values, especially where they were embodied in personal, sociological, institutional and ethical edifices. For those that can see then, the damage done to us after the physical hostilities had ended is of far greater damage than any done to us during the burning blitz.

Humanly speaking, I have to tell you that all is lost. For the church is presently like a one legged veteran gathering a petition for a sick friend, trying to find its own way home in the cold dark rain, trembling at the thought that the rubber wheels of its invalid carriage might be punctured by the sharp and ignorant teeth of politically correct and drug empowered, drunken youths.

But God. Yes, but God! And I tell you that it is only those two words that get me up in a morning. But God! Let us leaders all make prayerful and practical ways in this current death sentence, for those two most marvelous words to be redemptively expressed. BUT GOD! Let us rip the heads of the nodding dogs of our sick society and pray that God might raise up to us some spiritual war mongers, some new Churchill's, ready, at whatever the cost to fight the good fight once more. Now then is the time for us to pray and implore, that those troops of the Empire of The Son, who were birthed in the New World by the bloody efforts of the soldiers of the old, now long gone missionary people of these islands, would with all their power and might come to the aid, rescue and liberation of the old.

A gherkin is a sweet little vegetable suitable for the hamburger generation. A Gurkha is a soldier. Fierce, formidable, fanatical.

Listen: *"----- We shall defend our Island, whatever the cost may be, we shall fight on the beaches, we shall fight on the landing grounds, we shall fight in the fields and in the streets, we shall fight in the hills; we shall never surrender, and even if, which I do not for a moment believe, this Island or a large part of it were subjugated and starving, then our Empire beyond the seas, armed and guarded by the British Fleet, would carry on the struggle, until, in God's good time, the New World, with all its power and might, steps forth to the rescue and the liberation of the old." (Winston Churchill)*

Pray: Lord, from the sown seeds of the saints of old who from these islands took Your Word abroad, please send back to us the fruit of spiritual sustenance and deliverance, in Jesus name we pray, amen and let it be so.

| Vol 01 | Q4 | NW00316 | November 11th |

Night-Whisper | **REMEMBER**

Of bread and blood red wine,

and how to keep from falling on our "R"s

The 5.00am signing of the Armistice document which put an end to the ongoing hostilities of WWI between the Allies and Germany was signed today at Compiègne in France. Armistice Day is the anniversary of that symbolic end of World War I in 1918, and is brought to mind each and every year on the eleventh hour of the eleventh day of the eleventh month, when the guns stopped firing and at a long and much hoped for last, it finally became "all quiet on the Western front."

In England this act of remembrance is fully celebrated on Remembrance Sunday and in America it is celebrated on the 11th November and is called Veterans Day. The central symbol of this remembrance is the flower which proliferates itself all over the churned up grounds of Western Europe, that is, the blood red Poppy. There is no more fitting flower or color to remember the veterans of and "The Glorious Dead" of all our wars.

Granted, on the one hand, there is little glory in the manner of mass and industrialized killing. On the other hand, this term, 'Our Glorious Dead' is found on most

Revelation 19:11-16

"Now I saw heaven opened, and behold, a white horse. And He who sat on him was called Faithful and True, and in righteousness He judges and makes war. His eyes were like a flame of fire, and on His head were many crowns. He had a name written that no one knew except Himself. He was clothed with a robe dipped in blood, and His name is called The Word of God. And the armies in heaven, clothed in fine linen, white and clean, followed Him on white horses. Now out of His mouth goes a sharp sword, that with it He should strike the nations. And He Himself will rule them with a rod of iron. He Himself treads the winepress of the fierceness and wrath of Almighty God And He has on His robe and on His thigh a name written: KING OF KINGS AND LORD OF LORDS."

major war memorials all over these lands of ours, and is a testimony to the sacrifice they made against the onslaught of tyranny and also an especial testimony to the high regard the survivors placed upon the sacrifice of their fallen comrades, their families and their loved ones. Their Glorious Dead.

So, in symbols of stones and flowers all draped in silence, around our lands, there used to be a nationally observed two minute testimony to the Remembrance of that sacrifice. This quiet Remembrance brought with it a Respect for the valuable, sacrificial and dutiful offering of those lives. This was important, for you see, when the situations which led to the conflict were most thoroughly Recalled they led to a Resolve not to let it happen again. Unfortunately it is here that we all fall on our R's as it were, for not only is this silence now forcefully disdained by the ungrateful living but on the whole, such Resolve not to let the carnage happen again, when placed in the hands of the self-Righteous and sinning forgetful blind, has led to a peace at any price mentality, instead of a Righteousness at any cost way of life. Inevitably, such un-Righteous Resolve of "peace at any price," will lead to our Removal from the map and our Replacement on the scene by the onslaught of old evils dressed in new clothes. It's happening even now. Unfortunately, this generation is totally unable to meet the enemy. All of this is because we have forgotten that peace at any price is no peace at all. We have failed to remember this.

When such a Resolve not to let the carnage happen again is placed in the hands of the self-Righteous and sinning forgetful blind, it has led to a peace at any price mentality, instead of a Righteousness at any cost way of life.

Right Remembrance will lead to Real Respect coupled with accurate Recollection and therefore a Righteous Resolve to Re-arm our forces and Replenish our Reserves. My politics are not to the far right of Genghis Khan but rather, they are Rooted in Reality, for it is dreadfully obvious that darkness and evil take no prisoners in this world and so, for the flowers of peace and freedom to be enabled to continue to flourish, there must always be war, until once and for all, evil is finally ripped and removed from the hearts of nations and of men. Yes, there is such a thing as a righteous war. Evil shall be ripped from the planet and only Jesus can do this thoroughly and last I read, He is coming back, and this time is booted, spurred and armed to the teeth, to wage a final battle against the darkness. Until that time, He too calls us His people to Remembrance, and a such a Remembrance that it continually fuels our forgetters with dripping Red Reminders. Yes, the central symbols of this Remembrance for Christians are not stones and poppies but are the common a day items of the kitchen larder, even pure white bread and blood Red wine. So Christian when you are remembering the Lord in quiet reflection, remember that the purchase of righteousness was paid for at the ultimate cost. *Righteousness was won at the greatest of cost.* It always is. Let us not fail and fall on our R's but let us this day, REMEMBER.

Listen: *"Put on the whole armour of God, that you may be able to stand against the wiles of the devil. For we do not wrestle against flesh and blood, but against principalities, against powers, against the rulers of the darkness of this age, against spiritual hosts of wickedness in the heavenly places. Therefore take up the whole armour of God, that you may be able to withstand in the evil day, and having done all, to stand." (Ephesians 6:11-13 NKJV.)*

Pray: Lord, help us to stand against all unrighteousness even and especially if it is within our own beloved lands. We remember today then, the immense cost of our present freedom and so resolve in righteous ways, by Your grace and power, to wage war against all evil and all the works of darkness. Especially O Lord, we do not forget but most sincerely remember even Your great sacrifice for us. Thank you, thank you, thank you. Amen.

| Vol 01 | Q4 | NW00317 | November 12th |

Night-Whisper | **PASSION**

Where are the Ogres?

Some people have said, and I am one of them, that God is a poet. Others have said that up to 75% of the Old testament is Hebrew Poetry in some form or another? Friends, before we get to the whys' and wherefores' and sidestepping the vivisection of the technicalities of verse, let's try to answer this simple question of just 'What is poetry?'

For me, poetry is a combat combination of verbal punches, all arriving swiftly from different angles, with interlocking tempos all, and all delivered with but two purposes: first to open up the opposition and to get his guard down, maneuvering him rightly into a poleaxe position, and then secondly, to quite simply, knock his blooming block off!

What is poetry, but the occasional nod to the knowing intellect whilst most thoroughly massaging and messaging another soul. It is a racing heartbeat loosed of beta-blockers. It is 'Screaming Lord Such' in a long black topper singing about Jack the Ripper. It is hitting, moving, and unforgettable instruction, it is a hot chili that makes you go 'Wow!' and then repeats itself all the way through before searing the exit hole in hot remembrance.

Ezekiel 23:17-21

Then the Babylonians came to her, to the bed of love, and in their lust they defiled her. After she had been defiled by them, she turned away from them in disgust. When she carried on her prostitution openly and exposed her nakedness, I turned away from her in disgust, just as I had turned away from her sister. Yet she became more and more promiscuous as she recalled the days of her youth, when she was a prostitute in Egypt. There she lusted after her lovers, whose genitals were like those of donkeys and whose emission was like that of horses. So you longed for the lewdness of your youth, when in Egypt your bosom was caressed and your young breasts fondled. NIV

What is poetry? Well Robert Graves in an introduction to his poems about love says,

"Even nowadays an archaic sense of love-innocence recurs, however briefly, among most young men and women. Some few of these, who become poets, remain in love for the rest of their lives, watching the world with a detachment unknown to lawyers, politicians, financiers, and all other ministers of that blind and irresponsible successor to matriarchy and patriarchy — the mechanarchy."

….he goes on….

"Poets look forward to a final reign of love innocence when the so called impractical will once more become the inevitable, when miracles are accepted without surprise or question and when the patently illogical machine has at last performed its reduction 'ad absurdum,' by disintegrating."

I like that.

Certainly, the rise and rule of the machine is soon to reach its Zenith in iron and clay, and 'mechanarchy,' or as we call it today, transhumanism, shall become the wonder and way of the world. God will, never the less, destroy it and any entity that shall inhabit it. Meanwhile, despite decline on steroids, despite another Pastor found with his hand down a trouser, up a skirt or in a pocket, the 'mechanarchy' of the legacy church still continues to kill its 'prophet-poets,' for it finds them large, offensive, onerous and Ogre like in their munching of error and truth like burping ways. Graves in comparing 'Ogres to Pygmies' in his poem of the same name says,

> ***They dug great pits and heaped great cairns,***
> ***Deflected rivers, slew whole armies,***
> ***And hammered judgments for posterity***
> ***For the sweet cupid-lipped and tassel-yarded***
> ***Delicate-stomached dwellers***
> ***In Pygmy Alley, where with brooding on them***
> ***A foot is shrunk to seven inches***
> ***And twelve-pence will not buy a spare rib.***
>
> ***And who would choose between Ogres and Pygmies***
> ***The thundering text, the sniveling commentary***
> ***Reading between such covers he will likely***
> ***Prove his own disproportion and not laugh.***

The legacy church has long ago chosen between Ogres and Pygmies and populated her pulpits with small men and little women who sniveled out a talk for ten minutes on any odd Sunday when folks decided to turn up. Pygmy preachers they are who minimize the Most High and confine Him to the Phantom Zone of ten minutes of pure inconsequential drivel. Their mantra has been, "For God's sake let us make sure we never offend anyone!" To this they have been true and in such truth have lost the Kingdom.

What us Poetry? It is the preached word. It is a man with a black Geneva preaching gown clutching a .44 Magnum high above his head and firing it into the ceiling just to get people's attention. BANG! BANG! BANG! It is the passion and fire of well-set jewels delivered by grey haired men sporting purple hearts and dueling scars.

> *What us Poetry? It is the preached word, it is a man with a black Geneva preaching gown clutching a .44 Magnum high above his head and firing it into the ceiling just to get people's attention,*

What is Poetry? It is pure joy, that keeps you awake all night in happy expectation of the coming Lord's day all dressed in the glorious red of the Great David sacrificed, the rich russet of little David's redeemed hair, and the blue and white of that other Prince with God who was sometimes crackers. Poetry is quite simply the fulfilled expectation of delightful food for the soul. It is food that is full of light.

I tell you once again then, that if your visit to 'church' and the preaching of God's word, does not either leave you offended nor mended, yes, if it does not leave you neither broken in pieces nor crushed to powder, if it does not leave you neither set on fire nor taken higher, then my friend you have been in the presence of a Pygmy, even a small pulpit monkey, a failure in a frock, an effeminate weasel that surrendered to the snake a long, long time ago. I say again to you then, get out of there! Yes, get out and go and find an Ogre Poet, a Preacher who will reach ya! Go find a lover of God's Word who has remained in love with both it and Him, and where true signs and remarkable wonders are expected without surprise or question.

Ah, but where are the Ogres of today? I have found that the few that remain are banished and have gone to the high country to watch the flood of judgement fire come sweeping through the land.

Listen: *"Arise, shine; For your light has come! And the glory of the Lord is risen upon you. For behold, the darkness shall cover the earth, And deep darkness the people; But the Lord will arise over you, And His glory will be seen upon you. The Gentiles shall come to your light, And kings to the brightness of your rising. "Lift up your eyes all around, and see: They all gather together, they come to you; Your sons shall come from afar, And your daughters shall be nursed at your side. Then you shall see and become radiant, And your heart shall swell with joy; Because the abundance of the sea shall be turned to you, The wealth of the Gentiles shall come to you. The multitude of camels shall cover your land, The dromedaries of Midian and Ephah; All those from Sheba shall come; They shall bring gold and incense, And they shall proclaim the praises of the Lord. All the flocks of Kedar shall be gathered together to you, The rams of Nebaioth shall minister to you; They shall ascend with acceptance on My altar, And I will glorify the house of My glory. "Who are these who fly like a cloud, And like doves to their roosts? Surely the coastlands shall wait for Me; And the ships of Tarshish will come first, To bring your sons from afar, Their silver and their gold with them, To the name of the Lord your God, And to the Holy One of Israel, Because He has glorified you. (Isaiah 60:1-9 NKJV)*

Pray:

Arise my body, my small body, we have striven
Enough, and He is merciful; we are forgiven.
Arise small body, puppet-like and pale, and go,
White as the bed-clothes into bed, and cold as snow,
Undress with small, cold fingers and put out the light,
And be alone, hush'd mortal, in the sacred night,
-A meadow whipt flat with the rain, a cup
Emptied and clean, a garment washed and folded up,
Faded in colour, thinned almost to raggedness
By dirt and by the washing of that dirtiness.
Be not too quickly warm again. Lie cold; consent
To weariness' and pardon's watery element.
Drink up the bitter water, breathe the chilly death;
Soon enough comes the riot of our blood and breath.

'After Prayers, Lie Cold,' by CS Lewis

Night-Whisper | **CONTINUE**

The six measurements of a real man

A man is measured first by the size of his wallet, second by the size of possessions, third by the size of his genitals, fourth by the size of his muscles, fifth by his ability to conquer other men, and sixth by his philanthropy. Yes, in the world, a man is measured by these six things. Size and acceptable overcoming power is everything in the world. However, this scale of the earthly man's six points of measurement are set upon all things that are passing. For how can money, materials, muscle and might, be appreciated and seen to be of eternal value and consequence in a liver spotted bald and crooked old vegetable, or a corpse, a trust fund, or a broken down and moss covered old stone plinth?

1 Timothy 5:8

But if anyone does not provide for his own, and especially for those of his household, he has denied the faith and is worse than an unbeliever. NKJV

In the legacy church a man is measured first by his size of his congregation, second by the size of his social media following, third by the quiet breadth of his all-embracing non boat rocking ecumenism, fourthly by his maintained outward respectability, fifthly by the worldly success of his family, and sixthly by his outward compassion. Yes, in the legacy church, the respect of Sodom, the admiration of Babylon, size and impact, and therefore by extension, untainted worldly influence, is everything. For what is a 'ministry man' without worldly influence?

God's tape measure is marked with a very different scale to these two, however, and His six points on His scale of true manliness encompass all eternal depths!

God first measures a man then, is by the tensile strength of his personal adhesiveness. The Bible calls this faithfulness. God measures a man first by his faithfulness. Above all a man must be found faithful to the Word of God, faithful to the callings of God, faithful to the directions of God, and faithful to his wife!

God secondly measures a man by his willingness and action to provide for his own family. This is an extension of faithfulness to those in the immediate circle of his personal responsibility. Such willingness to work, must come before any ability to do so, for there are many lazy losers who have squandered their ability. Willingness coupled with action, shows a man's responsibility to provide for his own family.

God thirdly measures a man by his personal integrity. He is true to God and he is true to himself. He may well have right aspirations to improve his position, but concerning his own condition, he knows himself. He has a sober view of who he is. He is who he is. In him is no inward self-deluding guile, and no outward deceiving subterfuge. In him is no pretense nor pretentiousness. He is a truly honest man.

> *God thirdly measures a man by his personal integrity…… In him is no inward self-deluding guile, no outward subterfuge, no pretense nor pretentiousness. He is a truly honest man*

God fourthly measure a man by his daily contentment with necessities. This is a measure of thankful joy, it is a measure of knowing the passing of time, it is a measure of personal preparation for eternity, it is a measure of thankfulness, it is a measure of the acknowledgment of the true source of all things. For sure, a faithful man providing, should have both treasure and have store. But his joy and therefore his contentment is in the present day provision of food and clothing, of sustenance and covering. He is thankful in the basics, and without shirking his responsibilities of personal provision, acknowledges God for the ultimate providing of both his daily bread and his daily breath and also of God's continued morning mercies in any of his coming tomorrows. He is therefore a thankful and a happy man and is content with what he has today.

God fifthly measures a man by his long suffering patience, his continuance on the path of obedience and honor, and by extension therefore, of his well observed courage. This courage is not noted in a moment of glory, but is seen to be manifest in the minutes of each passing day. It is the outward expression of applied faithfulness and integrity, of work willingness, of contentment and joy, and of hope for the future. Courage is continuance on the path of God.

God lastly measures a man by his actions of sacrificial love. This is the binding cord of the former 'five a day,' and without such sacrificial love, everything else is become but a banging gong, an eternally unprofitable parade, and a foundation of sand which provides no lasting support for anything eternal. God's ultimate measure of a man, is of that man's actions in loving sacrificially.

Let me ask you tonight then. In God's eyes, are you a man?

Listen:

If you can keep your head when all about you
Are losing theirs and blaming it on you,
If you can trust yourself when all men doubt you,
But make allowance for their doubting too;
If you can wait and not be tired by waiting,
Or being lied about, don't deal in lies,
Or being hated, don't give way to hating,
And yet don't look too good, nor talk too wise:

If you can dream—and not make dreams your master;
If you can think—and not make thoughts your aim;
If you can meet with Triumph and Disaster
And treat those two impostors just the same;
If you can bear to hear the truth you've spoken
Twisted by knaves to make a trap for fools,
Or watch the things you gave your life to, broken,
And stoop and build 'em up with worn-out tools:

If you can make one heap of all your winnings
And risk it on one turn of pitch-and-toss,
And lose, and start again at your beginnings
And never breathe a word about your loss;
If you can force your heart and nerve and sinew
To serve your turn long after they are gone,
And so hold on when there is nothing in you
Except the Will which says to them: 'Hold on!'

If you can talk with crowds and keep your virtue,
Or walk with Kings—nor lose the common touch,
If neither foes nor loving friends can hurt you,
If all men count with you, but none too much;
If you can fill the unforgiving minute
With sixty seconds' worth of distance run,

Yours is the Earth and everything that's in it,
And—which is more—you'll be a Man, my son!

'If' – by Rudyard Kipling

Pray:

Disturb us, Lord, when We are too well pleased with ourselves,
When our dreams have come true
Because we have dreamed too little,
When we arrived safely
Because we sailed too close to the shore.
Disturb us, Lord, when
With the abundance of things we possess
We have lost our thirst
For the waters of life;
Having fallen in love with life,
We have ceased to dream of eternity
And in our efforts to build a new earth,
We have allowed our vision
Of the new Heaven to dim.
Disturb us, Lord, to dare more boldly,
To venture on wider seas
Where storms will show your mastery;
Where losing sight of land,
We shall find the stars.
We ask You to push back
The horizons of our hopes;
And to push into the future
In strength, courage, hope, and love.

A prayer attributed to Sir Francis Drake

| Vol 01 | Q4 | NW00319 | November 14th |

Night-Whisper | **FOCUS**

The 'Category 12 Demographic' of the modern day legacy church

The 'Cat. 12' demographic of the modern church is a testament to its imminent departure from the European scene. Why? Because we are NOT reaching virtually any of the majority of the vast indigenous population. This is very important to note. Sure, here and there and now and then, there are some slight exceptions but on the whole we are failing to engage and impact the majority indigenous people within the nations of Europe. Why is this? Well, I wonder if we examine the 'Cat. 12 demographics' of the current local British church whether we can find some reasons as to why?

James 1:23-25

For if anyone is a hearer of the word and not a doer, he is like a man observing his natural face in a mirror; for he observes himself, goes away, and immediately forgets what kind of man he was. But he who looks into the perfect law of liberty and continues in it, and is not a forgetful hearer but a doer of the work, this one will be blessed in what he does. NKJV

Here are some (very) general descriptors then of who we have become. Oh, and please note that these are general observations and not criticisms. However, no matter that the truth being that the local church provides millions of combined service hours to those in our communities, it is still an impossible task of getting those we serve to be converted and become part of the local church. This, it seems, has proved a virtual impossibility to us. It also goes without saying that those 'majority' folk we are serving, if they do become part of the congregation, that they are a very small segment of the same.

First then, the local church consists of the physically and mentally disabled. A loving, caring and safe environment will always attract many such folk living in the community to the local church. Because the Government, long time ago now, began embedding 'care in the community,' this has afforded loving local church communities the opportunity to provide, at the very least, emotional care and company for the disabled and the lonely. Some of these folks often do transition to regular Sunday services, however, I wonder if this is an extension of getting further emotional care and company? Therefore, should the majority indigenous people ever take a look at the their local church, it is seen to be there mostly for hurt and disabled people. It's not for them.

Secondly, the local church consists of grandmothers. These are usually the older ladies of the church. (Well, they would be!) They will provide the backbone of 'Kitchen services,' the toilet cleaning, the dusting and baby-sitting. 'Mums and Tots' will usually be managed by them as will the 'child care' on Sundays. Indeed, the grandmothers of today will usually have their own grandchildren in tow. Therefore, should the majority indigenous people ever take a look at the local church it is seen to be there mostly for hurt and disabled people, and old grannies with their screaming grandkids. It's not for them.

Thirdly the local church consists of the hairy-eared grandfather. Balding, going blind and often sporting an offensive halitosis, he's usually smiling and greeting people as they come into the church. He might even be a token elder

It might be because they have been looking for a fine Christian husband (good look with that one!)

sitting on the very old elder board, or a tight fisted trustee. Therefore, should the majority indigenous people ever take a look at the church, it is seen to be there mostly for hurt and disabled people, old grannies with their screaming grandkids, and funny old grandfathers. It's not for them.

Fourthly the local church consists of the odd lone single woman or the even more not too odd lonely wife. The lone woman, for whatever reason, has no mate beside her. It might be because they have been looking for a fine Christian husband (good look with that one!) or some other reasonable reason. Whatever, though they are still looking, they are now even older and lonelier. The lonely wife is very simply, one of a multitude of those desperate and self-deceived women who married the wrong bloke. He was not interested in Christ then or Christianity, and he isn't now either, though being a wee bit wise, he sure appreciates the benefits of a good looking, loving and ever faithful Christian wife. Therefore, should the majority indigenous people ever take a look at the church it is seen to be there mostly for hurt and disabled people, old grannies with their screaming grandkids, funny old grandfathers and lonely and hurt women. It's not for them.

Fifthly, the local church consists of the 'just out of spots' youths and early twenties, 'Giza job' Christian 'Yosser Hughs' types. If talented, they are leading the 'band' or the dwindling youth group. If they are not talented, they are taking care of the light and sound desk. They are mostly there because their mum goes to the church and so does their current batch of mates. When they move to college or university, they will usually never go back to any church, and if they do, it's because they hope to make it big in Christian music, 'find themselves' in Christian altruism or both. Therefore, should the majority indigenous people ever take a look at the church it is seen to be there mostly for mostly for hurt and disabled people, old grannies with their screaming grandkids, funny old grandfathers and lonely and hurt women, and young people struggling with guitars of relationships or both. It's not for them.

it's run by old Tory's and folks who want their kids to be like David Cameron

Sixthly, the local church consists of immigrant and asylum seekers. They are there to learn English and to be seen to be part of the Christian community. Whether their journey to this point has been fleeing, fearful, fraught or economic fantasy, should the majority indigenous people ever take a look at the local church, it is seen to be there mostly to provide succor and sustenance to those folks now 'over here,' taking their jobs and their housing, while imposing yet another non-indigenous culture upon them. The local church is seen to be there mostly for hurt and disabled people, old grannies with their screaming grandkids, funny old grandfathers, lonely and hurt women, just out of spots and into pants young people struggling with guitars of relationships, and foreigners destroying their culture and taking their jobs. It's not for them.

In at number seven of the local church demographic comes the ever hopeful middle class occasional male. They are like occasional tables and are just as solitary and separate. These are, never the less, the financial givers. The folks keeping the doors open for 'when God moves.' Therefore, should the majority indigenous people ever take a look at the church it is seen to be there mostly for hurt and disabled people, old grannies with their screaming grandkids, funny old grandfathers, lonely and hurt women, just out of spots and into pants young people struggling with guitars of relationships, foreigners destroying their culture and taking their jobs, and to top it all, it's run by old Tory's and folks who want their kids to be like David Cameron. It's not for them.

In at number eight, nine and ten are the homeless, the indigent, and the PC Walla (gay or otherwise) there to always prove a point. Eleven and twelve are of course Pastor Victoria, who it seems has no secrets whatsoever now, and the Rev. Och-Aye McKay, formerly of the Gay Gordons. Therefore, should the majority indigenous people ever take a look at the church, it is seen to be there mostly for hurt and disabled people, old grannies with their screaming grandkids, funny old grandfathers, lonely and hurt women, just out of spots and into pants young people struggling with guitars and/or relationships, foreigners "destroying our culture and taking our jobs," and to top it all, it's run by old Tory's and folks who want their kids to be like David Cameron, who, like the country, are all overrun with the poor, the poverty stricken, the homeless, a far too good a sprinkling of PC Walla's, fancy fairies with all their fans, women leaders and male leaders who wish they were women, all of whom seem to have become de-facto unpaid workers for continually failing government parties of every flavor, who long time since have emptied the pension funds and cut to destruction the funding of any former true social and national security. For the majority indigenous population, the local church is just not for them.

> ....*a far too good a sprinkling of PC Walla's, fancy fairies with all their fans, women leaders and male leaders who wish they were women.*

I would like to say that my 'Category 12 Demographic' was simply a fictional caricature for your amusement or annoyance and was created purely to foster in you a considered reflection. However, these are no caricatures, no, they are our very own repulsive nightmare! The present truth is stranger than fiction.

Some of you will say, "Well Robert, I am proud to be part of a church that ministers to the underdog, the underprivileged, the outcast and the underclasses." And I will stand and salute your endeavors as you slip beneath the waves of national inconsequentiality.

No, the two fold question remains for our urgent consideration: 1) How did we lose the majority population? 2) Maybe when we can answer that question, we can then ask, how do we win them back?

I would suggest that we lost the majority population when we lost our Biblical integrity and moved from a 'love us or loathe us we will not change in these Biblical imperatives' mentality, to a 'we will become whatever you want of us just so long as you like us' mentality. If this is indeed how we lost them, then, if there is a remnant left within this totally corrupt and compromised mess, it is time to for you to step outside and go set up a no nonsense stall once more, and start telling the Gospel of God to the majority population. Oh, and should there be a remnant in the compromised rubbish that want to stay within it, then you had better start a bloody revolution and a civil war whilst you are there to try and 'oik' out those terrible tares. If you do not, then you will be counted along with them and die in that same city of destruction.

> *If you do not, then you will be counted along with them and die in that same city of destruction*

Remnant, look around you now. Would you really want to bring a non-believer into this? Do you want them to become like everyone around you or even you, your very own person, which maybe even now you are beginning to loathe and despise for all these years of past compromise?

These are very hard words my friends, but I write them for those in very, very hard times. Don't hate me for these words. If I am wrong, then in ten years' time, you can laugh at how wrong I am now and was back then. If I am correct however, then in ten years' time, it will be far too late to make the necessary corrections. The fat lady of present willing blindness will have sung her last.

Listen: *And what accord has Christ with Belial? Or what part has a believer with an unbeliever? And what agreement has the temple of God with idols? For you are the temple of the living God. As God has said: "I will dwell in them And walk among them. I will be their God, And they shall be My people." Therefore "Come out from among them And be separate, says the Lord. Do not touch what is unclean, And I will receive you." 'I will be a Father to you, And you shall be My sons and daughters, Says the Lord Almighty." (2 Corinthians 6:15-18 NKJV)*

Pray: Father, is this what it has come to? Is this Your will? Then so be it. However, if there is any chance of winning the majority indigenous people, help us turn attention to the how. In Jesus name I ask it, amen and let it be so.

Night-Whisper | CONTINUE

Of suicidal spit and the true signs of salvation

Just in case you didn't know, the collective name for a gathering of prophets, is in fact "a school of prophets!" Now from our text tonight please note that there appears to be no geographical place called Naioth, which is currently known. However, as the Hebrew word here word means "dwellings" some believe that it is likely that Naioth was in fact the name of the collegiate residence of this school of prophets, in, or maybe just outside, Ramah. The great water cisterns in that place, I believe could be seen as metaphors for the gathering of that same spirit of prophecy that resided there, like an enveloping cloud. So much so that people entering the cloud became wet with capacity, overwhelmed with propensity, and overcome by the ability to speak forth words from God. The old questioning saying of, "Is Saul also among the prophets?" is resurrected here because of the manifestation of this gift upon him in particular. My answer to that question is a resounding no!

1 Samuel 19:18-21

"So David fled and escaped, and went to Samuel at Ramah, and told him all that Saul had done to him. And he and Samuel went and stayed in Naioth. Now it was told Saul, saying, 'Take note, David is at Naioth in Ramah!' Then Saul sent messengers to take David. And when they saw the group of prophets prophesying, and Samuel standing as leader over them, the Spirit of God came upon the messengers of Saul, and they also prophesied. And when Saul was told, he sent other messengers, and they prophesied likewise. Then Saul sent messengers again the third time, and they prophesied also. Then he also went to Ramah, and came to the great well that is at Sechu. So he asked, and said, 'Where are Samuel and David?' And someone said, 'Indeed they are at Naioth in Ramah.' So he went there to Naioth in Ramah. Then the Spirit of God was upon him also, and he went on and prophesied until he came to Naioth in Ramah." NKJV.

There was a man sent by Jesus who also gathered himself into another collective grouping, the assembly of the apostles. This man was sent to heal the sick, raise the dead, and in the so doing, he lived by faith, enjoying the life of an itinerant minister, eating frugally and thankfully, yes, blessing the people and heartily preaching the coming of the Kingdom of God. (Matthew 10:1-13). His name was Judas and he sold his Master for thirty pieces of silver.

I have lived long enough to see a number of nationally applauded, well-loved and well respected preachers, teachers and so called miracle workers, all go to the wall. Yes, I have seen their suicidal spit drench the cheek of Christ. I tell you tonight friends, that even though the whole of the Christian world would in embarrassed shame rather forget these symbols of our own culpable gullibility, these dreadful disasters are nevertheless of great importance to us, for they teach us that neither gifting nor anointing is a sign of true salvation. No, there are in the end only two real signs of this: The Fruit of The Holy Spirit and perseverance in the Faith. Scary, but true.

> *Yes, I have seen their suicidal spit drench the cheek of Christ. I tell you tonight friends, that even though the whole of the Christian world would in embarrassed shame rather forget these symbols of our own culpable gullibility, these dreadful disasters are nevertheless of great importance to us, for they teach us that neither gifting nor anointing is a sign of true salvation*

Listen: *"And when they had preached the Gospel to that city and made many disciples, they returned to Lystra, Iconium, and Antioch, strengthening the souls of the disciples, exhorting them to continue in the faith, and saying, 'We must through many tribulations enter the kingdom of God.'" (Acts 14:21-23 NKJV.)*

Pray: Stick with me O Lord my God and then I shall indeed stick at it. Lord, if You are not with, let me not even open my mouth. Amen and let it be so.

Night-Whisper | **REST**

Quiet Querencias

Hemmingway, in his 1932 published book *Death in The Afternoon*, writes a treatise on the source and descriptions of courage and fear, as displayed through the spectacle of the Spanish bullfight, and in so doing, highlights the most dangerous place for the Matador in his attempt at slaughter, and that is, the Querencia.

Psalm 27:4

"One thing I have desired of the Lord, That will I seek: That I may dwell in the house of the Lord all the days of my life, to behold the beauty of the Lord, and to inquire in His temple." NKJV

There are in effect three phases to a bullfight.

First the Levantado, where the giant bull arrives on the scene, proud and angry, its giant neck holding high its impaling horns. At this point the bull's mighty musculature of a neck is lanced repeatedly by the Picadors and the sharp knives of the razor Banderilleros. The bleeding neck muscles cause the bull to slowly lower its horns.

The second phase is the Parado where the bull is now slowed and kept at bay.

Eventually the slaughter moves to the final phase, the Aplomado, where the exhausted bull now transfixed on but one red object straight ahead, is thrust through by the matador, his sword plunging down through the center of the sorry bulls now tired neck, severing in two its pumping heart. The crowd cheers, Roses and seats are thrown in the arena, people applaud profusely!

Observers will notice that in each stage the fighting bull will keep returning to one particular point in the ring. That one point of constant return is it's Querencia, its defendable position of felt safety. All animals and all humans have this kind of returned position, this home as it were, this defendable place of felt safety. It is said that if the matador tries to kill the bull whilst it is in its Querencia, then undoubtedly the matador will be badly gored, even killed. The matador's intent then, is always to get the bull out of its Querencia. Do you see my point?

Friends, tonight this bullfighting picture may be a very uncomfortable contemplation for some of you, but nevertheless, it is a very necessary one. If the Devil is the matador that plays us each to death, then let us note that we each have our own Querencia, our defendable place of felt safety. This is a place from which we gain sustenance, from which we gain strength, from which we gain respite from the heat of our days. Your personal Querencia maybe a physical place, it may be an occupation, it may be a group of acquaintances, or it may be as simple as a hot bath or as profound as a week in a monastery, but for you it is your Querencia!

> *If the Devil is the matador that plays us each to death, then let us note that we each have our own Querencia, our defendable place of felt safety.*

Get regularly to your own Querencia and make it the secret place of your fellowship with the Mosh High, for be sure of this: If you are tired, bloodied, and walking with your head and horns down and not in your Querencia, then the devil is out to kill you and it will be by a piercing through your heart. The devil will slice your heart in two. Remember this.

Listen: *"For in the time of trouble He shall hide me in His pavilion; In the secret place of His tabernacle He shall hide me; He shall set me high upon a rock. And now my head shall be lifted up above my enemies all around me" (Psalms 27:5-6 NKJV)*

Pray: Oh lead me, to the place where I can find You. Oh lead me, to the place where You will be. Lead me to the cross, where we first met, draw me to my knees, so we can talk. Let me feel Your breath, let me know You're here with me. Oh lead me, to the place where I can find You. Amen, and let it be so. (Delirious)

Night-Whisper | **FAITHFUL**

God the Grandfather and N.O.M.A.N.

In the Coen brothers' 2003 film *Intolerable Cruelty*, George Clooney stars as Miles Massey, the cynical attorney who is highly specialized in breaking marriages apart and making the divorce as profitably as possible for his client, regardless of their own personal culpability in the divorce! The leading lady in the film is Catherine Zeta Jones who plays Marilyn Rexroth, a woman choosing to marry men who are exceptionally rich and astonishingly silly and therefore very likely to commit adultery, thus giving her the excuse to divorce them so she can in turn then win a massive financial settlement from them, which will make her independent of all men! The dialogue, the acting, the timing, the humor of the movie is in my opinion, all quite brilliant and very Coen-esque.

The main speech of the *Intolerable Cruelty* concerning all the possibilities and vulnerabilities of true and selfless, sacrificial love, is made by the character Miles Massey at his keynote address which is given at the annual convention of his professional association. The association is cleverly called: The National Organization of Matrimonial Attorneys Nationwide. I remember watching the movie and seeing their organizational logo and motto in the background of the main

Malachi 2:13-16

"So He does not regard the offering anymore, Nor receive it with goodwill from your hands. Yet you say, 'For what reason?' Because the Lord has been witness Between you and the wife of your youth, With whom you have dealt treacherously; Yet she is your companion And your wife by covenant. But did He not make them one, Having a remnant of the Spirit? And why one? He seeks godly offspring. Therefore take heed to your spirit, And let none deal treacherously with the wife of his youth. 'For the Lord God of Israel says That He hates divorce, For it covers one's garment with violence,' says the Lord of hosts. 'Therefore take heed to your spirit, That you do not deal treacherously.'" NKJV

dialogue and emblazoned underneath it was the fictional association's most hilarious tag line, here it is... "What God hath joined, let N.O.M.A.N. put asunder." It was a most clever and hilarious contrivance and I laughed considerably!

In the real world however, divorce is not funny and it remains exceptionally painful for many, many years, often times even a lifetime. There is very little laughter in it, I can tell you that. Divorce remains financially painful, it remains emotionally painful, it remains relationally painful, and in my Pastoral observance of it over the years, it remains painful for the rest of a person's life. Friend, there is no condemnation in my writing this tonight because the saying, **"there but for the grace of God go I"** most certainly applies to me and my wife. We each have ten things, which have kept our marriage together: our fingernails! God has been very gracious to us. Indeed, I say to all people who are still married to their first spouse, **"God has been very gracious to you!"** Be careful then in your often unwarranted and sometimes very ignorant judgment of others, for none of us really knows what goes on behind closed doors.

> *Divorce remains financially painful, it remains emotionally painful, it remains relationally painful, and in my Pastoral observance of it over the years, it remains painful for the rest of a person's life.*

Nevertheless in our text for this evening God says several important things to us and hangs them all on one massive nail! "I hate divorce!" Listen to how "The Message" brings this climactic statement to our attention:

"And here's a second offence: You fill the place of worship with your whining and sniveling because you don't get what you want from God. Do you know why? Simple. Because God was there as a witness when you spoke your marriage vows to your young bride, and now you've broken those vows, broken the faith-bond with your vowed companion, your covenant wife. God, not you, made marriage. His Spirit inhabits even the smallest details of marriage. And what does he want from marriage? Children of God, that's what. So guard the spirit of marriage within you. Don't cheat on your spouse. "I hate divorce," says the God of Israel. God-of-the-Angel-Armies says, "I hate the violent dismembering of the 'one flesh' of marriage." So watch yourselves. Don't let your guard down. Don't cheat.

Divorce is indeed, the violent dismembering of the 'one flesh' of marriage. So watch yourselves tonight. Don't let your guard down. Don't cheat on your mate. To help you and heal you, I have three things for your consideration this evening:

In any event, to men in particular the Scriptures clearly speak tonight, don't be a traitor. Don't cheat on your wife!

First, if you are divorced, there is no need to keep adding to your existing pains. Self-condemnation, anger at your former spouse and a multitude of other leather tails of self-flagellation, will only fan the flames of hurt and keep the blood flowing and the wounds from healing. It's time to heal. Get with God and get it sorted. Forgive yourself.

Secondly, I want to tell you, especially those of you struggling in your marriage, that God is interested in marriage. Indeed, God is interested, immersed and inhabiting all aspects of your marriage. Be aware of that. Prayerfully seek Him then in every part of your marriage. Every part of it I say, for He will indeed help you in every part of your marriage.

Thirdly, don't mess up the covenant and if you've messed up, then please don't keep messing up. The Bible here I think is particularly speaking to men and I wonder if it is speaking to older more well off men especially. I mean older men who compared to their wives are more well-off financially, more well-off opportunistically, more well-off physically, more well-off health wise maybe? I wonder? Don't cheat on your wife! With great sadness, I note how many Pastors have been discovered on the hacking of the Ashlely Maddison cheating website. What the flying fish is going on here! It seems even the men of God are caught in the epidemic of infidelity*!* In any event, to men in particular the Scriptures clearly speak tonight; don't be a traitor.

If you are a called Pastor involved in this stuff tonight. May I say to you, "Judas! Get out."

Listen: *"And He answered and said to them, 'Have you not read that He who made them at the beginning "made them male and female," and said, 'For this reason a man shall leave his father and mother and be joined to his wife, and the two shall become one flesh'? So then, they are no longer two but one flesh. Therefore what God has joined together, let not man separate." Matthew 19:4-6 NKJV*

Pray: Mercy Lord, please forgive us our many sins and our traitorous hearts. Mercy Lord, and despite our many sins, we ask that you wash us and make us clean, that You change us from traitors into people of honor and integrity and courage. Make us new O Lord and make us stronger too. Yes, make us a testimony to Your grace and to Your love and to Your redemption, do it in such a renewing, regenerating and revitalizing way that our offspring would rise up, and be amazed! Indeed, that they would rise up refreshed and call us Godly parents! Mercy Lord, mercy, for we wish to be Godly and to give You the Godly offspring of Your heart's desire. In Jesus name we ask it, amen and let it be so.

| Vol 01 | Q4 | NW00323 | November 18th |

Night-Whisper | **REPENT**

Of silver foxes and the strangulation of all our secret sins

Folklore has it, that the devil himself made the black fox, that it might hide in the shadow of a man, an invisible presence, an unseen foe that will bring nothing but woe.

Luke 13:32a

"And He said to them, 'Go, tell that fox,-------'" NKJV.

Actually, the black fox is better known as the silver fox and it is thought that when they were originally bred in captivity for the purpose of the fur trade, their offspring were, whether by accident or with intent, eventually let loose upon the wild population. In any event, the black fox is indeed an aberration of nature.

Though they can be seen in the day and early evening, foxes are predominantly creatures of the night and for tonight, I think the black fox is a fitting metaphor for all our pet sins, which we have bred in secret captivity, for they too are creatures of the night.

Whenever we think we have control over a particular sin, and in secret fondle it, take it out and pet it, even hold it to our heart, it may only seem to us to be but a small and black little thing which we can easily control, but I tell you, it will grow and it will grow. It will get loos and it will breed! Now tell me, what are you thinking about when you breed that particular of a sin? Surely, though it cannot bear its teeth, (no, foxes cannot bear their teeth and snarl) its nevertheless soft and silver fur, coupled with its slit like yellow eyes, which make navigation in the darkness a slippery and simple thing for the cat like dog, surely they should tell you something of its haunting intent? Surely, they should tell you something of the danger. Don't you even smell it yet? Are you a dummy?

Friends, you must never make pets of these little black fox sins, for they will escape and for long time to come, even though you thought yourself rid of the tiny little thing, they shall dog your steps, skulking in the shadow of yourself and destroying all your vines. If you have any secret silver foxes tonight, I suggest you strangle them quickly with a certain confession and then bury them deep with the spade of true repentance. If you do not, then be assured they will grow up into Herod and make all your Rachel's weep.

Listen: *"Catch us the foxes, the little foxes that spoil the vines, for our vines have tender grapes." (Song of Solomon 2:15 NKJV)*

Pray: Lord tonight, help me to strangle all my silver foxes and bury them deep. Lead me from the stinking cages of all my self-contempt, in Jesus name I ask it, amen.

| Vol 01 | Q4 | NW00324 | November 19th |

Night-Whisper | ACTION

The soon coming 'Wonders of The Lord'

Contrary to the thoughts and prayers and desires of many good people, I do not believe God will revive the church in the West. Frankly, there is nothing left to revive in much of it, and worse than that, I do believe the Lord of the church is projectile vomiting the majority of it out of his mouth. Have you noticed how the outside of empty church buildings, and there are many in the UK, all look like a pile of pavement vomit, wretched from a high heeled 'ladette' after a Saturday night binge and cold comfort curry?

Job 14:7-9 NKJV

"For there is hope for a tree, If it is cut down, that it will sprout again, And that its tender shoots will not cease. Though its root may grow old in the earth, And its stump may die in the ground, Yet at the scent of water it will bud And bring forth branches like a plant.

Some bright-eyed professional middle-class brother (they are always middle class) accosted me yet again just the other day regarding my millennial position asking, "Are you pre-millennial?" He asked. "That would account for your pessimism regarding the influence of the church in this present age?" My response was to simply to ask him, "Are you on heavy anti-depressant medication?" Forgive me brethren, but if you are 'Post-mill' or 'A-mill' in your millennial position, well nowadays, not only do I believe your eschatological conclusions are hermeneutically and historically incorrect, but I think you need psychological counselling! Now I have offended a large number of you, my medical instructions to you are even so, by the by. You see, the real purpose of this particular Night Whisper is to point out the greatly positive aspect of my historical pre-millennial, and present non-revival position. In brief, I want to tell you that I have a growing hope for the immediate future. Why?

Personally, I dislike the Biblical term 'remnant.' For me, in its present Christian cultural usage I find it far to exclusive. It may be a matter of simple semantics, but I much prefer the unusual phrase of 'Holy

stump!' The picture of a tree stump, fully rooted, flowering and fruited gets me so excited that I can let the present expressions of church drown in the vomit of her Lord. I can let the closures come, let the buildings be turned into pubs. Let Mosques occupy what were long time ago now, places of true worship to the one and only Triune God. I can do this because I see Christ is judging the church.
THEREFORE, LET THE FIRE FALL! Let the branch loping begin. Let the leaf-burning make our eyes water and the crackle of dry twigs fill our ears. Let the ground clearance be brought to a speedy conclusion and in it all, let only a holy stump remain. Bring in the bulldozers Lord and let no tears be seen to fall. Yes, let there be no mourning for the dead, for

> *One great sign of their abandonment by God is this, that they only contain rats, willful women and abandoned children.*

the judgment of the Lord is right; the judgment of the Lord is good, the judgment of the Lord is altogether necessary. When the morning comes, in the clearance of the misty grey, let us see the Holy stump. Solitary, firm, immovable, flowering, fruitful, rooted, ready and waiting. This my friends, is what I am looking for, and I do not think we shall find it in the present expression of the Western church.

Indeed, should God move in a most gracious and unprecedented way in our nations, my deep suspicion is that it will be outside of our present infiltrated and corrupt church systems. These messy and sticky old fungus filled wine skins could never hold the New Wine of God. Therefore, not only do we need to look and pray for a 'move' of God outside of the church structures, but the Holy people of God need to leave the corrupted structures and preach the Word in the deeps. I believe when we do this, we shall need other Holy partners to help us pull in the catch. If this is the case my friend, why are you still manning dead men's boats? No wonder you have fished all night and caught absolutely nothing. You have been part of the crew of the Marie Celeste, the Baychimo, the Octavius, or of the Flying Dutchman, or even the Titanic! Can these ships of the line ever be repaired? No. Leave them alone. Indeed, one great sign of their abandonment by God is this, that they only contain rats, willful women and abandoned children. I hope that most terrible picture makes you think a little deeper and act a lot more decisively.

To remain sane, to remain hopeful, to remain energized, is to leave the rotten hulls of the past, get in some new boats and go and fish in the regions beyond you. Yes, I see it now, it is *"Those who go down to the sea in ships, who do business on great waters, they see the works of the Lord, and His wonders in the deep." (Psalms 107:23-24 NKJV.)*

Listen: *Then He got into one of the boats, which was Simon's, and asked him to put out a little from the land. And He sat down and taught the multitudes from the boat. When He had stopped speaking, He said to Simon, "Launch out into the deep and let down your nets for a catch." But Simon answered and said to Him, "Master, we have toiled all night and caught nothing; nevertheless at Your word I will let down the net." And when they had done this, they caught a great number of fish, and their net was breaking. So they signaled to their partners in the other boat to come and help them. And they came and filled both the boats, so that they began to sink. When Simon Peter saw it, he fell down at Jesus' knees, saying, "Depart from me, for I am a sinful man, O Lord!" For he and all who were with him were astonished at the catch of fish which they had taken; and so also were James and John, the sons of Zebedee, who were partners with Simon. And Jesus said to Simon, "Do not be afraid. From now on you will catch men." So when they had brought their boats to land, they forsook all and followed Him. (Luke 5:3-11 NKJV)*

Pray: Deliver us O God our Father, from the prison hulls of our own choosing, from the wrecks of our own making, from the cold rocks and breaking waves of Your own destructive and righteous actions. Lord Jesus, these terrible calamities have been whistled downed the wind by Your own sweet lips. Thank you. Now Lord send some men of war, some bright-flagged salts from afar, to come and pick up the survivors. Then together, let us push out into the deeps to see once again 'The Wonders of the Lord.' Amen and let it be so.

Night-Whisper | **TOUGH**

Praying Until You Taste The Blood

Ah, what can ail thee, knight-at-arms,
Alone and palely loitering?
The sedge is withered from the lake,
And no birds sing.

(John Keats - La Belle Dame Sans Merci)

I used to live just a five-minute walk away from the former playground of Georgian gentry and Royalty. This Colonnade Walkway I speak of is called The Pantiles and was originally paved with S-shaped roofing tiles of the same name. The place is now so famous that the area of The Pantiles was proposed to become a world heritage site! The main reason for the existence of this area, indeed the whole town around it, is the discovery made by a drunken Nobleman called Dudley Lord North, who, upon returning home after getting smashed out of his skull with his friends, then being dry mouthed and drooping from his horse, happened to spot a reddish water, seeping out of the ground. He drank it, felt revived, informed his friends of the red water's properties of rejuvenation and "hey voila!" An iron rich watery star was born.

John 7:38-39

"'He who believes in Me, as the Scripture has said, out of his heart will flow rivers of living water.' But this He spoke concerning the Spirit, whom those believing in Him would receive; for the Holy Spirit was not yet given, because Jesus was not yet glorified."
NKJV

I have sipped the water of that famous spring, drinking from a glass stained red by the high iron content of the water. It tasted like blood. Did you know that same living water springing from the belly of the Christian, the center of our being, also tastes of blood for it is also full of iron. I mean the waters of His life, of eternal life, are just jam packed full of iron. The precious blood of Jesus you see, is fortified with ferrous from the nails upon the tree!

From this great fact, I need to remind you tonight, that Christ never yet bred anemic Christians. There are no chocolate soldiers in His ranks and no one that will not be fortified by the springs from heaven bubbling up within them. You see, the springs of heaven are Chalybeate springs, tasting of His blood, putting iron in your backbone and strength in your veins. So, if you cannot taste His blood in your mouth tonight, if you are stooped and not upright, if you are frail and palely loitering fair knight of the King, then I tell you, I'd suspect that so called spring in you, for it just might not be His! Yes, if you are that pale and wretched knight, that poor human being, that pitiful Christian, then you need to pray tonight! Yes, you need to clear the well and then pray and pray again, yes, you must keep on praying until you taste the blood.

> *The springs of heaven are Chalybeate springs, tasting of His blood, putting iron in your backbone and strength in your veins.*
>
> *KEEP ON PRAYING UNTIL YOU TASTE THE BLOOD!*

Listen: *"And in that day you will say: 'O Lord, I will praise You; Though You were angry with me, Your anger is turned away, and You comfort me. Behold, God is my salvation, I will trust and not be afraid. For Yah, the Lord, is my strength and song; He also has become my salvation.'" Therefore with joy you will draw water from the wells of salvation. (Isaiah 12:1-3 NKJV.)*

Pray: Let the living waters testify of Your presence within me! So, spring up O iron waters and fill my mouth with the taste of blood, the taste of nails pulled from the wood. Amen and let me know I am Yours.

| Vol 01 | Q4 | NW00326 | November 21ˢᵗ |

Night-Whisper | **COMMIT**

Sweet smiles and sheer lies

The title of tonight's Whisper is how Eugene Peterson's "The Message," translates our opening text. I think it most accurate, for I have found both ever and always, that a divided heart can be nothing else but a deceptive heart full of sweet smiles masking sheer lies.

Hosea 10:2a

"Their heart is divided; Now they are held guilty." NKJV.

Whenever we are of two minds, whenever we are indecisive, we shall become full of deception. We shall deceive ourselves into thinking anything but the truth about the situation, and while this most selfish of self-deceptions continues, we shall inevitably deceive others regarding our directions, actions and intentions. Deception will inevitably mean a spreading of the legs and of placing a foot in two camps. Aer YOU listening! This trepidatious condition will put us off balance and shall inevitably result in a fall and the frightening thing is that this spreading of the legs can begin to happen so very subtly indeed. Fortunately, there is a telltale sign for us to watch out for. Attend to this, and the slow slippery leg spreading will be reversed. I am of course talking about the sign of 'Disguise.'

Take note within yourselves, that whenever you are disguising your true feelings, whenever you are disguising your true heart intentions, with your false countenance, your suspect whereabouts, your hidden bank account, your altered sale amount, then you are donning a disguise. Careful now, for your legs are spreading.

The double answer of course to the symptom of Disguise is that of focus and integrity. Whatever the task, whatever the purpose, whatever the relationship, there is great safety in a singleness of heart, a singleness of heart that decisively pursues, loves and commits to the leaving of all other things. This is true integrity of purpose. So, if your legs are beginning to spread tonight then you had best drop the disguises and come to a focused and safe, most singleness of heart.

Listen: *"You shall love the Lord your God with all your heart, with all your soul, and with all your strength." (Deuteronomy 6:5 NKJV.)*

Pray: Lord, forgive my spreading legs and help me to be a one camp person, focused and solid, steadfast and sure, lest I be found guilty before Your throne, in Jesus name I ask it, amen and let it be so.

| Vol 01 | Q4 | NW00327 | November 22ⁿᵈ |

Night-Whisper | **PREPARE**

Suited, booted and ready. Having no sympathy for the Devil.

It was in Dallas today in 1961 that President John F Kennedy was assassinated. Nearly forty years on from this event it is interesting that over 70% of Americans believe that this assassination of the president was a conspired removal plot.

Revelation 19:19-20

"And I saw the beast, the kings of the earth, and their armies, gathered together to make war against Him who sat on the horse and against His army."
NKJV

Though intriguing, the roots of these many conspiracy theories are at best, tangled. Yet nevertheless, they all point to some form of secret and shadowy forces hid in the background of world affairs moving and manipulating for their own sordid means, protection, greed and gain. For what it's worth, before Jackie said a word, I was told it was Lyndon B Johnson who had Kennedy assassinated. (You heard it here first!)

Evil has been around for a long time friends and Lucifer, it's not so hidden head, has been waging war against the saints and more particular against their Lord, for unknown ages. We are privileged to have access to the high points of this long battle if not its intricate historical developments but make no mistake, this long war has developed and is developing still.

Be assured that the enemy though thoroughly defeated at Calvary, is not convinced of its ultimate demise and Lucifer in his anger and in his pride continues to marshal his forces, his satraps, his own 'blood bought' dynasties against the marvelous moving of the Most High God.

Evil has been around a long, long time. It has big plans, big people in its pay and big bad things at its heart. We may all mostly be but little players on this present stage, poor foot soldiers as it were, warriors only for the working day maybe but be assured of this, that the devil is out to take you out!

Like it or not, we all have a gun pointing at our head, so watch out dear friends, watch out. Get booted, suited and ready for your part in the fight which is so surely to come upon us with an even greater ferocity than ever before in history. Are you ready soldier?

Listen: *"The Beast had a loud mouth, boastful and blasphemous. It could do anything it wanted for forty-two months. It yelled blasphemies against God, blasphemed his Name, blasphemed his Church, especially those already dwelling with God in Heaven. It was permitted to make war on God's holy people and conquer them. It held absolute sway over all tribes and peoples, tongues and races. Everyone on earth whose name was not written from the world's foundation in the slaughtered Lamb's Book of Life will worship the Beast. Are you listening to this? They've made their bed; now they must lie in it. Anyone marked for prison goes straight to prison; anyone pulling a sword goes down by the sword. Meanwhile, God's holy people passionately and faithfully stand their ground." Revelation 13:5-10 from, THE MESSAGE*

Pray: Lord, deliver me from paranoia into the truth of Your word and let Your peace reign in my open eyes. Blessed be the Lord my Rock, who trains my hands for war and my fingers for battle, my loving kindness and my fortress, my high tower and my deliverer, my shield and the One in whom I take my refuge. Amen!

| Vol 01 | Q4 | NW00328 | November 23rd |

Night-Whisper | **WATCH**

Destroying distraction

The dumbing down of television continues, but evidence of its global dimension to dumb down so thoroughly and with such entertaining zest, was found in the 1980s CBS Television series called *Dallas*. The story of a corrupt and powerful, wealthy family in the rich oil business was encapsulated by the seedy and steely lead character, a Mr. John Ross Ewing as he was known to both his friends and his enemies. Like all evil characters in pantomime, John Ross Ewing got his comeuppance when a secret assassin tried to kill him. Today in 1980, many estimate that some 350 million people tuned in their television sets to find out just who shot JR Imagine that! 350 million people!

1 Corinthians 16:13-14

"Watch, stand fast in the faith, be brave, be strong." NKJV

Distraction is a key form of attack in the devil's plan to keep people in utter blindness. Entertainment has always been a key conduit for disinformation, disarmament, disability and distraction to be drip fed to the masses. Now don't get me wrong here, it works both ways in that entertainment is also a conduit for truth, armament, endowed ability and focus! Yes and because of this, it has always been and will increasingly become a key battleground for the truth. I am not against entertainment but want you to become aware tonight that when you open yourself to it, you are indeed being warred upon.

Time is short and the coming of the Lord draweth nigh. Do not be distracted by silliness, do not be misled or misinformed, Do not be pacified, petrified or putrefied by little pixels of every kind because I tell you this, whenever the enemy gets you distracted, he shall try and rip your bowels out with a blunt and rusty knife. Watch how you watch. Watch what you watch. Watch where you watch. Watch who you watch.

Listen: *"Remember therefore how you have received and heard; hold fast and repent. Therefore if you will not watch, I will come upon you as a* *thief, and you will not know what hour I will come upon you."* Revelation 3:3 NKJV

Pray: Guide me in my looking Lord, Savior, show me what to see, in all my fretful glances God, may my watching eyes alight on Thee. Amen.

| Vol 01 | Q4 | NW00329 | November 24th |

Night-Whisper | **CONSIDER**

Shocking Roman Catholics and the problem of pain

It was Oxford University, which, in 2008, despite the dire economic climate, showed to the world that they had more money than sense, when they took a dozen Roman Catholics and a dozen atheists and stuck them in an MRI brain scanner. While these two dozen, desperate for a few quid in their pocket sets of guinea pigs lay cocooned in the resonator, scientists gazed astonishingly at the part of the brain which modulated the mechanisms of neural pain reception, for whilst administering electric shock therapy to them, they discovered that whilst the Roman Catholics meditated on a picture of *The Madonna*, they were able to withstand more pain than the atheist, who by the way, were simply gazing at an old Da Vinci's painting of *Lady With An Ermine*. Conclusion: It is far easier to burned at the stake of you're a believer providing you have a positive image to focus on. The response from an Anglican Bishop was typical when he said, "Of course we should expect this, for faith changes people's perceptions." "Admittedly," one psychologist later remarked, "we could probably get the same results in atheists, providing we shocked them when they themselves had a more personal and positive image placed in front of them!" Say, Madonna or maybe Maradonna, or even a Mars bar. I tell you, the world has gone mad.

1 Corinthians 10:13

"No temptation has overtaken you except such as is common to man; but God is faithful, who will not allow you to be tempted beyond what you are able, but with the temptation will also make the way of escape, that you may be able to bear it." NKJV

No, you don't have to have faith in Jesus Christ or God The Father to learn how to control pain. However, as I write, though I do have faith in Christ right now, my lower left molar is still throbbing like a red-hot rivet! Looking at Oxford's declared faith and pain conclusions, I have to conclude that, either my mind control techniques are awful, or my faith in Jesus Christ is pitiful. If that is the case, then I find it all rather discouraging for despite all those Christians running around Toronto now able to eat peanut brittle chocolate because of new heavenly gold fillings, it would appear the master dentist Himself, refuses to fix my very own present throbbing molar. It's painful, it's not fair and frankly in my opinion, teeth are a terrible design flaw anyway. What's a man to do? Also, why does God give Gold fillings and not put new everlasting batteries in heart pacemakers, or change the prescription of my spectacles for me without a visit to the optician? Just asking.

In this fallen world, I am thankful for every incidence of the relief of personal pain in whatever form it takes. Yes, in this fallen world, the relief of any pain is a great mercy for which we should all be thankful for. You see, despite its beauty and the short seasons of pleasantness this present life and world may offer, old age, worn out-ness, accident, madness, selfishness, loss and all the horrors of war, are all our most present and most miserable lot. It is only the future life in Jesus, indeed, with Jesus in heaven, which offers a place where the present tears of pain shall cease to flow forever. Selah.

It is only the future life in Jesus, indeed, with Jesus in heaven, that offers a place where the present tears of pain shall cease to flow forever. Selah.

Meanwhile, we daily seek His mercy, daily seek His miracle of the relief of all our present pains, and whether it is in the form of the direct administrations of the Paraclete, or the form of the indirect applications of the famous Paracetamol, we are thankful.

The always rising and ever falling temples of youth and health are not those we should seek to permanently inhabit, but rather, whilst enjoying these two most hallowed and temporary of halls, we are encouraged to look from their bright windows and out into our inevitably gumsy and immanent futures of decrepitude, and get our lives sorted out right now for the service and worship of God. Yes, get it sorted out right *now* whilst the morning dew still rests refreshingly on our two most sparkling eyes and whilst we still have teeth. You see, despite the silly shenanigans of all our Oxford Dons, the preacher still calls the considering of our future and painful demise, wisdom! So tell me, how wise are you tonight?

Oh and if at last I might make a broad and sweeping statement regarding the coming controversies, may I say that you need to avoid all forms of transhumanism. It's just the devil trying to get you to live forever without God. The lie continues. Oh the odd pacemaker, electronic arm and heart valves are all OK, even knees and hips and such…but when you get A.I. mixed up with your brain and opened up to other consciousness's, I tell you, your headed for hell. Mark me well. The coming decades, should the Lord tarry, will prove the warning of this last paragraph.

Listen: *"Honor and enjoy your Creator while you're still young, before the years take their toll and your vigor wanes, before your vision dims and the world blurs And the winter years keep you close to the fire. In old age, your body no longer serves you so well. Muscles slacken, grip weakens, joints stiffen.The shades are pulled down on the world. You can't come and go at will. Things grind to a halt.The hum of the household fades away.You are wakened now by bird-song. Hikes to the mountains are a thing of the past. Even a stroll down the road has its terrors.Your hair turns apple-blossom white, adorning a fragile and impotent matchstick body. Yes, you're well on your way to eternal rest,While your friends make plans for your funeral. Life, lovely while it lasts, is soon over. Life as we know it, precious and beautiful, ends. The body is put back in the same ground it came from.The spirit returns to God, who first breathed it." (Ecclesiastes 12:1-7 -from THE MESSAGE: by Eugene H. Peterson.)*

Pray: The days of our lives are seventy years; and if by reason of strength they are eighty years, Yet their boast is only labor and sorrow; for it is soon cut off, and we fly away. Who knows the power of Your anger? For as the fear of You, so is Your wrath. So teach us to number our days, that we may gain a heart of wisdom. Return, O Lord! How long? And have compassion on Your servants. Oh, satisfy us early with Your mercy, that we may rejoice and be glad all our days! Make us glad according to the days in which You have afflicted us, the years in which we have seen evil. Let Your work appear to Your servants, and Your glory to their children. And let the beauty of the Lord our God be upon us, and establish the work of our hands for us; yes, establish the work of our hands. Amen and let it be so. (Psalms 90:10-17 NKJV)

Night-Whisper | **HOPE**

One foot in the grave

The South of France has always been a place for British ex-pats seeking solace in the sun. It was a few years ago when I flew into Nice on that same Cote D'Azur and it is here in this 2000-year-old French city, that the Anglican church there has one of its most famous of European churches. For me the beauties of Holy Trinity lies not in its Neo-Gothic majesty or in its rich stained glass, lit majestically above the high alter and warmed by the afternoon sun, but outside, in the green graveyard where lies the mortal remains of a famous Scottish Poet. Today in 1847, the Revd. Henry Francis Lyte died of tuberculosis and was buried in graveyard of Holy Trinity in Nice.

Genesis 3:19

"In the sweat of your face you shall eat bread Till you return to the ground, For out of it you were taken; For dust you are, And to dust you shall return." NKJV

Since 1927, along with the British national anthem, millions of cheering fans at each and every Football Association Cup Final have sung Lyte's most famous of poems. How wonderful is that! Indeed, it is even more wonderful when you understand the life that this man led, for it was indeed a life ever and always lived, with one foot in the grave.

Evelyne Millar writes of the second son of Captain Tomas Lyte of the Royal Marines. Henry, born in Scotland, together with his mother and two siblings, followed his father to Ireland. Captain Lyte had been sent there to help put down the 1798 Irish rebellion. Shortly after this, his father deserted the family taking with him Henry's older brother, whilst his mother also returned to England with his other brother. There they all died and Henry aged but nine years of age, was left in Ireland, alone, orphaned and destitute.

It was the headmaster of Lyte's school, the Revd. Dr Robert Burrows, who took pity on young Henry and took him in and cared for him, even to the point of paying for his education. It was money well spent for Henry, whilst at Trinity College Dublin, was awarded the Chancellor's Prize for English Verse for three successive years!

Henry was ordained into the ministry and worked so fervently at his parochial duties and writing that he wore himself out and contracted a lung disease that would bother him the rest of his life. Indeed it was his doctor that told him that if he did not seek easier and warmer climates of Europe, he would die. Throughout his life Henry Lyte would spend long and torturous absences from his duties and family, whilst recovering from these recurring bouts of debilitating illness.

Ministering to the sailors of his parish he wrote them hymn books, prayers to be said whilst at sea and of course, sea shanties!

Henry's last Parish was Brixham on the south coast of England where he served the last twenty-three years of his life, living always with one foot in the grave. Ministering to the sailors of his parish he wrote them hymnbooks, prayers to be said whilst at sea and of course, sea shanties!

It was just three weeks before his death that he penned his most famous of poems and he sent the finished manuscript to his wife, from Avignon in France. It seemed that he knew that it was very unlikely that he would ever return home. The poem was first sung at his memorial service which was held at his home parish in Brixham and from the lips of a man who spent all his life with one foot in the grave, we have left for us one of the most immortal and moving of prayers full of his own personal testimony and jam packed with life's observances. Never flowed more marvelous words from the pen and heart of man that was deeply in love with his Savior, despite the sorrows of his life.

Listen: May Lyte's most famous poem, be our daily and most ardent prayer.

Pray:

Abide with me; fast falls the eventide;
The darkness deepens; Lord with me abide.
When other helpers fail and comforts flee,
Help of the helpless, O abide with me.

Swift to its close ebbs out life's little day;
Earth's joys grow dim; its glories pass away;

Change and decay in all around I see;
O Thou who changest not, abide with me.

Not a brief glance I beg, a passing word;
But as Thou dwell'st with Thy disciples, Lord,
Familiar, condescending, patient, free.
Come not to sojourn, but abide with me.

Come not in terrors, as the King of kings,
But kind and good, with healing in Thy wings,
Tears for all woes, a heart for every plea—
Come, Friend of sinners, and thus bide with me.

Thou on my head in early youth didst smile;
And, though rebellious and perverse meanwhile,
Thou hast not left me, oft as I left Thee,
On to the close, O Lord, abide with me.

I need Thy presence every passing hour.
What but Thy grace can foil the tempter's power?
Who, like Thyself, my guide and stay can be?
Through cloud and sunshine, Lord, abide with me.

I fear no foe, with Thee at hand to bless;
Ills have no weight, and tears no bitterness.
Where is death's sting? Where, grave, thy victory?
I triumph still, if Thou abide with me.

Hold Thou Thy cross before my closing eyes;
Shine through the gloom and point me to the skies.
Heaven's morning breaks, and earth's vain shadows flee;
In life, in death, O Lord, abide with me.

Night-Whisper | **PREPARE**

The dagger men

It was the eight times wounded and highly decorated American hero, General Robert Tyron Frederick, who not only founded the first and joint Canadian US Special Forces Brigade in WWII, but also helped design their close combat weapon of choice, the sharp and triangular shaped, V42 Stiletto commando fighting knife.

Luke 22:35-38

"And He said to them, 'When I sent you without money bag, knapsack, and sandals, did you lack anything?' So they said, 'Nothing.' Then He said to them, 'But now, he who has a money bag, let him take it, and likewise a knapsack; and he who has no sword, let him sell his garment and buy one. For I say to you that this which is written must still be accomplished in Me: "And He was numbered with the transgressors." For the things concerning Me have an end.' So they said, 'Lord, look, here are two swords.' And He said to them, 'It is enough.'"

This Stiletto fighting knife, is at one end designed to easily pass through the rib cage to pierce the major organs and sharp enough to slice and not raggedly severe any artery, and at the other end, it is hard enough to act as skull cracker. The Stiletto knife still remains the fearful insignia for most special forces units. Indeed, the terror activities on the battle field of Frederick's fighting men led them to be dubbed by their enemies as the Devil's Brigade, for their secret, special and black ops antics meant they also left their calling card on all their sliced and diced, assassinated corpses which simply read, *"Das dicke ende kommt noch!"* - *"The worst is yet to come!"*

It was the Muslim, Hassan-i Sabbah, who became the founder of the Islamic sect, which in turn became known as the Hashshashin, who were, according to Marco Polo's observations, a drug induced, mass of murderer's intent on martyrdom. Nevertheless, it was these same (Sounds very familiar does it not.) These are the Hashshashin killers who would become the intriguing assassins of both fiction and film. However, they were not the first assassins by any means, for it was the first century Jewish Sicarii, who by the way, also especially enjoyed doing their knife murdering in public, that were the much feared and infamous assassins around the time of Christ. Yes, we must acknowledge that assassins are not new and that there is something both secret and silently terrifying about the dark infiltration of these most dangerous of dagger men.

> *It was the Jewish Sicarii, who by the way, also especially enjoyed doing their knife murdering in public, that were the much feared and infamous assassins around the time of Christ.*

Of course, the apostles were also knife carriers themselves. Yes, even when Jesus was with them! The lost ear of Malchus would be a clear indication of that! Some would also suggest that Judas had not only previously been a Zealot, fighting against the Romans, but that his very name, 'Iscariot,' might also be construed to show that he was also once a Sicarii himself, a political assassin, a sleek and silent terrorist if you will, striking not only at the Romans but publicly at any Jewish leader, political or religious, who were deemed to be in collaboration with their sworn enemy.

You will also possibly remember the left-handed judge assassin named Ehud, who leaps from the old Testament narrative, brandishing a concealed and specially designed knife, to spill all the "dirt" from the Moab King Eglon's oversized belly, onto the floor of his then, not-so-fine bathroom, and in the so doing begin an uprising which would in turn free his people from the oppression of their Moabite enemies. Yes, dagger men have been around a long, long time.

In our much-misunderstood text for tonight, I believe the Lord may be saying two things.

First, it is obvious that even in the disciple's present inventory of protective weapons, that even if you were trained and proficient in their use, two daggers were probably not enough for a decent defense! Indeed, the subsequent command of Jesus to desist from physical defense whilst He got to the repair of Malchus's ear, is indicative that He had *no* intention of their being used that night. With all this dagger counting and talking going on then, Jesus quickly says **"Enough already!"** Meaning either that He had no wish to continue down that line of conversation as it bore no reference to the actions of the present distress, or, that the presence of the two swords would be more than enough to have the possibility of trumped up political charges of insurrection brought against Him, that He might then fulfil the prophecy of Isaiah and indeed be counted as being among the transgressors.

The second and most practical of meanings is that that, where previously the disciples were to make no provision for their mission, from this point on, they were now to make *every* provision for the Great Commission and that included protecting themselves from attackers. I wonder if Jesus says, **"Even if you have to pawn your most important clothing, get a sword, for the battle is truly on!"** Surely, there is no metaphor here? Jesus simply says, **"Get yourself a dagger because you are going to need it."**

It was the Jewish Sicarii, who by the way, also especially enjoyed doing their knife murdering in public, that were the much feared and infamous assassins around the time of Christ.

While we have no record of the early church disciples protecting themselves against the indiscriminate attacks of robbing and murderous scum, we do have a clear record of there being no personal physical defense whatsoever being taken against political or religious attack. Where physical attacks occurred, it is clearly seen that where possible, full recourse was taken to initiate all necessary protection from the existing system of civil law. Paul surely shows us that?

Tonight, I say that within God's law, we must make proper defense of ourselves and our family from any murderous attack. Tonight, I say that without preclusion to the life of faith, we must also make every practical provision to ensure the fulfilment of the Great Commission. This Gospel message then, must not be delivered via the means of any Gunboat diplomacy, but nevertheless, I wonder if the carriers of this message might also make sure that they maybe have some kind of Gunboat in their travelling bag? As for me, at the moment, if possible, I personally would carry a weapon. Those big preachers that refuse to do so, should also get rid of their bodyguards.

Listen: *"For if the trumpet makes an uncertain sound, who will prepare for battle?" 1 Corinthians 14:8 NKJV*

Pray: Lord, help us to make better preparations for the promoting and proclamations of the Gospel of The Great Commission of Your Son and our Savior, Jesus Christ the Lord. Amen and let it be so!

| Vol 01 | Q4 | NW00332| November 27th |

Night-Whisper | **PREPARE**

Avoiding the disappointment at the end of a gushing tap

Luke 9:62

"But Jesus said to him, 'No one, having put his hand to the plow, and looking back, is fit for the kingdom of God.'"
NKJV.

At the end of a long day, usually when my old bones are stiff, my joints are a creaking and my muscles are contracted with stress, sometimes, instead of a shower I long for the long therapeutic relaxation that only a hot bath can provide. It never ceases to disappoint me then, even to the point of utter disgust, when while sitting naked and slightly cold, longingly and expectantly waiting in the running water for the final filling up of the bath and the covering of the watery shroud of my warm death, that just before you get to the point where you can slip beneath the bubbles and even cover your hairy and white blubbery old belly, the hot water sometimes just runs out! I stand abruptly. Naked, angry, cursing the waves, while whipping out the plug and letting go the lukewarm water down the wasteful drain. What a waste of time and effort. Now I am even more tense, even more spent and more in need of relaxation than when I first disrobed. What disappointment can be found at the end of a running tap.

I do not think our Jesus likes to find disappointment at the end of a running tap either. For I wonder if there is something, which He finds 'appily anticipatory and even ecstatically expectant at the end of our long ploughed furrows? So much so, that should we fail to reach the end, that is, when the hot water of our hot beginnings runs out before His ever-watching eyes, it leaves Him very disappointed. If so, then I think He might wish then, that He never even bothered to get ready to relax in enjoyment with us, never even bothered to prepare to bathe with us in all the hot Jacuzzi like completions of our many started endeavors.

So I say to you tonight, keep your water piping running hot and make sure, the tank is full and bubbling. You must complete all you started out with God to do. If not, neither you nor the Lord will be satisfied.

Listen: *"Now the just shall live by faith; but if anyone draws back, My soul has no pleasure in him." (Hebrews 10:38 NKJV)*

Pray: Lord, give me fuel and ignition and an ever-burning fire in the center of my soul, in Jesus name I pray, amen and let it be so.

Night-Whisper | **TRUTH**

Flick, click, crush

When truth is set aside, men believe anything. So, for some time now at the beginning of the 21st Century we have been bombarded by a multitude of ever-growing parapsychology programming, their attractiveness being not just in their seeming entertainment value, but on their uncovering dark, hidden and malevolent forces. One of the most telling of tag lines for one these television series says something like this: "If you look into the dark, sometimes, the dark looks back!" Now this is a tag line that not only I believe has an ominous tone to it but I think speaks some truth to us as well.

Ephesians 5:11a

"And have no fellowship with the unfruitful works of darkness" NKJV.

There are two ways to deal with darkness, that is to either Disdain it or to Discover it.

We disdain any darkness by offering to it the high and cold shoulder of our abject haughtiness. After all, what is the value of darkness, its power and its fruit, to the sons and daughters of the light. We should not investigate the darkness, stare at the scuttling cockroach or even consider its ways. The Bible is scant on its revelation of the metaphysical and dark spiritual realms for a very good reason. It is currently a very dangerous place for us to be. To that end, the Scriptures are very clear with both judgements and warnings that we should have no involvement with it whatsoever!

Now just to contradict myself most thoroughly may I say that there are times, however, that we have to Discover it. I do not use this verb in the sense of a continual action of going deeper into the manifestations and ways of darkness, but rather, we need to discover it by a simple click of an action of turning on the light. I am of course simply talking about the Discovery which light exposure brings. Concerning the cockroaches of darkness then, when we suspect their scurrying, we should simply, flick, click and crush.

Brother, sister, live in the light and whatever you do, do not look into the darkness, for yes indeed, it will look back at you. Remember, when you hear the scurrying, flick, click, crush. If you don't, your openness to them will bring infestation. Remember, resisting the devil is crushing him. Cast him out and do not look into the darkness.

Listen: *"For you were once darkness, but now you are light in the Lord. Walk as children of light (for the fruit of the Spirit is in all goodness, righteousness, and truth), finding out what is acceptable to the Lord. And have no fellowship with the unfruitful works of darkness, but rather expose them. For it is shameful even to speak of those things which are done by them in secret. But all things that are exposed are made manifest by the light, for whatever makes manifest is light. Therefore He says: 'Awake, you who sleep, Arise from the dead, And Christ will give you light.' See then that you walk circumspectly, not as fools but as wise, redeeming the time, because the days are evil. Therefore do not be unwise, but understand what the will of the Lord is. And do not be drunk with wine, in which is dissipation; but be filled with the Spirit, speaking to one another in psalms and hymns and spiritual songs, singing and making melody in your heart to the Lord, giving thanks always for all things to God the Father in the name of our Lord Jesus Christ, submitting to one another in the fear of God." (Ephesians 5:8-21 NKJV)*

Pray: Our Father in heaven, hallowed be Your name. Your kingdom come. Your will be done on earth as it is in heaven. Give us this day our daily bread. And forgive us our debts, as we forgive our debtors. And do not lead us into temptation, but deliver us from the evil one, for Yours is the kingdom and the power and the glory forever. Amen. (Matthew 6:9b-13 NKJV)

Night-Whisper | **CLEAN**

The plays, and all the picture painting of redemption

It is Shakespeare in 'Hamlet,' Act 2 Scene 2, who has the Danish Prince, seeking to gain visible proof that his uncle, King Claudius, had indeed murdered his dear father, the former king. To this end, Hamlet himself turns playwright, constructing a picture wherein he impregnates the play with references to regicide. Knowing that the present King, his uncle Claudius will be watching the play at court, Hamlet looks and waits for the flinching signs of sin. Hamlet is so confident of this happening that he says, "The play's the thing, wherein I'll catch the conscience of the King."

2 Samuel 12:1-4

"Then the Lord sent Nathan to David. And he came to him, and said to him: 'There were two men in one city, one rich and the other poor. The rich man had exceedingly many flocks and herds. But the poor man had nothing, except one little ewe lamb which he had bought and nourished; and it grew up together with him and with his children. It ate of his own food and drank from his own cup and lay in his bosom; and it was like a daughter to him. And a traveller came to the rich man, who refused to take from his own flock and from his own herd to prepare one for the wayfaring man who had come to him; but he took the poor man's lamb and prepared it for the man who had come to him.'" NKJV.

In the first instance, I find it profitable, if not uncomfortable, to examine my own reactions to all the stories, scenes and sentiments which I might find in the many plays and pictures which I expose myself to. Sometimes when I do this, the overt glance of a long since silenced conscience, often creeps across my barrier mountains and meets my eyes once more, inviting confession and even demanding repentance and restitution. Hamlet was right. "The play's the thing, wherein I'll catch the conscience.."

In the second instance it is also of interest to observe another person's reaction to stories, scenes and sentiments which they are also exposed to, for these reactions, especially if the response is grossly out of proportion to the pictorial ignition point, show large a person's pain in terms of them either being victim or villain. Every time I preach, every time I paint pictures with my words, here and there in the congregation of the listeners, it is often in the well-shuffled buttock, the wet eye, and the bowed head, where I too see that 'the play is the thing which shall catch the conscience of the King.'

All good pictures call forth truth, confession and repentance, restitution and restoration. Yes, in all good pictures, unlike the heart of Hamlet who was only intent on self-justified revenge, there always lies the possibility of redemption. If God keeps bringing pictures across your petrified path, I tell you, He is but seeking your redemption.

> *Every time I preach, every time I paint pictures with my words, here and there in the congregation of the listeners, it is often in the well shuffled buttock, the wet eye, and the bowed head, where I too see that 'the play is the thing which shall catch the conscience of the King.'*

Listen: *"So David's anger was greatly aroused against the man, and he said to Nathan, 'As the Lord lives, the man who has done this shall surely die! And he shall restore fourfold for the lamb, because he did this thing and because he had no pity.' Then Nathan said to David, 'You are the man!'" (2 Samuel 12:5-7a NKJV)*

Pray: Lord, in all Your drawings on the wall of my soul, lead me to those places of restoration and redemption in Jesus name I pray, amen and let it be so.

A time of true thanksgiving

At some point this date in our calendar will fall on the final Thursday of November, which of course is the competitively recently newly dedicated day in America for the celebration of 'Thanksgiving.' Harvest Celebrations are, however, not new. No, not at all. For an innate thankfulness to a 'Higher Being,' the ultimate giver of food and fertility is found in almost all indigenous peoples, even amongst the once flourishing native Indian tribes of America. Yes, the need to say 'Thank you' is a human trait, not a Christian one.

Luke 14:26-28

"If anyone comes to Me and does not hate his father and mother, wife and children, brothers and sisters, yes, and his own life also, he cannot be My disciple. And whoever does not bear his cross and come after Me cannot be My disciple." NKJV.

Such polity to a 'Supreme Being' however, might be offered by pagan peoples more out of relief and fear rather than be a thankfulness which is offered out of the relaxed joy of a gifted prized possession. Relief in the sense that a seemingly capricious God has finally come through with the goods once more and fear, in the sense that that we must be thankful lest He not continue to come up with the goods next year if we don't acknowledge His present and most beneficent goodness. If we have to sacrifice an odd virgin to maintain this fertile flow, then let it be so. Whatever it takes.

It was a commercial decision to regulate the specific start date of 'Thanksgiving' and was overtly chosen by this other 'nation of shopkeepers' to make sure that the selling days before Christmas were as long and as profitable as they could possibly be. To this end then, the Virgin Mary and her son Jesus are regularly sacrificed on the altar of commerciality each and every year, for tomorrow in America, is the start of the Christmas period and all the fun and all the feasting, all the selling and all the competing will now get under way with the earnestness gobble of a chocoholic waking up in the Hershey's factory.

I was told yesterday of a Christian man who after years of serving his local church and heading a very successful ministry to children had one day, just up and left his calling, his duties and his responsibilities. Apparently a tornado had gone through and damaged his own church so badly that one Sunday the doors had to be left shut for that Lord's day and so, he had opportunity, for the very first time, to go and visit another church nearby. In his opinion, this "other church" was bigger, better and shinier in oh so many ways than his own, that he just "up'd sticks" and decided he would go there instead. Now, we all would like to see this seemingly fickle move as being indicative of some much deeper reasons for the abandonment of years of profitable ministry but no, there was nothing deeper. The reasoning and the decision was as shallow and as a fickle as that. It was very simply, a much more nicer deal.

I think if we are honest, we could acknowledge that much of our church choices are commercial ones. Yes, much of our church choices are from a 'what's the best deal I can get for my kids and my marriage, for my future and my personal happiness' sake, rather than for any other. Pastors know this and so all their programming panders to these 'spiritually' commercial needs. So much so, that Pastors have become the high priests of the annual sacrifice of the Virgin and her Son. Oh don't worry and please don't be too upset, for this sacrifice can be justified in oh so many ways, that in this now commercialized and man centered religion which we have created, we leaders spend most of our time making sure we are lining our shelves with so much shiny and cut priced Christianity, just to make sure that our shameful sheep might never actually be seduced to go and shop elsewhere. Yes, most church leaders in America especially, actually live under the dark cloud of a commercial fear, where the Shekinah stenched breath from the mouths of disappointed founding member stockholders, fill the air with the condemnation of commercial loss, the like of which should only be found in the boardrooms of K-Mart and the once great

> *Pastors have become the high priests of the annual sacrifice of the Virgin and her Son. Oh don't worry and please don't be too upset, for this sacrifice can be justified in oh so many ways, that in this now commercialized and man centered religion which we have created, we leaders spend most of our time making sure we are lining our shelves with so much shiny and cut priced Christianity, just to make sure that our shameful sheep might never actually be seduced to go and shop elsewhere.*

American car industry. Unfortunately though, it is this same cloud of "fear and condemnation of loss" that most of the time fills both the pastor's leather bound studies during the day and their horror-filled dreams during the night. Yes, like all good shopkeepers, pastors face daily the questions of "What do I need to do to keep my shoppers and then go and get me some more!" So, should the congregation numbers drop and with it the fertile flow of money, materials and manpower suddenly cease to flow, then in the face of such commercial condemnation from remaining members, inevitably, the virgin and her Son shall be sacrificed again. Whatever it takes you see? Whatever it takes.

> *To break the sacrificial commercialism of the church, the question we must ask of our own local churches is this, "What can I give?" Not "What can I get?"*

To break the sacrificial commercialism of the church, the question we must ask of our own local churches is this, "What can I give?" Not "What can I get?" The question we must ask of our own local churches is this, "What will it cost me to serve here?" Not, "What can they offer to keep me here?" You see, real Christianity, the heaven branded stuff, is never cut price! Pastors, don't you know that the possession of something valuable and costly brings with it such a great care and thankfulness from the possessors of the same, that their words and their lives will inevitably ooze with the relaxation and joy of a true thanksgiving. No fear you see, no manipulation, just a confident and heartfelt thankfulness.

This Thanksgiving then Pastor, leader, commercial sacred and spiritual feeder, why don't you stop the annual sacrificing of both virgin and her Son on the altar of competitive cut price commercial Christianity and simply begin to offer them the real deal? Stop cutting Him down and selling Him cheap! Rather, go raise Him high and make Him costly. Maybe then, maybe in a few years' time, we as a nation can then begin to live in a time of true thanksgiving. Tell me tonight then, just how valuable is Your Jesus? Don't ask yourself, "What will they have to do to keep me?" But rather ask yourself, "What has it cost ME to follow Him?"

Listen: *"Then the king said to Araunah, 'No, but I will surely buy it from you for a price; nor will I offer burnt offerings to the Lord my God with that which costs me nothing.'" (2 Samuel 24:24a NKJV)*

Pray: I am persuaded, Lord to love You, for I have been changed to bless Your name. I am constrained by this great Gospel, forever to worship Thee. (From 'Precious Jesus' by Thomas Whitfield)

It's time to order your next Quarter of

Night Whispers

& maybe order one for a friend as well!

Check us out at

www.NightWhispers.com

Order at | WWW.TheologyShop.com

---------------------------0---------------------------

Night-Whispers is authored by Victor Robert Farrell, produced by WhisperingWord Ltd and licensed for the sole use of:

The 66 Books Ministry

A modern day,
Back to the whole Bible,
Boots on The Ground,
Proclamation Movement.

www.66Books.tv

Night-Whisper | **CONSIDER**

Gestation times

From conception to birth, the gestation period for a human being is around nine months. Of course the gestation time varies greatly across God's other creation, from 33 days in rabbits to 600-660 days in elephants. In any event, there are definite time differences between conception, full formation and the following birth. It has been my observation that the same is true for ideas. All ideas have conception but all ideas need formation before fruitful birth. Often, trying to bring good ideas, even great ideas to birth before proper formation leads inevitably to abortion.

Luke 14:28-31

"For which of you, intending to build a tower, does not sit down first and count the cost, whether he has enough to finish it — lest, after he has laid the foundation, and is not able to finish, all who see it begin to mock him, saying, 'This man began to build and was not able to finish.'"
NKJV

Since the early 1800s, there have been many suggestions, many ideas on how to build a tunnel under the English Channel thus connecting Britain to mainland Europe. All have been interesting conceptual ideas, and one of the better ones was proposed and put forward in 1880 by Sir Ed Watkin, the chairman of the then South Eastern Railway, who for this project gained acts from both the British and French parliaments approving of the project. Indeed, two shafts had been sunk in both Dover England and Sangatte France and tunnels from both the British and French sides, had begun to stretch hundreds of yards under the channel. Unfortunately, British military fears of invasion from mainland Europe through a completed tunnel led to the halting and destruction of years of work. Portions of these very expensive and dead ideas are still accessible today. What a waste.

From this night onwards, when a good idea, when a great idea is conceived in your head and heart, do not start pushing straight away! Let it lay a while, let it gestate in a prayerful and protective environment.

Thoroughly prepare for its arrival, make provision for its support and plan thoroughly for its implementation. If you do this, then it shall take even greater shape in your womb and have a greater chance of life when it is given birth too.

132 feet below the English Channel, shortly after 11am today in 1990, workers drilled an opening the size of a car through a wall of rock. This hole connected the two ends of an underwater tunnel linking Great Britain with the European mainland for the first time in many thousands of years. A birthed idea had received a giant slap on the 'Heini' and began to scream itself into life.

From now on then, why not make sure your gestation period gives every chance for your ideas to live!

From now on then, why not make sure your gestation period gives every chance for your ideas to live!

Listen: *"Or what king, going to make war against another king, does not sit down first and consider whether he is able with ten thousand to meet him who comes against him with twenty thousand? Or else, while the other is still a great way off, he sends a delegation and asks conditions of peace. So likewise, whoever of you does not forsake all that he has cannot be My disciple." Luke 14:30-33 NKJV*

Pray: Lord, help me to count the cost of all my ideas of Christian service, indeed, of all my many ideas. Then Lord, will you please bring to pass those, which might live, and also, will You come and help me in the bringing of these dreams to maturity, no matter what the cost and for Your eternal glory, In Jesus name I pray, amen and let it be so!

| Vol 01 | Q4 | NW00337 | December 02ⁿᵈ |

Night-Whisper | **CONTINUE**

Right declarations of death

Tomorrow and if not, then someday, most of us will take up pole position. The leader we have been shadowing will have gone. Gone maybe in terms of physical death, gone maybe in terms of sickness, gone in terms of retirement or relocation, in any event, they are now gone for good! When this happens, it is we, their near followers who are left to take up the fallen baton and when this happens, many of us need the assurance that it is in fact we who should be leading, that it is we who now have the authority to continue to lead.

Joshua 1:1,2a

"After the death of Moses the servant of the LORD, it came to pass that the LORD spoke to Joshua the son of Nun, Moses' assistant, saying: 'Moses My servant is dead.'" NKJV

There are many folk leading without the God-approved authority to do so. The baton has not been theirs to pick up but rather, with ignorant blindness, they have taken upon them a task, which is beyond them or with arrogant culpability, they have assumed a role of their own proud heart's desire. When this happens, disaster is in the making for both them and the blind sheep that now follow them. It is only a matter of time.

So then, in light of such terrible and misguided leadership endings, how may we be assured that it is indeed us, who must take up the fallen baton and move on with it?

The body of Moses was never found. It was never found because God was his undertaker and the Archangel Michael was the hefty bodyguard that kept Satan from discovering its whereabouts, less even the rotting flesh of this great man and the brittle bones of this dead prophet, should be set as a place of homage and sinful worship! The problem for Joshua was that there was no body and consequently because of that, maybe many people thought that one day, Moses would just mosey on back on in the camp and pick up where he left off! After all, he had gone AWOL before! I wonder then if our text for tonight indicates that there was uncertainty about the formers leader's plans and presence to fulfil them, even now playing on the heart of Joshua and that because of that, the LORD Himself had to come to Joshua and verify the case, clarify the new situation and certify Joshua's role in full. The baton was his to pick up.

Friends, in our text for tonight, this right and opening declaration of death was necessary because a new leader is being birthed and with this new leadership, a new authority. This authority though linked to the past, is of necessity fresh and independent of the past. A living leader is now needed for Israel, one facing forward, one facing the future, one quickened for action, one fully free to operate with no reference save to God himself. Moses is Dead.

> *A living leader is now needed for Israel, one facing forward, one facing the future, one quickened for action, one fully free to operate with no reference save to God himself. Moses is Dead.*

So, how may we be assured that it is indeed we, who must take up the baton and move on with it? Well, only when God speaks to us of the 'death' of the person we are replacing, for this is the foundation of all future revelation, which we will receive concerning "the how" of all our present leadership. Without this declaration of death from the most High God, our face will always be looking over our shoulder instead of looking ahead.

If the leader you think you are replacing is not in some sense declared dead, then rather than mighty manifestations, you are in for some mighty problems.

Listen: *"Be strong and of good courage, for to this people you shall divide as an inheritance the land which I swore to their fathers to give them. Only be strong and very courageous, that you may observe to do according to all the law which Moses My servant commanded you; do not turn from it to the right hand or to the left, that you may prosper wherever you go. This Book of the Law shall not depart from your mouth, but you shall meditate in it day and night, that you may observe to do according to all that is written in it. For then you will make your way prosperous, and then you will have good success. Have I not commanded you? Be strong and of good courage; do not be afraid, nor be dismayed, for the LORD your God is with you wherever you go." NKJV*

Pray: Lord, for each new role You place me in, declare the death of the past and then quicken my whole body, soul and spirit for the task ahead, in Jesus name I ask it, amen!

Night-Whisper | **BELIEVE**

Miracle aid

Like it or not, and many Christians will not, our text for today clearly shows a direct link between miracles, the glory of God and belief in Him!

John 2:11

"This beginning of signs Jesus did in Cana of Galilee, and manifested His glory; and His disciples believed in Him." NKJV

These disciples, newly called to the ministry *of* Jesus Christ, newly called to a ministry *with* Jesus Christ, enjoyed His 101 training, reveling no doubt even in His one-on-one training and had heard His words most thoroughly. These words, these words of knowledge, these words of wisdom, these words of life, had ignited in them such a desirous passion that they had moved with watching and waiting wonder, along the road with Him. Yes, they were His boys, yes, they were the growing posse of His possession and now, yes right now, over a few drinks and a couple of dances, they would become the believing people of His power!

Words, even Bible words, are simply not enough to walk along the road with Jesus! Now before you cry me down as a heretic, you need to know that even our Lord Jesus testified to that fact, indeed, even the Word itself testifies that of itself! Words are not enough. What is written, what is said, must cause people to take up their bed and walk or else we who are already walking, we who are already watching and we who are already waiting, might just stop believing! Indeed, we will never even begin to truly and consistently believe unless we see the miraculous. Yes, miracles are necessary to see the glory of God among us and necessary to our continued and growing belief! I know that sounds heretical to some of you but never the less, it is true.

I have observed that where the belief in the present practice of miracles has ceased, where the acknowledgement of miracles is simply within the confinement of a very short period of time, after the resurrection of Christ and the death of apostles, that there is a grey sickness that settles upon such folk, leaving many of them granite like in both face and heart. Furthermore, where miracles are never seen, they cease to be expected and the Word itself becomes but dark type, set on powerless pieces of paper and the practitioners and even the preachers of such powerless words, will even themselves eventually leave the fold and they shall leave it disappointed, they shall leave it distraught, they shall leave it disconsolate, they shall even leave it destroyed. Yes, we must have miracles for our day, for this day!

Now having said that, let me tell you folks, that miracles are like Chinese food. They are monosodium glutimately tasty, they are fulfilling, they are satisfying, they are definitely of some nutritional value but I tell you what, in just such a short time, you are going to want another and then another and yet another! Miracles are tasty, miracles are the vitamins of the healthy spiritual life of faith and very necessary but by themselves, they are insufficient in nutritional value to sustain the consistent spiritual life.

> *Miracles are tasty, miracles are the vitamins of the healthy spiritual life of faith and very necessary but by themselves, they are insufficient in nutritional value to sustain the consistent spiritual life. -*

In the end then, our belief and hope, though validated by the miraculous, must be as thoroughly rooted in the Word of God, as was the belief of these early disciples. Yet nevertheless, here in Cana of Galilee, God the good puts feats to His Words and in so doing, He is glorified and the disciples are believing, even believing in this very particular and strengthened way, and that, for the very first time.

Some of you tonight, are also for the very first time, waiting to believe in such a way. May God grant you such a miraculous feast both tomorrow and the next day and many times thereafter, amen.

Listen: *"For the kingdom of God is not in word, but in power." 1 Corinthians 4:20 KJV*

"Who being the brightness of His glory and the express image of His person, and upholding all things by the word of His power, when He had by Himself purged our sins, sat down at the right hand of the Majesty on high..." Hebrews 1:3-4 NKJV

"We give no offence in anything, that our ministry may not be blamed. But in all things we commend ourselves as ministers of God: in much patience, in tribulations, in needs, in distresses, in stripes, in imprisonments, in tumults, in labours, in sleeplessness, in fastings; by purity, by knowledge, by long suffering, by kindness, by the Holy Spirit, by sincere love, by the word of truth, by the power of God, by the armour of righteousness on the right hand and on the left, by honour and dishonour, by evil report and good report; as deceivers, and yet true; as unknown, and yet well known; as dying, and behold we live; as chastened, and yet not killed; as sorrowful, yet always rejoicing; as poor, yet making many rich; as having nothing, and yet possessing all things."
2 Corinthians 6:3-10 NKJV

Pray: Lord, may the dynamite of Your Word explode in our lives tomorrow. In mighty miracles of marvelous testimony, come turn all our water into wine so that our hearts may be gladdened once more, in Your great name I pray, amen!

| Vol 01 | Q4 | NW00339 | December 04th |

Night-Whisper | DESTINY

Chocolate, churches and Christ

As I write these thoughts, I am visiting Louisville Kentucky at the moment, a city that prides itself on its College sports. I flew in recently, late on a crispy clear dark winter's night, to find its American football stadium lit up like a Christmas tree, packed to the gunnels with cold and screaming fans. The Louisville Cardinals were at play on their well-supported and intimidating home turf of The Ville! Getting to go to school, going to college, is an honor and for these big football scholarship boys, made even bigger still by protective packing. Yes, it is a very big deal indeed. To the TV-watching millions though, denied the opportunity by simple lack of funding, it grates somewhat that muscle and speed, put simply in the right place at the right time has brought the chosen few an excellent education.

Colossians 3:16

"Let the word of Christ dwell in you richly in all wisdom, teaching and admonishing one another in psalms and hymns and spiritual songs, singing with grace in your hearts to the Lord." NKJV

Now, if you think not being able to pursue an education through financial lack is tough, then imagine a world in which because of your religious beliefs you were not allowed to attend any form of higher education and neither were you allowed to enter into any profession such as medicine or law! This was indeed the case in 19th century England for any members of the Quaker movement, which was founded by George Fox, over two centuries before but unlike those times, has today come to embody, faith, integrity, equality and simplicity.

The Quakers, a once marvelous Christian sect, denied by government these simple rights and having not many lucrative sporting opportunities available at that time, pursued the only other avenues available to them, that being, creating good personal businesses! Many of these good and gentle folk took them to becoming the best business entrepreneurs ever produced in England. For sure, many of their fledgling companies are today still carrying high value stock in the global market place. One such entrepreneur was a Quaker called John Cadbury, the inventor of the finest chocolate ever produced on this planet. Indeed, did not Paul himself speak of "the mystery of the chocolate, which even the angels desired to look into?" Maybe not, but he should have!

John Cadbury looking at 19th Century England, saw the evils of the addiction of alcohol as being the main source of poverty amongst the poor. Being part of the temperance movement, he took social action by choosing to invent a drink, which would become a substitute for alcohol. These replacements were hot cocoa and hot chocolate and I must confess, that I have been addicted to them both ever since I first tasted them!

Today, Bourneville may be the only town in the United Kingdom that has no pub but it has three things we all need and those are chocolate, churches and Christ.

John Cadbury had seven sons and it was Richard and George who continued to build the business, moving it to a suburb of Birmingham England called Bourne brook. Here they again made revolutionary changes to their product, its production and most importantly of all, to their workforce! Here they gave birth to a model town if you will, a Ville, a living place so extraordinary for its time that Bournbrook became Bourneville and its flowing dark richness would permeate the whole world and that my friends is by no means a silly understatement.

Here at "the Ville," in the darkness of England, an astonishingly bright revolution in community housing took place in terms of mutual respect, high wages, pension schemes, excellent living conditions, organic vegetable gardens, places for sport, recreation, reflection and recovery. It was quite simply, Christ in the Cadbury family that brought these "heaven on earth" conditions to the dark industrial factories of England. Today, Bourneville may be the only town in the United Kingdom that has no pub but it has three things we all need and those are chocolate, churches and Christ.

Tonight then, let me leave you with three dark pieces of chocolate goodness for your consummation and consideration.

First, that your unfair and unrighteous circumstance may in fact be squeezing you into an entrepreneurial, profitable and life-giving direction. This is no bad thing! You might end up giving Quaker oats to a starving world!

Secondly, that your relationship with Christ means very little to this world and even to heaven, if it has not got legs to go and feed the poor, to change the world and to glorify the God of heaven. The Gospel has always been a social Gospel. Hear me now! Not to the detriment of preaching! Not to the cowardice of a closed mouth! But preaching the Gospel is words and deeds. It is truth in action.

Thirdly, that the Cadbury ripple of Christian good works, once cast into the sea of humanity is still travelling and changing the world, maybe even the galaxy as we know it, even today. Goodness has a knock on effect, you see, even from generation to generation.

> *The Cadbury ripple of Christian good works, once cast into the sea of humanity is still travelling and changing the world, maybe even the galaxy as we know it, even today. Goodness has a knock on effect, you see, even from generation to generation.*

Dear friends, just what ripples of creamy goodness are you sprinkling upon this most needy of seas upon which we sail together.

Listen: *"I am dark, but lovely, O daughters of Jerusalem, Like the tents of Kedar, Like the curtains of Solomon." Song of Solomon 1:5 NKJV*

Pray: Lord may all our works in every place, be rich and dark and beautiful to You, in Jesus name I ask it, amen.

Night-Whisper | **OBEY**

Chocolate pockets and Ripples of goodness

John Cadbury was outdone in terms of the seven children he had, in that his son Richard had eight! One of these good chocolate soldiers, the granddaughter of the famous founder of the best chocolate company in the whole world, (before our American cousins got hold of it and changed the taste) was a young lady called Helen Cadbury.

1 Corinthians 1:27-29

"But God has chosen the foolish things of the world to put to shame the wise, and God has chosen the weak things of the world to put to shame the things which are mighty; and the base things of the world and the things which are despised God has chosen, and the things which are not, to bring to nothing the things that are, that no flesh should glory in His presence." NKJV

Helen's father Richard was a practicing Christian (is there any other?) and had set up a mission hall outside of the then most Heavenly Ville, in one of the slum districts of Birmingham. Helen, used to the regular visitors of evangelical Christians to her home, used to the family's daily morning prayer and Bible readings led by her father, was moved to accompany him one night to that same little Christian mission hall. Here, Helen was well aware of the two kinds of people in the hall. The first kind was the hopeless, the hurt and the destitute. The second kind was those who used to be the hopeless, the hurt and destitute! The source of change in these latter folk of hope, purpose and presence was Christ alone. The invitation from the preacher that night for people to come forward and believe on Christ was met by the trembling legs of Helen. It was her father, in the little back room of the Christian mission hall that led the quaking hearts of men and women to faith and peace in Jesus Christ. That particular and blessed night, his daughter Helen was among them. How wonderful.

Helen, aged just thirteen, finding it difficult to share her faith and experience with her peers, found that simply reading the Bible in front of them solicited many questions from, which in the answering, she could then read the Scriptures to them. Ever the organizer, she founded a club with her friends called the Pocket Testament League. Together, this little group of girls issued handmade membership cards and sewed pockets in their dresses to carry the small Bibles. Their goal was simply to "Read, Carry and Share." Little did she know, but Helen, through this small collection of female friends was in process of making another chocolate ripple on the dark surface of humanity.

The well-focused child became a lovely and organized, wealthy single woman. Just then, as often happens in stories, a single and well-connected man came upon the scene that was associated with Moody and Torrey and Chapman, all prominent World Wide Evangelists of the time. The man was Helen's soon-to-be husband, the Gospel singing Charles McCallon Alexander, who had also become a Christian aged just thirteen, and had been involved in innovative citywide simultaneous mission meetings for many years. It was this same Charles, who with love and connectivity, helped take the once schoolgirl organization of the Pocket Testament League into an official body which on this day of my writing, has over 170,000 members and has distributed over 100 million Pocket New Testaments to people around the world. Amazing! You see, it was God, who joined up the dots. It was God, who hooked Helen up with the right man at the right time with all the right connections. It was God who also no doubt answered exceedingly abundantly, all that could be asked and thought of, in the prayers of that young and quaking little chocolatier.

> *Helen Cadbury founded a club with her friends called the Pocket Testament League. Together, this little group of girls issued handmade membership cards and sewed pockets in their dresses to carry the small Bibles. Their goal was simply to "Read, Carry and Share." Little did she know, but Helen, through this small collection of female friends was in process of making another chocolate ripple on the dark surface of humanity.*

How did this little schoolgirl cause such a splash through the depression and two world wars? Well you see, Helen didn't just have any old chocolate in her pockets dear friends, no, she had a Cadbury's Ripple tucked away in there as well, which in obedience and faith, she cast upon the waters of the world. What ripple effect of good might it have on the world if the God inspired ideas of your Christ subjected heart were also cast on the waters of your life in obedience and faith? Tell me, what's that in your pocket tonight?

Listen: *"Now to Him who is able to do exceedingly abundantly above all that we ask or think, according to the power that works in us, to Him be glory in the church by Christ Jesus to all generations, forever and ever. Amen." Ephesians 3:20-21 NKJV*

Pray: Lord, come join up my dots. Lord, help me to strike the waters in such mighty believing faith that lives in this and coming generations will be touched and changed forever. In Jesus name I ask it, amen and let it be so!

| Vol 01 | Q4 | NW00341 | December 06ᵗʰ |

Night-Whisper | **CONSIDER**

The bat out of hell

Tonight, if you listen very quietly, moving your neck to the left slightly and opening your ears to history, you might just hear the silent steaming of a Japanese carrier force moving into striking distance of Pearl Harbor and the waiting but still floating, lame duck, American Pacific Fleet. The bombs and torpedoes dropped from the sky tomorrow shall form the force of another sucker punch that will lay America reeling to the canvas floor once more. A stunned nation and an embarrassed American military, will from this point now quickly move in determined desperation to put together such a counter punch, that be it even ever so pitiful, its audacious boldness shall both cause the enemy to step back a little and its sunken homeland fans, to become buoyed up again with hope and courage once more. Enter then, stage left, aviator and aeronautical engineer, Lieutenant Colonel Jimmy Doolittle carrying his cunning plan.

1 Thessalonians 1:6-8

"And you became followers of us and of the Lord, having received the word in much affliction, with joy of the Holy Spirit, so that you became examples to all in Macedonia and Achaia who believe. For from you the word of the Lord has sounded forth, not only in Macedonia and Achaia, but also in every place. Your faith toward God has gone out, so that we do not need to say anything." NKJV

In just four months' time, Doolittle and his raiders will be the only bomber crews in US Army Air Force military history to launch from US Navy Carriers on a combat mission. The USS Hornet was given the honor to host these one-way flight crews to Tokyo and Jacob DeShazer, was on the last of the sixteen modified B-25s to leave its heaving deck. Corporal DeShazer was the bombardier of the B-25, named 'Bat Out of Hell.'

Jacob DeShazer had been brought up in a Christian environment but as a teenager, like so many others, had "kicked over the traces" and had purposefully wandered from God and now at the beginning of his mission, unlike some of his crewmates, DeShazer no longer even prayed. Fortunately for Jacob though, his mother did still pray. Mrs. DeShazer recalls how she *"awakened suddenly one night with a strange feeling like being dropped down, down, down through the air and with a terrible burden that weighed upon my soul! I prayed and cried out to God in my distress. Suddenly the burden was gone, and I drifted off into an untroubled sleep, something unusual for me. Later,"* she says, *"when comparing the time I prayed in America with the time in occupied China, it was just the time when Jacob had had to parachute from his falling plane. How I praise the Lord now, but of course then I didn't realize or know what was taking place so far away. When we heard in the war news that our airmen had been over Tokyo dropping bombs, little did I realize that my own precious boy was in the crew of one of the planes."*

The Japanese supposedly murdered 250,000 Chinese in their search for the downed Doolittle raiders, it's not surprising then that on his incarceration, he would see three of his fellow captives shot and he would see another die of starvation before his eyes.

Yes, Jacob DeShazer had to bail out of a fuel-empty plane trying to reach its recovery base in eastern China. DeShazer would spend 40 months as a Japanese prisoner of war. Noting that the Japanese supposedly murdered 250,000 Chinese in their search for the downed Doolittle raiders, it's not surprising then that on his incarceration, he would see three of his fellow captives shot and he would see another die of starvation before his eyes. Being on starvation rations himself, DeShazer suffered dysentery, beriberi fever, body engulfing boils, and various other bodily and mental conditions, which mostly came from the aftermath of being beaten, tortured, mocked, hung, and intolerably and incessantly abused. DeShazer remarked that his hatred for his captives was *"all consuming and knew no bounds."*

During the course of those forty months, the Emperor of Japan directed that prisoners should be treated "somewhat better" and so DeShazer asked for a Bible and he got one. *"When I got that Bible,"* he recalls, *"I thought about how the Christians believed the Bible -- believed it was the Word of God, and God didn't lie. So I read that Bible to find evidence that it is the Word of God and right away I found the evidence."*

On June 8, 1944, DeShazer received assurance of his salvation when his eyes fell once again on Romans 10:9. *"Boy, that hit me! It was the best news I'd ever heard in my life. There are just two things: you confess with your mouth and believe in your heart. And I did! I believed at that time -- and I do yet – it's God's Word. I believe heaven came down there in that prison cell."* The bat may have been a Japanese POW but he was at last, now out of hell.

The bat may have been a Japanese POW but he was at last, now out of hell.

Yet DeShazer's hatred for his captors continued. He knew that Christ commanded him to love His enemies and amazingly despite the continued beatings and mistreatment, he was instructed by the Holy Spirit in just how to love them! Now that is a miracle friends, let me tell you!

DeShazer came to love the Japanese so much that immediately after the war, he earned his theology degree and married and in 1948, he returned to Japan with his wife and growing family to labor there for many more years, even settling and planting a church in the very place he dropped his bombs all those years before! Tens of thousands are reported to have become Christians because of DeShazer's ministry and he even preached to some of his former prison guards who subsequently became Christians. Miracle after miracle friends, miracle after miracle and you know, it was the Pocket Testament League that greatly aided DeShazer in his Free Methodist ministry right there in Japan, even helping produce and distribute a pamphlet of his personal story called **"I was a Prisoner of Japan"**.

What a rich, dark, chocolatey goodness was spread through Japan by Helen Cadbury, that little ol' chocolatier.

The night is for bats and this night, DeShazer, that once bat out of hell returned to his terrible roost and in his claws he held not hatred but he held light and life and love, and many that were blind, as blind as bats out of hell themselves, were given eyes to see and hearts to receive.

Listen: *"For they themselves declare concerning us what manner of entry we had to you, and how you turned to God from idols to serve the living and true God, and to wait for His Son from heaven, whom He raised from the dead, even Jesus who delivers us from the wrath to come." 1 Thessalonians 1:9,10 NKJV*

Pray: Then sings my soul, my Saviour God, to thee, how great Thou art, how great Thou art! Then sings my soul, my Saviour God, to thee, how great Thou art, how great Thou art!

Night-Whisper | **HOPE**

A chocolate pearl, from the fiery harbor

Today in 1942 at 07:40 precisely, Mutsui Fuchida, one of Japan's most skillful flyers, opened the canopy of his Nakajima B5N2 Type 97 Model 3 torpedo bomber and fired a green flare to signal the attack on Pearl Harbor. It was this same Mutsui Fuchida, who just nine minutes later, ordered the code words "Tora, Tora, Tora" to be sent back to the Akagi, the flagship of the First Japanese Air Fleet. Complete surprise had been gained in the Japanese attack on Pearl Harbor.

1 Corinthians 6:9-11

"Do you not know that the unrighteous will not inherit the kingdom of God? Do not be deceived. Neither fornicators, nor idolaters, nor adulterers, nor homosexuals, nor sodomites, nor thieves, nor covetous, nor drunkards, nor revilers, nor extortioners will inherit the kingdom of God. And such were some of you. But you were washed, but you were sanctified, but you were justified in the name of the Lord Jesus and by the Spirit of our God." NKJV

Fuchida was first over the bombing zone at Pearl and after personally sinking the battleship Maryland, was the last to leave the bombing zone. Now, although Pearl Harbor was a cowardly attack, Fuchida himself was no coward. Leading many attacks during the war, he crashed six times at sea. Indeed, it was only an emergency appendectomy before the battle of Midway that kept him grounded but not out of the fray, for whilst trying to fight fires in an American bombing attack, he broke both his legs there in a bomb blast. Consequently, he was thus kept out of the battle of Guadalcanal, where he would have undoubtedly died. At the end of the war, Fuchida was the sole surviving officer of the seven commanders and thirty-two squadron leaders whom he led in the Pearl Harbor raid.

After Pearl Harbor, Fuchida became the Japanese national hero, and had a personal meeting with the Emperor himself! Like most of his compatriots, drunk on Victory sickness, it was the hangover after the defeat of Japan that led him to later question his whole existence and role in the war.

Fuchida concluded that it was proud nationalism and cultural hatred of others that had led in all nations and in his nation in particular, to a terminal lack of brotherly love for one another! In his post-war book, *No More Pearl Harbor*, Fuchida's new driving life force, was that peace and brotherly love was the only direction for his post war Japan and that peace should be chosen by them no matter what directions the other nations pursued. "How though," he wondered, "could such brotherly love be achieved?"

> *Fuchida came to the conclusion that it was proud nationalism and cultural hatred of others that had led in all nations and in his nation in particular, to a terminal lack of brotherly love for one another!*

Fuchida, retired from the Japanese Navy and now a post-war farmer, was nevertheless required to give an account of his war activities to a war crimes tribunal. It was while in process of attending such an interrogation in Tokyo, that he alighted from a train onto a platform where a saw an American missionary handing out some information. There on Shibuya railroad station was a very public Pocket Testimony League meeting going on and it was right there, that Fuchida was given a pamphlet called, "I was a prisoner of Japan." This pamphlet was written by Sergeant Jacob DeShazer, bombardier of The Bat Out of Hell, who was shot down over Japan whilst participating in the reprisal Pearl Harbor Doolittle raid on Tokyo.

Fuchida devoured the contents of the pamphlet and having read that it was the Bible that had transformed Jacob DeShazer; he got his own copy and read it with ravishing deliberation. Here he found out how and who, was the only person, which could transform a heart of hatred into brotherly love. Jesus Christ the Lord! *"This is it!"* cried Fuchida, *"I was strongly convinced. I concluded that the true realization of my book, 'No More Pearl Harbor' was no other than to expect Christ's second coming and to endeavor to prepare men from all over the world to welcome Christ's return. As a first approach towards this, I was convinced that I should first of all become a good Christian. Thus, I contacted the Pocket Testament League representatives who showed me from the Bible how to become a Christian. I then opened my heart and accepted Jesus Christ as my personal Savior on April 14, 1950."*

Fuchida went on to work as a Christian missionary, for the Pocket Testament League as well as joining his friend and Christian brothers, as a member of the Worldwide Christian Missionary Army of Sky Pilots!

Now tell me tonight, dear friends, just how amazing is it, that a little girl's Cadbury's chocolate fancy, could tickle all the blood bathed sandy shores of both the Atlantic and Pacific oceans? Therefore, I ask you again tonight then, "What's in your pocket?"

Listen: *"We know that we have passed from death to life, because we love the brethren. He who does not love his brother abides in death. Whoever hates his brother is a murderer, and you know that no murderer has eternal life abiding in him." 1 John 3:14-15 NKJV*

Pray: O Lord, You have searched me and known me. You know my sitting down and my rising up; You understand my thought afar off. You comprehend my path and my lying down, and are acquainted with all my ways. For there is not a word on my tongue, but behold, O Lord, You know it altogether. You have hedged me behind and before, and laid Your hand upon me. Such knowledge is too wonderful for me; It is high, I cannot attain it. Where can I go from Your Spirit? Or where can I flee from Your presence? If I ascend into heaven, You are there; If I make my bed in hell, behold, You are there. If I take the wings of the morning, and dwell in the uttermost parts of the sea, Even there Your hand shall lead me, and Your right hand shall hold me. If I say, "Surely the darkness shall fall on me," Even the night shall be light about me; Indeed, the darkness shall not hide from You, but the night shines as the day; The darkness and the light are both alike to You. For You formed my inward parts; You covered me in my mother's womb. I will praise You, for I am fearfully and wonderfully made; Marvelous are Your works, and that my soul knows very well. My frame was not hidden from You, when I was made in secret, and skillfully wrought in the lowest parts of the earth. Your eyes saw my substance, being yet unformed. And in Your book they all were written, The days fashioned for me, When as yet there were none of them. How precious also are Your thoughts to me, O God! How great is the sum of them! If I should count them, they would be more in number than the sand; When I awake, I am still with You. (Psalm 131:1-18 NKJV)

Night-Whisper | **TRUST**

Oh me, oh life

This of course is my least favorite of Bible verses. All the difficulties of life and death, from kids to cancer, from marriage to murder, from want to plenty, yes, all and everything is included in the "all things" that seemingly work together for our good! I do not like that one bit. Let me tell you why.

Romans 8:28

"And we know that all things work together for good to those who love God, to those who are the called according to His purpose." NKJV

I would much prefer a clear delineation of those things, which are blessed to me, and those things, which are cursed to me. Romans 8:28 however, allows no such delineation and consequent avoidance for the child of God but in undaunted forcefulness, screams and stands steadfast against all the storms of this life's journey of ours in its statement of utter confidence, that yes indeed, "all things work together for our good." The stunning encapsulation of God's utter Sovereignty that this statement makes, still troubles me rather than comforts me tonight, because this verse above all other verses, clearly *demands* that I trust Him in "all things" and in the so doing, questions my personal ability to trust God and thank Him in "all things." Now, if you think in the middle of personal devastation that this is an easy task for the Christian, if you think that this is not the greatest works of faith in our life to "trust God in all things," then my friend, you are a youngster in both the things of God and this world, yes, you are still wet behind the ears!

As I reflect on our recent evening meditations since the beginning of December, I nevertheless have to agree with the real life and intricate applications of Romans 8:28. I have to stand amazed at its ability to reveal itself as an enticing and demanding act of faith, fully alive in verdant veracity, even through the crowding complexities of terror and torture, of want and war as they manifest them self across both space and time. Yes, as I reflect on this month's meditations thus far, it is evident that many people contributed a link in the chain of the ever-unfolding goodness of God towards the people of this world, thus in turn, truly working all things together for good!

I don't know about you but when I consider these things and my place in the universe as intertwined with both the first and last Adam, with both sinners and saved, with both the carnal and the Christ, I am overwhelmed and struggle to find a little solid ground to stand on. It is truly amazing that God can and does work "all things" for our good.

> *Tomorrow then O poet of God, for all true Christians are the truest of poets...*

It is that quirky and ever so slightly strange Walt Whitman that might aid us in finding some solid ground to view this great verse of Romans 8:28 and maybe engage it, just a little, in its overwhelming complexities......

O me! O life!... of the questions of these recurring;
Of the endless trains of the faithless--of cities fill'd with the foolish;
Of myself forever reproaching myself,
(for who more foolish than I, and who more faithless?)
Of eyes that vainly crave the light--of the objects mean—
of the struggle ever renew'd;
Of the poor results of all--of the plodding and sordid crowds
I see around me;
Of the empty and useless years of the rest--with the rest me intertwined;
The question, O me! so sad, recurring--What good amid these, O me, O life?

Answer.

That you are here--that life exists, and identity;
That the powerful play goes on, and you will contribute a verse

Tomorrow then O poet of God, for all true Christians are the truest of poets, you too will have the opportunity to contribute a verse to this never-ending symphony regarding the goodness of God toward us in Christ Jesus. Watch with wonder then friends, listen in awe and consider very carefully just what and how you might write a verse in the book of the goodness of God. As we with consecrated pen, then so carefully write, even so circumspectly walk and examine our ways, maybe we pilgrims might then begin to possess to ourselves, some of the vast peace, which the knowledge of God's goodness towards us, actually working through "all things" could truly bring to our hearts? This is indeed, great faith indeed. This, indeed, is a great gift to possess.

Listen: *"And we know that all things work together for good to those who love God, to those who are the called according to His purpose." Romans 8:28 NKJV*

Pray: Lord, Your vastness, Your great goodness worked out in the times and lives of men and women, scares me, worries me, perturbs me, confuses me. Oh my God, I ask that Your goodness would become comfort to my heart and steadiness to my sailing soul in the year to come, in Jesus name I ask for it to be done, amen and amen and let it please be so!

Night-Whisper | **LIVE**

The real new man's bones

I do believe that "Praise to the Lord, the Almighty the King of Creation" is one of the greatest hymns of praise ever written! Though the German poet who penned these astonishing lines, Joachim Neander, died of tuberculosis aged only thirty years of age, he still speaks today and in speaking with such majesty, turns our hearts again to praise!

2 Kings 13:20-21

"Then Elisha died, and they buried him. And the raiding bands from Moab invaded the land in the spring of the year. So it was, as they were burying a man, that suddenly they spied a band of raiders; and they put the man in the tomb of Elisha; and when the man was let down and touched the bones of Elisha, he revived and stood on his feet." NKJV

It was Joachim's grandfather, a musician, who, following a popular trend at that time in Germany, had changed the family name from the original Neumann ("new man" in English) to the Greek form of "Neander."

The poet Joachim Neander then, didn't only take his new name from his grandfather but inherited also some of his grandfather's linguistic and musical talent, penning at least 60 hymns and putting them to music before his death from TB.

In 1674, Joachim, considered now by many to be one of the first important German hymnist after the Reformation, became a teacher in a Latin school in Düsseldorf. While living there and knowing he was always inspired by the wonders of nature, he liked to go the nearby valley (the German for which is, "thal" or "tal") of the Düssel. In this same beautiful tal, Joachim also held gatherings of informal praise services, at which he also addressed his hearers from the Bible. This same tal, this famous and poetic valley of vision, this same valley of prayer, praise and proclamation, was in the 19th century renamed by the German people in Joachim's honor, changing its name from the Düssel Tal to the Neander Tal.

In 1856, in this same renamed valley, skeletal and seeming humanoid remains were found and given the name Homo Neanderthalensis, or Neanderthal Man. The famous valley of heartfelt prayer, singing praise and powerful proclamation, had now been hijacked by doubt, cynicism and deception.

Tonight, whatever you think about the bones of this late Neanderthal Man, its genetic linkage or lack of, its skull size, its pelvic area, its controversy and cuckoo-like disposition, let me tell you but one thing, that Joachim, the first Neanderthal, the first new man of this valley of prayer, praise and proclamation, and in his threefold poetic power, he gave life to his hearers and yes indeed, Joachim though being dead, still speaks today in the same life giving manner and power in which he lived back then! You see, bones touched by God, always give life to others and at the last day, we shall see that it is Joachim's bones that shall finally come together, be clothed upon in Jesus and be found in all the eons yet to come, to be still and always upright and praying, upright and praising, upright and proclaiming. Tell me tonight then dear brother, dear sister, down in the valley of doubt and worldly cynicism, are your bones still rattling with prayer, praise and proclamation?

> *The famous valley of heartfelt prayer, singing praise and powerful proclamation, had now been hijacked by doubt, cynicism and deception.*

Listen: *"Again He said to me, 'Prophesy to these bones, and say to them, O dry bones, hear the word of the Lord! Thus says the Lord God to these bones: 'Surely I will cause breath to enter into you, and you shall live. I will put sinews on you and bring flesh upon you, cover you with skin and put breath in you; and you shall live. Then you shall know that I am the Lord.' So I prophesied as I was commanded; and as I prophesied, there was a noise, and suddenly a rattling; and the bones came together, bone to bone." Ezekiel 37:4-8 NKJV*

Pray:

> *Praise to the Lord, the Almighty, the King of creation!*
> *O my soul, praise Him, for He is thy health and salvation!*
> *All ye who hear, now to His temple draw near;*
> *Praise Him in glad adoration.*
>
> *Praise to the Lord, Who over all things so wondrously reigneth,*
> *Shelters thee under His wings, yea, so gently sustaineth!*
> *Hast thou not seen how thy desires ever have been*

Granted in what He ordaineth?

Praise to the Lord, Who hath fearfully, wondrously, made thee;
Health hath vouchsafed and, when heedlessly falling, hath stayed thee.
What need or grief ever hath failed of relief?
Wings of His mercy did shade thee.

Praise to the Lord, Who doth prosper thy work and defend thee;
Surely His goodness and mercy here daily attend thee.
Ponder anew what the Almighty can do,
If with His love He befriend thee.

Praise to the Lord, Who, when tempests their warfare are waging,
Who, when the elements madly around thee are raging,
Biddeth them cease, turneth their fury to peace,
Whirlwinds and waters assuaging.

Praise to the Lord, Who, when darkness of sin is abounding,
Who, when the godless do triumph, all virtue confounding,
Sheddeth His light, chaseth the horrors of night,
Saints with His mercy surrounding.

Praise to the Lord, O let all that is in me adore Him!
All that hath life and breath, come now with praises before Him.
Let the Amen sound from His people again,
Gladly for aye we adore Him.

Joachim Neander

Night-Whisper | **CONTINUE**

Merry makrothumia and happy hupomonee

I refuse to allow anyone to pray for me that I would have more patience. I hate the patience most of my fellow believers wish on me, for it always reminds me of a reluctant acquiescing to either depressing disappointment, or to a soul shattering suffering, or maybe to a worthless waiting of some kind and most of all, to a wimpish acceptance of a never-ending and fun-less frustration! That kind of patience, thank you very much, you can keep!

Romans 15:5-6
"Now may the God of patience and comfort grant you to be like-minded toward one another, according to Christ Jesus, that you may with one mind and one mouth glorify the God and Father of our Lord Jesus Christ."
NKJV

To compound my refusal of such prayer for patience, one ancient commentator remarks that, "Patience is that calm and unruffled temper with which a good man bears the evils of life." What rubbish and when I get to heaven I am going to find that brother and slap him! For you see friends, such silly and unruffled remarks, actually dehumanize the Christian, actually make us less biblical, less like Christ and sometimes force us into such an unreality, that it morbidly molds us into a kind of quiet and acquiescing, religious madness! Remember, that when the winds of life sweep down onto the sea of Galilee, it heaves in disappointment, crashes against the shore in anger, slaps its waves together in desperation and weeps its salty lament across the watching shores, and in the same way dear friends, in the same way, you the cruelly betrayed, you the hurt and disappointed, you the robbed and rubbished Christians of this world, are allowed to be that sea. Unruffled indeed! What poppycock! That's not biblical patience, it's dehumanized, dysfunctional madness.

In all your venting hurt and in all your disappointment though, what you are not allowed to be, is a deserter of Christ. No, you must endure for you are not allowed to become an unbeliever in His goodness. Yes, what you are not allowed to be, is one who turns his back on all the duties of

His love. What you are not allowed to be, is a teeth gritting and angry charlatan, kicking the sheep of His pasture. What you are not allowed to be is miserable, unfocused, faithless and hopeless, and I tell you this, without God's gift of "happy hupomonee," that real biblical patience, (not the rubbish that other Christians want so often to 'oik on me) then you shall most certainly become and do all these nasty things.

> *Thank God that He is patient! Indeed, He is all patience!*

Thank God that He is patient! Indeed, He is all patience! His "merry makrothumia" (the other Greek word we have translated as patience) that is, His long forbearance and faithful fortitude in holding back the pouring out of His righteous, hot and burning cup of molten anger upon us all, allows us time and affords us opportunity to change our minds and our direction and return to Him. God is happy to exhibit this long-suffering and forbearing patience with humanity because the end of it, is both our repentance and His shared and singing joy. How wonderful! We have a patient God.

Yes, thank God that He is patient! Indeed, He is all patience. His happy hupomonee (the other Greek word we have translated as patience) is a gift, which He freely gives His children, for as His merry makrothumia is related to His love, happy hupomonee is related to our continuing hope. Now this hopeful patience is one I both need and want, is one I both like and practice. This hopeful patience is one you can pray down from heaven upon me anytime dear friends, for this happy hupomonee is not a miserable swim in the sea of Christian Karma, no! It is a warrior-like attitude that rejoices in the attacks of the foe. It is a fruit-bearing gift from on High, that flowers in the face of all adversity. It is a courageous and continuing persistence, even endurance in all well doing, when we've been well done in! Not only is this hupomonee kind of patience, this kind of miraculous and joyful perseverance a gift to us but it is an obligation for us to both put on and to walk in and in the so doing, we shall be found to be that most sweetest fragrance of heavens hopefulness, rarely found but greatly prized among the hosts of smelly and disappointed humanity. A truly patient people of vast and biblical proportion.

I say again, that this truly biblical patience, this happy hupomonee is both encased in soulish humanity and expressed in spiritual faithfulness. So, let me patiently encourage you tonight then dear friends, that in all your expressed and sometimes violent storms, you still remain focused, you still remain faithful, you still remain joyful and you still remain in even apostolic mode in the continuance of your mission! Now that's biblical patience.

Listen: *"Truly the signs of an apostle were accomplished among you with all perseverance,(happy hupomonee) in signs and wonders and mighty deeds." 2 Corinthians 12:12-13*

Pray: Lord, grant me this gift of warrior like, joyful and focused endurance. Despite the wind at my face and the clouds above my head, help me to press on with the hope of reaping a fruitful crop. Grant me then this so great a gift of patience, and help me to put it on and walk in it, in Jesus name I pray, amen and let it be so!

Night-Whisper | **CONSIDER**

God's bloody hands

As General Joshua begins now to thoroughly take possession of the promised land, of the land flowing with milk and honey, make no mistake about it, that at this point, the land was flowing with the blood of the slaughtered inhabitants. Three times in this one chapter, after we read accounts of God's genocidal and God's ethnic cleansing of the land, we hear the refrain regarding Joshua that "he left none remaining."

Joshua 10:40-42

"So Joshua conquered all the land: the mountain country and the South and the lowland and the wilderness slopes, and all their kings; he left none remaining, utterly destroyed all that breathed, as the LORD God of Israel had commanded. And Joshua conquered them from Kadesh Barnea as far as Gaza, and all the country of Goshen, even as far as Gibeon. All these kings and their land Joshua took at one time, because the LORD God of Israel fought for Israel." NKJV

Our text for tonight however goes even farther and points out that not only was General Joshua acting under the expressed command of God Almighty but the Lord Himself, was intimately involved in the bloody conflict. Indeed, just as the Lord had took part in the battle against the five kings in Joshua chapter 10, by raining down upon them His heavenly artillery, so in the same way, in the rest of this conflict, God was most thoroughly involved.

There is no doubt that under the terms of the present Geneva Convention and under International Law of today, that both God and Joshua, His earthly general, would face charges for crimes against humanity for there was no doubt whatsoever, about the full involvement of God in this total and bloody war. Think about that!

In your thinking tonight then, let me remind you of but five small things:

First that this utter destruction was not a matter of some religious fanatic, some mad murderer, some sorry psychopath, shouting out that "God made me do it!" No, but by His direct presence and actions, God Himself was clearly, intimately and actively involved! The presence and actions of God the Almighty were not in question by anyone, especially by those people upon which He waged war. Yes, God was seen by everyone to have "fought for Israel".

> *God Himself was clearly, intimately and actively involved! The presence and actions of God the Almighty were not in question by anyone, especially by those people upon which He waged war. Yes, God was seen by everyone to have "fought for Israel".*

Second tonight, please remember that it was God who had placed these murderous scoundrels, this totally corrupt society, in His judicial courtroom dock. The Canaanites as a whole had been on trial, not Him, and as judge and merciful jury, He had long since pronounced them guilty, even giving them centuries to amend their ways until finally, when they did not, He became most terrible in carrying out His righteous judgment upon them. It was God who was judging rebellious humanity here folks. It was fallen and mixed humanity that had been on trial here, not God! Remember that.

Thirdly, note that the diabolical possession of a manifest spiritual evil had undoubtedly taken root in the land, so much so that the people of the land had in many ways become less than human, maybe in some, more than human. Therefore, this earthly conflict was no doubt part of a much greater heavenly conflict. The two were and are always, most intimately intertwined. The land of promise has always been a touching ground, a tinder box of bloody conflict, if you will, to try and halt both the first and second coming of Jesus, King of kings.

Fourthly, note that this same diabolical possession of manifest evil has throughout history and even today, been clearly seen in the devastations of two World Wars, Rwanda, Cambodia, Western Europe, The Middle East, etc. etc. etc., and that God has been constantly fighting these evil manifestations so that His Gospel may be preached.

Yes, fifthly and finally tonight, note that though free forgiveness has been purchased through the shed blood of Jesus and that this good message has and is being proclaimed throughout the whole world and has been done so for some 2,000 years now, that I am along with many others, increasingly convinced that the grace of this proclamation is quickly drawing to a close. The time of the end battle lines are being drawn today. People and practices are raising themselves up against the Most High God and He is coming to meet them.

I hear the feet of Jesus pad deliberately toward the tops of Carmel tonight. I hear the wind sucked into His flared nostrils and see His great lungs fill with the hot air of His indignation. The Lion of the tribe of Judah is getting ready to roar dear friend, and when He does, well, you had better watch out and you had better take care because He is coming to judge the earth. Are you living in the reality of this? What difference would it make to your worries, your choices and your priorities if you were? Think about that.

Listen: *"The Lord roars from Zion, And utters His voice from Jerusalem; The pastures of the shepherds mourn, And the top of Carmel withers." Amos 1:2 NKJV*

Pray: Along with the Holy Spirit, we the Holy people align our voices with the pleading of all the centuries of saints and tonight so Great King, Mighty Master, Strong Saviour, Roaring Lion of the tribe of Judah, we say "Come! Yes even so! Come Lord Jesus!" Amen and let it be so.

Night-Whisper | **EXAMINE**

Are there fairies at the bottom of your garden?

I often drive through Crowborough and pass the small bronze statue of old A.C.D., who spent the latter part of his previously very productive life in fruitless exploits, fallacies and falsehoods. It's such a shame really that for the sake of simply 'wanting to believe,' old A.C.D. gave credence to the infamous hoax of the Cottingley Fairies, where two young teenage girls supposedly took photographs of the creatures at the bottom of their garden. Just how could the author of the inscrutable Sherlock Holmes be taken in by such a hoax?

2 Corinthians 13:5

"Examine yourselves as to whether you are in the faith. Test yourselves. Do you not know yourselves, that Jesus Christ is in you? — unless indeed you are disqualified." NKJV.

Sir Arthur Conan Doyle, an intellectual and brilliant man, like so many people at the end of WWI, had lost such a large number of his friends and relatives, that he fell into a deep depression and eventually took solace in the possibilities of connection and the continuing of relationship through Spiritism, even though the founders of which were themselves self-confessed hucksters and hoaxers! You see, the need to desperately want something can often lead to the necessity of a belief with big built in blind spots.

There are three things to say here tonight.

First, please note that unscrupulous people for personal gain in terms of power, prestige and pound notes will, without conscience, manipulate and make use of many depressed and desperate people. This happens in the wider Christian church far too much.

Secondly, that the devil and his hoards are also hucksters and will themselves join in the game for their own purposes of pleasure, muddying the waters of human hucksterism with some metaphysical manipulation of their own.

Thirdly, that Christianity should have no blinkers. Christianity questions. Christianity queries. Christianity makes room for people who demand a couple of nail holes to stick their fingers into!

So, if you are seeking answers to sincere questions tonight, then go straight to the top and ask them! For it is my experience and indeed, it is most clearly written, that those who seek, shall most surely find, that those who ask shall really receive and that those who knock righteously in naked openness, shall have the door of their knocking laid opened wide to them.

Examine yourself. Examine your faith. Examine the Bible. Don't be a gullible. Don't be a plank.

Listen: *"But let each one examine his own work, and then he will have rejoicing in himself alone, and not in another." Galatians 6:4-5 NKJV.*

Pray: Father, lead me to the truth, in Jesus name I pray, amen and let it be so.

Night-Whisper | **DESIRE**

Of hot lips, curvy hips and lovely eyes?

Now Jacob loved Rachel. There is no doubt that Rachel was red hot and ready to be plucked. There is no doubt that Rachel was a beauty, a curvy stunning beauty, indeed, the most desirable of all female propositions. Her sister Leah on the other hand, well, she had nice eyes and that my friends, says it all.

Genesis 29:16-17

"Leah had nice eyes, but Rachel was stunningly beautiful."(THE MESSAGE.)

When all of Jacob The Twister's chickens finally came home to roost, he, by Laban's great deceit, found himself married to both of these pairs of eyes and the Bible records that Jacob loved Rachel more than Leah. Well after all, why wouldn't he? Leah lacked the lusciousness of femininity, for after all, all Leah had was a pair of lovely eyes!

It is at this point that God steps in, closing Rachel's womb and opening Leah's, so much so, that it was Leah who was primarily the fruitful one and it would be through Leah's offspring that Messiah would come. Leah in the naming of her children and in the prayer of her desperation was certainly on first name and intimate terms with God. Leah, with the lovely eyes, was blessed by God and fruitful. Red-hot Rachel, all ready to be plucked, was not!

Despite having seemingly good eyesight, young men are mostly led by their loins rather than their head. Indeed, if truth were told tonight, most throbbing of the heart would be found to emanate some two feet further down the torso. All red-hot Rachel's, ready to be plucked, seem to have that effect on men. I need to tell you tonight then, that when it comes to peace and blessedness, yes, when it comes to fun and fruitfulness in all its mellowed and autumn glory, that it is the eyes that have it. If you are looking for a spouse, then look at their eyes? Where are they looking? Are they looking to God? Because if they are, they shall be lovely eyes, full of peace, blessedness and delightful fruitfulness.

Speaking as a man then, let me tell you tonight my boys, that is the eyes that have it! What a pair!

Listen: *"Who can find a virtuous wife? For her worth is far above rubies." (Proverbs 31:10 NKJV.)*

Pray: Lord, help me seek and search for You, desire and pray for you, to be found and be reflected even in the shallow's of both my lover's eyes. Amen and let it be so.

Night-Whisper | **INTEGRITY**

Mizpah monuments

Mizpah is a most misunderstood word. Of course over the centuries it has become at times more of a money making word than a mystical one, as Jewelers and retailers, all have taken their share of sales from trinkets and lockets, coins and bracelets all bearing the out-of-context but cute little phrase of, *"May the Lord watch between you and me when we are absent from one another....Mizpah."* It's all very lovey dovey, it's all very nice, it's very sweet and it's all very romantic, but it's all very wrong! The context of the covenant cairn of Mizpah was built on one of danger, threat and cursing.

Genesis 31:48-50

"And Laban said, 'This heap is a witness between you and me this day.' Therefore its name was called Galeed, also Mizpah, because he said, 'May the Lord watch between you and me when we are absent one from another.'" NKJV

You will remember that after over twenty years of well-reaped abuse, Jacob finally gets the green light from God to flee away. His old uncle, Fagin Laban, pursues after Jacob and his family with the total intent on doing him great harm and recovering everything Jacob had, which quite frankly, he regarded as his! Laban would have done this if it wasn't for the dream intervention from God, which in brief said, "Laban, shut it! Laban, watch it." It was after Jacob and Laban vented to one another their thoughts that an irreconcilable difference of opinion was finally vocalized. That being the case there was clear need for separation and a covenant promise not to return into the other person's life with a desire for revenge and hurt. This was the true context on the cairn at Mizpah. It was, in effect, a line of demarcation drawn in the deep desert sand, which underscored the past life, which was now never to be revisited without a consequent curse of judgement and retribution from God on high.

There is a need today for many a Mizpah cairn to be erected upon the mystical mountains of our minds and our hearts. There are lifestyles which we have previously held openly, but now carry in secret habit, thoughts and pernicious practices intruding into what should be the peaceful places of our lives. Yes, there are Teraphims of many kinds, which we have carried from the past into our present promised lands that have been the cause of all kinds of pursuant guilt and condemnation, even threats of disclosure and death. Despite the accompanying fear of both discovery and loss, sins still demand that we sit on them and protect them from discovery under the lying excuse of a monthly menstrual flow.

> *Despite the accompanying fear of both discovery and loss, sins still demand that we sit on them and protect them from discovery under the lying excuse of a monthly menstrual flow.*

Not a few of you tonight *must* set up some Mizpah cairns on the mystical mountains of your hearts and minds. It's time to leave the past; it's time to draw under it a line of demarcation. Yes, under all thoughts and practices, habits and lifestyles that continue to be destructive and binding to you in the here and now, you must finally draw a line under it. Build that cairn and then *never* again return to do yourself harm! Build that cairn and then *never* allow a visit from there to do you harm! Yes! Once and for all time, mark it with the word 'Mizpah!'

Listen: *"Then Laban said to Jacob, 'Here is this heap and here is this pillar, which I have placed between you and me. This heap is a witness, and this pillar is a witness, that I will not pass beyond this heap to you, and you will not pass beyond this heap and this pillar to me, for harm. The God of Abraham, the God of Nahor, and the God of their father judge between us.' And Jacob swore by the Fear of his father Isaac."* Genesis 31:51-54 NKJV.

Pray: Lord, I cast away my idols. Lord, I am sick of the dark pursuers, the intrusion of the black Nazguls of my sinful past. Help me set up this night, some Mizpah cairns over issues in my life, which I declare tonight, shall no longer bring me death, or be sought after by me for their oh so dark a sustenance. Find me some rocks O Lord, and then together, let us build me a Mizpah cairn. In Jesus name I pray, amen and let it be so.

Night-Whisper | **EXAMINE**

Avoiding substance abuse

I like very much the expression of dissipation found in our text for tonight as referring to someone who "wastes his substance." The idea around the Greek word translated as dissipation is that of substance abuse in terms of an abandoned and unthinking recklessness which leads to personal destruction. Yup! Dissipation is a terminal disease.

Luke 15:13

"And not many days after the younger son gathered all together, and took his journey into a far country, and there wasted his substance with riotous living."
KJV.

Maybe it is because I am getting older, but frankly I no longer have the energy I used to have, and so already I find myself gazing somewhat enviously on younger folk, who seem to have so much energy that they just don't know what to do with it! Unfortunately, the possessors of such a seeming abundance of time, energy and good looks, often unknowingly fritter their substance away. It might be frustrating to see the accidental dissipation of substance which is common to youth and fuller growth but it tell you, it is absolutely heartbreaking to see a young person purposely throw away their substance, bulimically vomiting up their life on the pavements of drugs and idleness. Be sure that I am not talking of wasting money here. No, money can be replaced. I am talking about wasting substance. Time, talents, gifting, and all the unpacked possibility of life. This kind of dissipation is a tragedy of untold proportion in the modern Western world. This kind of substance abuse is not irredeemable but it is irreversible. Think about that.

There is another kind of dissipation though which the more seeming wise and respectable unfortunately get themselves hooked into. It is dissipation of a better kind, but dissipation nevertheless.

You see, whenever we spend ourselves on that which does not last, we dissipate our very substance. There are two questions we can ask ourselves concerning the spending of our substance, to better then discern either the true worth of its wise expenditure or its wasteful abuse.

"What is there of any value which I shall leave behind me when all my substance is spent? What things of value do I look forward to, have I invested in even, in my eternal life to come?" We are moving speedily towards the end of this year and I tell you, if you want to have done with substance abuse then these are two of the best substantial and ethical questions you could ever bring to your life. Try them if you dare.

A new year is coming. Think and pray right now, how you might invest your time and talents to more eternal consequence in the year to come.

Listen: *"With her enticing speech she caused him to yield, With her flattering lips she seduced him. Immediately he went after her, as an ox goes to the slaughter, Or as a fool to the correction of the stocks, Till an arrow struck his liver. As a bird hastens to the snare, He did not know it would cost his life. Now therefore, listen to me, my children; Pay attention to the words of my mouth: Do not let your heart turn aside to her ways, Do not stray into her paths; For she has cast down many wounded, And all who were slain by her were strong men. Her house is the way to hell, Descending to the chambers of death." (Proverbs 7:21-27 NKJV.)*

Pray: Lord, do not let me dissipate my substance, even on a perfumed bed of myrrh and aloes, and sugar coated cinnamon. Deliver me from taking my fill of all false loves which bring with them nothing but the coming of that morning emptiness. Deliver me from substance abuse I pray, in Jesus name, amen!

Night-Whisper | **JEWELS**

Singing sapphires

"*I don't know what it is?*" said the neurologist as he examined the MRI of my brain. "*It's not a tumor, and it's not MS but you do have increased white matter in the left hemisphere. Have you ever had a stroke?*"

"*Not that I remember,*" says I! This neurologist didn't fill me with confidence, I can tell you! As a former faultfinding technician, you just know when folks haven't got a clue, yes; you know when folks are just "poking and hoping."

Jude 24

"Now to Him who is able to keep you from stumbling, And to present you faultless Before the presence of His glory with exceeding joy" NKJV

"*Well, come back in three months' time and we shall take another look, meanwhile, let's get some fluid from your spine and look for some more indicators.*"

I didn't go back. No, it was another neurologist that without even looking at any MRI results asked me, "*When you were boxing and when you're coaching, were you ever hit so hard that you saw stars?*"

"*Many times!*" says I.

"*Well that accounts for the white matter,*" says he, "*It's just a bit of brain damage.*"

"Just a bit of brain damage!" Good grief Charlie Brown! Now you can have just a bit of a tummy ache, you can fall and scrape your knee and have just a bit of a cut, but I'm sorry, how on top side of God's good earth, can anyone say to you with a smile, "*Oh don't worry about that, it's just a bit of brain damage!*"

The moral of this little episode in my life is quite simple. Don't get punched in the head! The memory of this little episode however, is something quite, quite different. You see, I'm getting older, life is getting busier, the ball juggling and plate spinning seems to be on the increase, and my memory is not what it should be, it certainly is not what it was. Maybe it's just a bit of brain damage that's the problem. Ha!

I am fascinated by the function of memory, both factual and emotional memory. One very small aspect of this most magnificent capacity to store and retrieve both factual and emotional information is the ability of comparison. "My," we say, "he's put on a lot of weight since the last time I saw him!" You see, comparison! Indeed, almost every decision we make is based on memorial comparison. In this one little aspect then, memory is so very important to both who we are and the directions in which we shall go, and I suppose then, that memory is eternally important!

You see, comparison! Indeed, almost every decision we make is based on memorial comparison. In this one little aspect then, memory is so very important to both who we are and the directions in which we shall go, and I suppose then, that memory is eternally important!

The problem with memory is that it stores every bit of experiential information about ourselves and others, and in a fallen world, that means it stores all the facts and feelings of our sins, both those we have initiated, and those sins of others in which we have participated. Indeed, every sin of thought and action, every sin of commission and omission is stored in our memory. The coming of the light of God in the face of Christ Jesus has brought repentance, remorse, maybe even some acts of restitution and please God, some gracious relief to us but what about the memories of those often atrocious acts? Ah well, the memories are still there, lodged in us, lodging with us, like some scabby, unwelcome and unwanted guests. Maybe this side of heaven, God's work in us will be deep enough to remove the power of these memories over us, if not their presence within us. I think so. I hope so. We all want it to be so, do we not?

Like it or not, our memorial experience shapes us, it helps make us. Therefore, our memories, both good and evil, are also part of our story, and I think maybe, part of our eternal story as well. Did you hear that? Part of our eternal story as well! Now if I am correct, shall we then carry these memories of both good and evil, forever with us? If that is the case, how in heaven, along with Jesus and all the rejoicing saints, shall the memories of past hurts, past failures, past sins, still find a lodging place in our being? It sounds grotesque doesn't it? Yet nevertheless, I think they must, for if they do not remain with us, surely we shall lose such a part of our shaping story, that we shall cease to be who we truly are, cease to be our authentic selves. Shall God allow our plastic false selves into heaven? Shall God ever allow plastic of any kind in heaven!?" I think not. I've read the book of Revelation friends and heaven is solid with God made materials. There is nothing plastic in heaven, absolutely nothing!

Spurgeon today, commenting on our text for tonight says, **"We shall be unblameable and unreproveable even in His eyes. His law will not only have no charge against us, but it will be magnified in us. Moreover, the work of the Holy Spirit within us will be altogether complete. He will make us so perfectly holy, that we shall have no lingering tendency to sin. Judgment, memory, will—every power and passion shall be emancipated from the thralldom of evil."** How wonderful!

> *In heaven, memory, — and every power and passion shall be emancipated from the thraldom of evil.*

Our text for tonight is talking about positional and experiential faultlessness. I tell you the truth, if God does not deal with our memories, then I do not how this faultlessness can ever exist! For surely, part of hellishness is an eternal and continual remembrance of all our sins and shortcomings and so, would it not be hell in heaven to have brain damage healed only to then remember even more of one's desperate shortcomings and sins? Of course it would!

I do not know how our great God will do it. I really don't, but nevertheless, somehow, I believe that God will, no He must, make diamonds from our dirty coal memories still carried with us, and produce some singing sapphires from all our sinly scars.

Memories must remain for us to maintain our stories, for us to be all we truly are. Yet this dark and transforming mystery of heaven shall change them all into such a glittering of golden dust, that they shall be forever and for always, to the eternal praise of His glory. I agree with Spurgeon tonight that, "Memory shall be emancipated from the thralldom of evil!" All our yesterdays shall be then present with us in heaven but dealt with. Present but forgiven, present but healed, present but released, present but transformed, powerful and glorious. They shall become God made miniscule diamonds, glittering in the magnitude of the heavenly diadem.

Now I tell you friends, that's a miracle worth the waiting for!

Listen: *"To God our Saviour, Who alone is wise, Be glory and majesty, Dominion and power, Both now and forever. Amen." Jude 24 NKJV*

Pray: Lord, all my pains and all my scars, all my shame and hurts are in Your hands and in Your hands, they become less like scars and more like character. Amen to that Lord and amen again!

Night-Whisper | **PRAISE**

The elixir of life

Well it is nearly Christmas, and that old Scrooge-like mentality is raising its ugly head within me again. Sometimes I think the Puritans had it right when they banned Christmas! That is until I get my presents on Christmas day. I am, it seems, forever fickle.

Romans 1:21-22

"...because, although they knew God, they did not glorify Him as God, nor were thankful, but became futile in their thoughts, and their foolish hearts were darkened." NKJV

In me, the root of this Scrooge-like attitude is a spirit that is unthankful. Yes, a spirit of unthankfulness is the root cause of so many ills. Bitterness, depression, refracted vision, hate, anger and all the associated physical manifestations of a multitude of spiritual ills can trace their root cause to a lack of thankfulness. The antidote of course is quite simple, which is to be thankful! However, once you're in one of those Scrooge-like funks, once you're angry at God, once you're bitter at your circumstance, once you're sick both spiritually and physically then even beginning to be thankful is a bitter pill to swallow. Indeed, I would go so far as to say, that the elixir of life, the great and brimming, full and frothing cup of thankfulness, is far too robust a drink to be swallowed by any restricted throat of praise. Yet I tell you, unless this medicine of thankfulness is taken, in its fullness mind you, then bitter emaciation and black and twisted death shall surely fill its abandoned place in our lives. That's a fact that you can have for free tonight.

Now allow me to speak to many a sick puppy that might be reading these pages right now, for you *must* get thankfulness inside you tonight and there is no better time to begin this new regime than Christmas time. "Well how?" you ask, and I am glad you did, because I'm going to tell you how to do it.

First, pick something you can be thankful for. Jonah was thankful for a worm and a gourd and cool east wind. There is always something you know. Begin with something little. "Thank you for this soft pillow upon which I am laying my most miserable of heads tonight. Amen."

For the restricted soul, thankfulness is hard to swallow, but the trick is to begin with little things, sips of soft and pulpy goodness. Once you get a little thankfulness down your gullet on a regular basis is tends to open up the passageways, and larger amounts of thankfulness can be taken in to you. Over a period of time, even a short period of time such thankful intake will bring health to the whole being.

> *Once you get a little thankfulness down your gullet on a regular basis is tends to open up the passageways, and larger amounts of thankfulness can be taken in to you.*

Let me finish tonight by reiterating the one most important thing. *Do not think that thankfulness is something that* you simply give out! Oh no, if you think that then you will have missed the whole point of it. Thankfulness is an elixir for the bitter souls, for the hardened heart, for the blind and the deaf, for those who have lost their voice. Thankfulness is a medicine for the soul and an elixir par excellence that the great curer of souls Himself insists we lay upon our lips a thousand times a day. I can assure of one thing, there is life in this frothing cup of thankfulness and it always bubbles and over flows to others. Let me ask you tonight then, have you taken your medicine of thankfulness today?

Listen: *"And let the peace of God rule in your hearts, to which also you were called in one body; and be thankful." Colossians 3:15 NKJV*

Pray: I reluctantly squeak before You Lord saying that I wish to serve You with gladness, saying that I would like to come before You with winning singing instead of whining loss, because You are God and it is You who has made me, not myself, it is You who has called me a 'sheep of Your pasture,' ha! So then help me to enter Your gates with thanksgiving, and go into Your courts with praise so I might be most thankful to You my God and bless Your name instead of cursing it. I ask You this, because You the Lord are good and You say that Your mercy is everlasting and that Your truth endures to all generations. So if it's true, then do this for me, yes, put a new song on my heart, in Jesus name I ask it, just to make doubly sure, amen.

Clouds of glory

A Wireless Fidelity or Wi-Fi enabled device is something like a personal computer, game console, cell phone, MP3 player or personal data assistant for example, that can connect to the internet when within range of a wireless network, which is itself, connected to the internet. The area covered by one or more interconnected access points is called a hotspot. Hotspots can cover as little as a single room with wireless-opaque walls or as much as many square miles covered by overlapping access points. Such a mesh of overlapping access points is called a Wi-Fi cloud, and when you are in the cloud dear friends then you are in an area of seamless wireless access! Bear with me now folks, for there is some spiritual application here.

Matthew 13:58

"Now He did not do many mighty works there because of their unbelief." NKJV

I always appreciate those brave folks who pray for miracles of healing. I think it takes brave and believing people to publically step out and in faith, both ask for and believe for a miracle of any kind, especially the healing kind. The problem I have with this "kind courage" is that it rarely, and in my experience virtually never, results in the miracle that was prayed for. Why?

I used to very comfortably base my life on the precepts of the Holy Scriptures rather than the fullness of its New Covenant practices, by conveniently confining all New Testament miraculous paraphernalia of any sort, to a doctrinal storage area of dispensational disposal! In other words, "All that miraculous stuff was for then, as for now, well, we have the Word of God in its power and fullness and frankly we now neither need nor have the privilege nor the access to the miraculous manifestations of the New Testament period." Well, I wish we did indeed have the Word of God in its fullness and power among us (I shall leave that for another evening) but I know this, there was never a time in my personal history, indeed, in our national history, when we needed a manifestation of the New Testament miraculous montage! Why don't we see it?

Some people would say it is because of the lack of individual faith. What a most hurtful statement to those whose faith inevitably lays its roots in the fields of desperation. No, I don't think that is the case. So, if we have an apostolic and prophetic five-fold, and not a threefold ministry, and if we do not have a doctrinal dispensational disaster on our hands and the lack of an individual's ability to most desperately 'faith it' is not a contentious issue, then why do we not see such Manifestations of the Miraculous as seen in the New Testament?

> *One cloud is damp and grey. It is occupied by the demonic and home to various evangelical 'settlednesses.' Settled hopelessness, settled smugness and especially settled for less-ness!*

May I suggest, and it is only a suggestion, that we are in the wrong kind of cloud. I do wonder if there are two kinds of spiritual clouds. One cloud is damp and grey. It is occupied by the demonic and home to various evangelical 'settlednesses.' Settled hopelessness, settled smugness and especially settled for less-ness! When you are in this kind of unbelieving cloud, your head is always bowed against the wind, your shoulders shrugged downwards to the waiting earth, and your hands kept firmly in the warmth of your desperate pockets. In this cloud of unbelief, you will rarely, yes so very rarely find a hot spot of miraculous happening.

I wonder if there is another cloud. A cloud of bright belief, a gathering together of meshed and seamless hotspots where the ambience and atmosphere is one of hope, is one of expectancy, is one of raised and openhanded certainty in the mighty name of Jesus, and is even one of bright and brightest glory! I wonder if camps of angels move in such a cloud and I wonder if it is such a cloud in which Abraham still walks and Moses and Elijah, indeed, all the fulfilment of the law of the prophets walks there, in the form of one like a son of man! How would you like to be in that cloud tonight?

If you are in the wrong cloud, then maybe you need to find a new service provider.

Listen: *"For who, having heard, rebelled? Indeed, was it not all who came out of Egypt, led by Moses? Now with whom was He angry forty* *years? Was it not with those who sinned, whose corpses fell in the wilderness? And to whom did He swear that they would not enter His rest, but to those who did not obey? So we see that they could not enter in because of unbelief." Hebrews 3:16-19 NKJV*

Pray: Lord, there are too many Christian corpses left rotting in the wilderness. Bring us Your "Hotspot" people of faith and power O Lord and mesh them together into a mighty cloud of glorious and seamless belief, in Jesus name we ask it, amen and let it be so.

| Vol 01 | Q4 | NW00354 | December 19th |

Night-Whisper | **CONTINUE**

Completing circles

Here's a free party trick for Christmas time. Do you know how to draw a circle with a dot in the center without removing your pencil from the paper itself? OK, let me tell you!

Exodus 4:19-20

"Now the Lord said to Moses in Midian, 'Go, return to Egypt; for all the men who sought your life are dead.'" NKJV

First, draw a dot in the middle of the paper. Now, fold over the edge of the paper so that it touches the pencil. No need to crease the paper or move the pencil off the paper. Now, draw a straight line up onto the fold and from there, draw a quarter circle, drawing right down off the edge of the fold back onto the original plane. Now, unfold the paper, and where you are right now, is exactly where you need to be. Now, simply draw a circle with the dot at the center. Simple!

The thing I like most about this neat little exercise, this trick in mental agility, is that the task can only be achieved, can only be completed, by first of all moving in an arc from the facing plane of the paper to the rear and unseen plane of the paper, brought near by a fold. The fold must occur and the journey must be travelled before you can re-enter the plane of your destiny and complete the circle around the central point!

Now whether you like it or not, life is really similar to this. Sometimes to complete the task, we have the leave the plane of our travels before re-entering it a more appropriate point in maybe both space and time. Sometimes, before you can lead Israel to the promised land, you have to spend forty years in the backside of the desert, drawing an unseen arc across the wilderness before you are drawn back onto your original plane to complete the circle of your calling. Think about that.

Listen: *"But when it pleased God, who separated me from my mother's womb and called me through His grace, to reveal His Son in me, that I* *might preach Him among the Gentiles, I did not immediately confer with flesh and blood, nor did I go up to Jerusalem to those who were apostles before me; but I went to Arabia, and returned again to Damascus. Then after three years I went up to Jerusalem to see Peter, and remained with him fifteen days. But I saw none of the other apostles except James, the Lord's brother. (Now concerning the things which I write to you, indeed, before God, I do not lie.) Afterward I went into the regions of Syria and Cilicia. And I was unknown by face to the churches of Judea which were in Christ. But they were hearing only, 'He who formerly persecuted us now preaches the faith which he once tried to destroy.' And they glorified God in me. Then after fourteen years I went up again to Jerusalem with Barnabas, and also took Titus with me."* Galatians 1:15-2:2 NKJV

Pray: Lord, I know the longer my arc, the bigger my circle. Let it be so O Lord, let it be so, in Jesus name, amen and let it be so.

| Vol 01 | Q4 | NW00355 | December 20th |

Night-Whisper | **SMELL**

Hungry waters

In the South of France, it is the city of Grasse that claims to be the perfume capital of the world. It is the industrial professionals of this ancient industry that at the time of my writing tonight, claims that although there may be 1,000 professional Perfumers in the world, there are only 50 "noses" and each of them have originated or been trained in the city of Grasse!

Song of Solomon 7:6-9

"How fair and how pleasant you are, O love, with your delights! This stature of yours is like a palm tree, And your breasts like its clusters. I said, 'I will go up to the palm tree, I will take hold of its branches.' Let now your breasts be like clusters of the vine, The fragrance of your breath like apples, And the roof of your mouth like the best wine." NKJV

A "nose" is a unique technical artiste, an inventor of perfumes with the ability to recognize up to 3,000 different smells. Working for months at a time, their task and calling is the ability to mix such a harmony of fragrances that the tone of their invention will set all other noses to dancing!

Of course perfume has been used for thousands of years in commemoration, medication, sanitation, seduction and sacrifice. Useful stuff. Knowledge of perfumery came to Europe from the East early on the 14th Century, but it was Queen Elizabeth of Hungary who ordered the making of the modern perfume made from scented oils blended in an alcohol solution. Indeed this first European perfume became so popular that is was known throughout the Western World as Hungarian Water.

I would like to suggest tonight, that the church has much more than 50 noses! Indeed, I wonder just how many folk have the capacity of leadership to orchestrate such a harmony of fragrances, fragrances of commemoration, healing, health, spiritual seduction and sacrifice, that when steeped in the preservative and powerful alcohol of the Holy Spirit, they will set the church to dancing! I suspect there are many and should such a ballad of fragrant forcefulness be let loose in the church and subsequently upon the world, that the top note of "wowness" would turn their necks in wonder, the middle note of "wooing" would win their hearts to Christ and the base note of "warmth and tenacity" would both bind them in the loving arms of the Father and keep them firmly and happily in His grip.

I reckon we need to picking a few noses and then putting them to work and making us some Hungry Water to sprinkle on a tired old church and a stinky world! What do you reckon tonight?

Listen: *"The fig tree puts forth her green figs, and the vines with the tender grapes give a good smell. Rise up, my love, my fair one, and come away!" Song of Solomon 2:13 NKJV*

Pray: Lord, lead us to the noses and help us to honor them and release them in Jesus name we pray, amen.

| Vol 01 | Q4 | NW00356 | December 21ˢᵗ |

Night-Whisper | PREPARE

Two more twin towers

I am writing tonight's Whisper from the village of Bolney in West Sussex. I just so happen to be a few miles from the village of Hassocks, where on the London to Brighton railroad line, the Clayton Tunnel, digs itself 1.5 miles into the chalky hills of the Sussex Downland! Today, the tunnel's north-facing black and open mouth is still bedecked by castle-like towers, where like some foul entrance to hell, it has for well over a century, vomited its cold and moaning commuters, all the way up to London's Victoria Station. I have passed this tunnel entrance thousands of times in my life and have always been intrigued regarding the possibility of living in these twin towers, above this pretty and steaming, black and gleaming, gory gate of hell.

Amos 4:11

"'I overthrew some of you, as God overthrew Sodom and Gomorrah, and you were like a firebrand plucked from the burning; Yet you have not returned to Me,' says the Lord."
NKJV

In 1873, on the death of missionary David Livingstone, a copy of one of CH Spurgeon's printed sermons "Accidents, Not Punishments" was found among his but few possessions. Grubby, much read and well worn, it bore a handwritten comment at the top of the first page which said, "Very good, DL." Livingstone had apparently carried this sermon with him throughout his travels in Africa, and upon his death it was returned to Spurgeon and apparently was much treasured by him.

Spurgeon preached this message, "Accidents, Not Punishments" in response to two disasters in 1861. One was a terrible collision between two trains in this same Clayton Tunnel, between London and Brighton and another train wreck in Kentish Town Fields, North London. In both these gruesome incidents, 38 people were killed and hundreds were injured.

The crux of Spurgeon's sermon was a call for Christians not to quickly attribute the judgement of God to terrible accidents. Wise advice! Indeed, in that same sermon Spurgeon makes reference to his first message preached at Surrey Gardens Music Hall in 1856 which was used for an event of his, and also was where seven people were killed in a human stampede and 28 more people were seriously injured. "I can say with a pure heart," says, Surgeon, "we met for no object but to serve our God, and the minister had no aim in going to that place but that of gathering the many to hear who otherwise would not have listened to his voice and yet there were funerals as the result of a holy effort *(for holy effort still we avow it to have been, and the after-smile of God hath proved it so). There were deaths, and deaths among God's people, I was about to say, I am glad it was with God's people rather than with others. A fearful fright took hold upon the congregation, and they fled, and do you not see that if accidents are to be viewed as judgments, then it is a fair inference that we were sinning in being there—an insinuation which our consciences repudiate with scorn?"*

> *Christians must not to quickly attribute the judgement of God to terrible accidents.*

The fact is that we are all dying. The fact is that both the righteous and the unrighteous, whether in planned or unplanned ways, whether in gruesome or gallant circumstances, shall all meet death. Spurgeon was right, that the ways of death and the providences of God in it, are mostly inscrutable! Indeed, I echo Spurgeon's call in that, "God Forbid we should offer our own reason when God has not offered His."

Death is coming. All you can do is be prepared for that passing. For all of us are already living in the twin towers above the Clayton Tunnel, above the black gates of death. Are we prepared tonight? For I tell you, that it is only if you have safely met with Jesus that you can safely meet with death.

Listen: *"Therefore thus will I do to you, O Israel; Because I will do this to you, Prepare to meet your God, O Israel!" Amos 4:12 NKJV*

Pray: Lord, each day I praise You. Lord, each day I give myself away to You. Lord, thank You that You have dealt with the cold of the grave by the heat of Your resurrection, that You have dealt with the sting of death by the Shield of Your salvation and that even I, yes even I am safe in You. For You are the Lord Christ, my Jesus, and my Savior. Amen!

Night-Whisper | **WISDOM**

Satan's claws

Two boys were walking home from Sunday school after hearing some strong preaching on the devil. One said to the other, "What do you think about all this Satan stuff then?" The other boy replies, "Well, you know how Santa Claus turned out don't you? So, it's probably just your Dad!" Well, I wish Satan was just your dad, but unfortunately he isn't. He is that old serpent, that old dragon and I tell you tonight that he is well armed with hook like claws and his most favorite time to come visit, is Christmas time. Now let me tell you why.

James 4:7

"Therefore submit to God. Resist the devil and he will flee from you."
NKJV

The jolly season has arrived, with all its vast expenditure and enormous expectation. The kids are coming, and the brothers the sisters, the aunts and the uncles and apart from the presents, guess what else they are bringing? Yes, you've got it! All their baggage. Now here is the thing you need to know this Christmas time; once their baggage meets your vast expenditure and your enormous expectations the kindled friction fire that is started in each other's hearts becomes redder than the eyes set in the long and scaly beast himself, waiting and warming himself by the log fire.

So, how do resist the devil at Christmas time? How do you stop the festive family fire from building and raging? Well, stop building it in the first place and stop stoking it in the second.

Don't over-extend yourself or over-expend yourself this Christmas time. Make sure your reserves are intact, yes, rest and retire as much as you can. Chill out! Getting rid of your (probably totally unrealistic) expectations on the family get together will help this no end as well. Don't have any expectations at all concerning other people. Let dogs be dogs and cats be cats and the rats, well you probably shouldn't have invited them in the first place! You know what I mean.

If you do not take my advice this Christmas and lower your expenditure and expectations, that you'd better watch out and you'd better take care, 'cause Satan's claws are coming to town!

Listen: *"Be sober, be vigilant; because your adversary the devil walks about like a roaring lion, seeking whom he may devour. Resist him, steadfast in the faith, knowing that the same sufferings are experienced by your brotherhood in the world. But may the God of all grace, who called us to His eternal glory by Christ Jesus, after you have suffered a while, perfect, establish, strengthen, and settle you. To Him be the glory and the dominion forever and ever. Amen." 1 Peter 5:8-11 NKJV*

Pray: Lord, help me to rest in You this Christmas time. Help me to give place and space to grace, both within me and through me in Jesus name I pray, amen and let it be so!

| Vol 01 | Q4 | NW00358 | December 23rd |

Night-Whisper | **FORGIVE**

Hook's 'Pure Poison' or 'Le Jardin Da'Amour?'

Sir James Matthew Barrie, 1st Baronet, Order of Merit, was the Scottish novelist best remembered for creating Peter Pan! The ninth of ten children, JM Barrie was just six years of age when his mother's favorite son, James, on the eve of his fourteenth birthday, died in a skating accident. His mother never got over this loss and spent the remaining 29 years of her life in deep depression, her only consolation being that her lost boy, would always remain a child. One time when the novelist entered her room, and heard his mother say "Is that you?" he knew it was the dead boy she was hoping to see and so he replied in a very little, lonely, rejected and dejected voice, "No, it's no' him, it's just me." All of this had such a profound impact on Barrie, that he himself never grew much beyond five foot! It would appear that J.M. Barrie was very familiar with malice, jealousy and disappointment. It resided in his stunted bones.

Ephesians 4:31-32

"Let all bitterness, wrath, anger, clamour, and evil speaking be put away from you, with all malice. And be kind to one another, tender hearted, forgiving one another, even as God in Christ forgave you."
NKJV

So, with that interesting and opening thought, let's get back to Christmas time and how to further avoid Satan's Claws, that old devil pirate captain's hooks.

Remember last night, that I counselled you in over-extending yourself in both expenditure and expectation. Now remember you must not do this, because as soon as you find your extravagance is neither appreciated nor reciprocated and worst of all, does not have the desired effect you hoped for, then a poison will build in the red corner of your eye!

Jason Isaacs plays the character of Captain Hook in the 2003 PJ Hogan version of *Peter Pan* starring a very young Jeremy Sumpter. The screenplay records that Captain Hook tried to take Peter Pan's life by poisoning his medicine, by corrupting that which should have been good for him. "Lest he should be taken alive, Hook always carried upon his person a dreadful poison distilled when he was weeping from the red of his eye. A mixture of malice, jealousy and disappointment, it was instantly fatal and without antidote." Did you get that? This poisonous mixture is instantaneously fatal to any relationship and to your own heart in particular.

I tell you, if you want to increase in stature this Christmas, if you want to stop the stunting rot settling into your bones, especially around your loved ones, then you had better empty out that poison you have secretly carried hidden away in your pocket for all these many a year, and dab on your welcoming cheeks, some fragrance of free and tender forgiveness, some love from the Garden of God, that very best perfume of Christmas time. Tell me, which fragrance will you be wearing this coming Christmas Eve? It's time to start forgiving.

> *You had better empty out that poison you have secretly carried hidden away in your pocket for all these many a year, and dab on your welcoming cheeks, some fragrance of free and tender forgiveness, some love from the Garden of God, that very best perfume of Christmas time.*

Listen: *"Therefore, laying aside all malice, all deceit, hypocrisy, envy, and all evil speaking, as newborn babes, desire the pure milk of the word, that you may grow thereby, if indeed you have tasted that the Lord is gracious."* 1 Peter 2:1-3 NKJV

Pray: Lord, help me not to neither poison nor disembowel myself or others this Christmas time, in Jesus name I ask it, amen and let it be so.

| Vol 01 | Q4 | NW00359 | December 24th |

Night-Whisper | **STRONG**

Libera me

Last night I attended a typical Christmas carol service. The theme of the short message began with asking the question, "What do Christmas carols say to us?" I found this to be both an interesting general question, and a most penetrating personal question.

Isaiah 7:14

"Therefore the Lord Himself will give you a sign: Behold, the virgin shall conceive and bear a Son, and shall call His name Immanuel." NKJV

As for me, I am mostly unmoved by Christmas carols. I can muster up just enough gusto to sing but one Christmas carol, and that may be but once a year! After that, my yawning boredom closes both my heart and mouth and I long for deliverance. There is, however, one Christmas carol that I would love to sing daily but because it moves my spirit so much, I am rarely able to do so.

The carol I am referring to is most interesting because the tune is in fact taken from a Roman Catholic Requiem Mass. Yes, the tune is taken from a 15th century French Franciscan nun, funeral procession, which in Latin is called the "Libera Me," or "Deliver me." How appropriate for bored old me and how amusing, that thousands of jolly carollers are completely unaware that they are in fact singing a funeral dirge! Hilarious!

The word "antiphone" is made from combining two Greek words, first "αντί" meaning "opposite", and then "φωνη" meaning voice. Antiphone refers to two choirs singing the same musical piece but in alternation. This style of singing is found in the early church, even in Israel of old and is most definitely a copy of the heavenly form of angelic style of praise and worship. From the earliest centuries of the church these antiphones have been sung on every Lord's day evening and those which are known as the "O antiphones" have always been sung just during the seven or eight days prior to Christmas.

Each of these "O antiphones" is titled by both one of the names of Jesus and one of His attributes:

December 17: O Sapientia (O Wisdom)
December 18: O Adonai (O Adonai)
December 19: O Radix Jesse (O Root of Jesse)
December 20: O Clavis David (O Key of David)
December 21: O Oriens (O Sunrise)
December 22: O Rex Gentium (O King of the nations)
December 23: O Emmanuel (O Emmanuel)

Now, when taken backwards, the first letters of these seven titles form a Latin acrostic of "Ero Cras" which translates in English to "Tomorrow, I will come." In medieval times, an eighth antiphone was added, entitled "O Virgo Virginum" or, "O Virgin of Virgins," with the acrostic now becoming "Vero Cras" or "Truly, tomorrow I will come!" How awesomely wonderful is that!

I am telling you this tonight because the Christmas carol which I would like to sing every day but cannot, is the translation of a 12th century Christian Latin text, which is thought to be a metrical version of a collation of these self-same Advent antiphones. The opening words of each stanza of my favorite carol was originally translated "Draw Near," today though we are more familiar with the translation which begins, "O Come." I cannot sing this carol, because my heart fails me by producing fountains of shuddering tears as my spirit weeps in the deep and desperate longing of the fulfilment of this most marvelous of Christmas carols.

I cannot sing this carol, because my heart fails me by producing fountains of shuddering tears as my spirit weeps in the deep and desperate longing of the fulfilment of this most marvelous of Christmas carols.-

The response of my spirit that the carol "O Come, O Come Emmanuel" produces within me a deep knowledge. Yes, it tells me that though I walk through the valley of the shadow of death, I am in fact a child of this Great and coming King and that above all things, my deepest being longs for His sunrise to dawn upon my soul. Longs for it I tell you, until I am sick with longing. Tell me tonight, "What do Christmas carols say to you?"

Listen:

O come, O come, Emmanuel,
And ransom captive Israel,
That mourns in lonely exile here
Until the Son of God appear.

Rejoice! Rejoice!
Emmanuel shall come to thee, O Israel.

O come, Thou Wisdom from on high,
Who orderest all things mightily;
To us the path of knowledge show,
And teach us in her ways to go.

Rejoice! Rejoice!
Emmanuel shall come to thee, O Israel.

O come, Thou Rod of Jesse, free
Thine own from Satan's tyranny;
From depths of hell Thy people save,
And give them victory over the grave.

Rejoice! Rejoice!
Emmanuel shall come to thee, O Israel.

O come, Thou Day-spring, come and cheer
Our spirits by Thine advent here;
Disperse the gloomy clouds of night,
And death's dark shadows put to flight.

Rejoice! Rejoice!
Emmanuel shall come to thee, O Israel.

O come, Thou Key of David, come,
And open wide our heavenly home;
Make safe the way that leads on high,
And close the path to misery.

Rejoice! Rejoice!
Emmanuel shall come to thee, O Israel.

O come, O come, great Lord of might,
Who to Thy tribes on Sinai's height

In ancient times once gave the law
In cloud and majesty and awe.

Rejoice! Rejoice!
Emmanuel shall come to thee, O Israel.

O come, Thou Root of Jesse's tree,
An ensign of Thy people be;
Before Thee rulers silent fall;
All peoples on Thy mercy call.

Rejoice! Rejoice!
Emmanuel shall come to thee, O Israel.

O come, Desire of nations, bind
In one the hearts of all mankind;
Bid Thou our sad divisions cease,
And be Thyself our King of Peace.

Rejoice! Rejoice!
Emmanuel shall come to thee, O Israel.

Pray: Deliver me, O Lord, from eternal death, on that awful day when the heavens and earth shall be shaken and you shall come to judge the world by fire. I am seized with fear and trembling until the trial is at hand and the wrath to come: when the heavens and earth shall be shaken. (The English translation of the "Libera Me".)

| Vol 01 | Q4 | NW00360 | December 25th |

Night-Whisper | **HONOUR**

Re-gifting ourselves to God

2 Samuel 24:24a

"Then the king said to Araunah, 'No, but I will surely buy it from you for a price; nor will I offer burnt offerings to the Lord my God with that which costs me nothing.'" NKJV

Now that all the business of the day is over and you have had the discipline to take the time to come aside a while and reflect upon Jesus and His Word, may I say to you that I hope your Christmas day has been both enjoyable and profitable. Of course, I do hope you got some gifts as well and that some of you even got some gifts that are going to be useful to you in the coming days! Oh and by the way, may I ask you what gift you gave to Jesus today? It's an interesting question isn't it? I mean, just what do you give to the God who has everything?

Unfortunately, God does not possess everything. For example, He may well be waiting for the fulfilment of some of those vows you made to Him in the oh so, long ago. Alternatively, He may not have the attention which He requires from you. Maybe, He does not possess the obedience which He would like to see from You. On the other hand, maybe, He does not see the fruit He expected in You. He may not see your wallet as open as much as he would like to. He may not have your ears and as yet, good grief Charlie Brown, He may not even have your heart. Imagine that. What have you given God for Christmas today?

Now, though some of these things I mention which God does not yet possess are frankly more our filial duty than gifts, more a farmers expectation, more a Master's demand if you will, or a friend's desire rather than a gift to be given to Him at Christmas time, nevertheless, may I ask you to consider your own heart's response to a gift you may have received yourself, which has been well thought out, tailored to your dreams, and costly to the giver. Surely such a gift would always warm and bless your heart. I wonder tonight then that the manner in which we give even that which is rightfully owed, will nevertheless be received as a great gift and that with great joy by the receiver?

I think tonight is a good night to apologize to Jesus for our forgetfulness by maybe deciding to deliver to Him tomorrow, something that will bless His heart. Christmas is always a good time to re-gift ourselves to God. Don't you think? Re-Gift yourself to God tonight.

Listen: *"My son, give me your heart..." (Proverbs 23:26a NKJV)*

Pray:

When the music fades, all is stripped away and I simply come
Longing just to bring something that's of worth
That will bless Your heart
I bring You more than a song for a song in itself
Is not what You have required
You search much deeper within through the way things appear
You're looking into my heart

I'm coming back to the heart of worship
And it's all about You. it's all about You, Jesus
I'm sorry Lord for the thing I've made it
When it's all about You, it's all about You, Jesus
King of endless worth no one could express
How much You deserve, though I'm weak and poor
All I have is Yours. every single breath

(Matt Redman)

| Vol 01 | Q4 | NW00361 | December 26th |

Night-Whisper | **COURAGE**

Blinded by the light!

In the United Kingdom and commonwealth, for centuries this day after Christmas has been called Boxing Day. The etymology of this term is mostly concerned with employees of various sorts, receiving what can only be termed as a Christmas bonus, which was given in compensation for their work during the last year, or their work of just yesterday. In any event, these goods, be they brand new or sumptuous leftovers, were given in a box to the less fortunate, hence the name, Boxing Day! I do hope you get a bonus gift this Boxing Day.

Isaiah 42:16a-d

"I will bring the blind by a way they did not know; I will lead them in paths they have not known. I will make darkness light before them, And crooked places straight." NKJV

Boxing Day in my time and culture is almost just as important as Christmas Day, in that it is a continuing of family get-togethers and yes indeed, another meal as big and if not bigger than Christmas Day has been served, incorporating most fully the tastier leftovers of Christmas Lunch! For the chefs of houses, and the constant cookers at Christmas time, having the means to produce new dishes and reheat those of yesterday is very important then, so you will understand my disappointment of today, when late last night, I had to turn off the Aga because for some unknown reason, it was popping and overheating. I did of course turn it on again early this morning! However, because of its design, the Aga took some eight to ten hours to get up to usable heating speed. Yes indeed, the Aga, the Swedish "stored-heat stove and cooker" invented by Nobel Prize for Physics winner, industrialist, Dr Gustaf Dalén, is really more of a living creature, or more of a way of living than a cooker! Siffice to say, we had an interesting boxing day lunch.

Now, although Acetylene was discovered in 1836 by Edmund Davy and was rediscovered in 1860 by French chemist Marcellin Berthelot, who in fact coined the name "acetylene," it was in fact Dr Dalén, who whilst working with this most explosive of gases, invented Agamassan

(Aga), a substrate of Acetylene, to absorb the gas itself and thereby allow safe storage and hence commercial exploitation. So, in 1906, the good Doctor became chief engineer at his Gas Accumulator Company (manufacturer and distributor of acetylene,) which industrialized the gas and commercialized its use! Not only was acetylene used in small old-fashioned motor vehicle carbide lamps, but also in the vast setting of lighthouses! Indeed, many Dalén lamp lighthouses are still in operation today. It was his invention of the "solar flow control valve" that allowed the acetylene lamps used in sea buoys and unmanned lighthouse to automatically turn themselves off when it was daylight. This invention not only saved 80% of fuel but also got Dalén his Nobel Prize for Physics. It was his brother, a most famous ophthalmologist, who collected Dalén's prize, because Dalén himself, had been injured and permanently blinded in an acetylene explosion earlier in the year. So, the man that discovered the brightest of lights in his time, was in fact made blind by it!

> *The man that discovered the brightest of lights in his time, was in fact made blind by it!*

Whilst Dr Dalén was recovering at home, he was exposed to the vast amount of work his wife did in trying to prepare and cook for the family. From this now well-informed and well-cared-for position, whilst blind remember, he invented the Aga cooker! Dr Gustaf Dalén, a remarkable philanthropist sharing his Nobel Prize money with his staff, a great optimist and humanitarian, left inventions in the world which are still being used in both large-scale commercial arenas and in the home even today. What he discovered and utilised both hurt him and blinded him but it did not stop him being a blessing to his family and to others both in his own time and there on after. Admittedly, he had help from his family and friends but Dalén did not allow his handicap to destroy him. Did you get that?

Many of us are going into a New Year handicapped in some way. Maybe the handicap is all the more bitter because it was gained whilst trying to do good, whilst trying to pursue and utilise the light? As far as I can ascertain, Dalén was not a Christian but you are! The Father said to Israel, the apple of His eye, that He will bring them by ways and lead them in paths not previously known and in so doing, He will make the crooked places straight. This is a great promise for the New Year. Take it, it's a bonus gift for you this Boxing Day.

Listen: *"These things I will do for them, and not forsake them."* Isaiah 42:16d NKJV

Pray: Lord, please be my Keeper, be my leader, be my light this coming year, in Jesus name I pray, amen and let it be so!

And I said to the man who stood at the gate of the year: "Give me a light that I may tread safely into the unknown."

And he replied:

"Go out into the darkness and put your hand into the Hand of God. That shall be to you better than light and safer than a known way."

So I went forth, and finding the Hand of God, trod gladly into the night. And He led me towards the hills and the breaking of day in the lone East.

So heart be still:
What need our little life
Our human life to know,
If God hath comprehension?
In all the dizzy strife
Of things both high and low,
God hideth His intention.

God knows. His will
Is best. The stretch of years
Which wind ahead, so dim
To our imperfect vision,
Are clear to God. Our fears
Are premature; In Him,
All time hath full provision.

Then rest: until
God moves to lift the veil
From our impatient eyes,
When, as the sweeter features
Of Life's stern face we hail,
Fair beyond all surmise
God's thought around His creatures
Our mind shall fill.

"God Knows" by Minnie Louise Haskins.

| Vol 01 | Q4 | NW00362 | December 27th |

Night-Whisper | **PEACE**

Proclamation, provision, peace and power

I was awoken in the night with these words in my ears and I believe it is because they mean something to me, indeed, they are special to many and to most.

Esther 6:6-9

"So Haman came in, and the king asked him, 'What shall be done for the man whom the king delights to honour?' Now Haman thought in his heart, 'Whom would the king delight to honour more than me?' And Haman answered the king, 'For the man whom the king delights to honour, let a royal robe be brought which the king has worn, and a horse on which the king has ridden, which has a royal crest placed on its head. Then let this robe and horse be delivered to the hand of one of the king's most noble princes, that he may array the man whom the king delights to honour. Then parade him on horseback through the city square, and proclaim before him: "Thus shall it be done to the man whom the king delights to honour!"'" NKJV

Our text for tonight is taken from the story of the wicked Haman! He hates the Jews but is about to have his hatred and jealousy found out and gruesomely rewarded. The evil which he intended for others and their families is about to be visited upon him and his family! It's historical fact, and yet it still makes a great operatic score and oratorio, and dare I say, that it would also make a fantastic pantomime! Maybe I go too far!

Haman, just a chapter previously has been boasting about being blessed by the king, most evidently seen in his richest, his children, his status and so forth. These things most certainly meant something to Haman, that's for sure. Now for tonight, let's lay aside Haman's megalomaniacal tendencies and obvious demonization and look at his desires. Speaking as a man, I find that frighteningly, his desires and satisfactions are in fact the same strong driving forces which I find in me and I tell you, their fulfilment are also seen as marks of blessing even in the church, for who does not want to be seen to be blessed by the King, seen to be honored by the King, seen to be provided for abundantly by the King, seen to be granted peace and seen to be given power to reign by the King? Yes, in our society, possessions are power but in the church, possessions are not only power, but they are affirmed to be outward proclamations of providential blessings and divine honor from the King, and Oh, what peace such possessions bring us, and Oh what accompanying power they can bring to us within the church. Maybe I go too far.

> *In our society, possessions are power but in the church, possessions are not only power, but they are affirmed to be outward proclamations of providential blessings and divine honor from the King!*

There is everything that is Biblical about laying up for ourselves treasure in heaven. There is everything Biblical about longing to hear in heaven those most marvelous of words ever spoken to any individual, "Well done you good and faithful servant!" Yes, there is everything Biblical about seeking crowns and commendations in heaven. In heaven, in heaven, in heaven! The New Testament is a heavenly book and for Christians all of this heavenly seeking, makes us otherworld people, makes us strangers and pilgrims, makes us true disciples of Christ.

It seems to me that we have, for convenience's sake, maybe even for covetousness's sake, taken the Old Testament material and the earthly promises and blessing made to Israel, and made them New Testament signs of accomplishment, badges of honor if you will, marks of a man of God in this world and I tell you, that the desire in me to possess these things, is a great one and it is fanned into roaring flames by the church of today. After all, these are the outward signs of God's blessing!

Tell me, just what is your rod of measuring success, both yourself and for other men? Might the following of this lie also get you hung on a gallows? Maybe I go too far. Maybe this is just my Christmas pantomime talk. What do you think?

Listen: *"These are the things I want you to teach and preach. If you have leaders there who teach otherwise, who refuse the solid words of our Master Jesus and this godly instruction, tag them for what they are: ignorant windbags who infect the air with germs of envy, controversy,* *bad-mouthing, suspicious rumours. Eventually there's an epidemic of backstabbing, and truth is but a distant memory. They think religion is a way to make a fast buck. A devout life does bring wealth, but it's the rich simplicity of being yourself before God. Since we entered the world penniless and will leave it penniless, if we have bread on the table and shoes on our feet, that's enough. But if it's only money these leaders are after, they'll self-destruct in no time. Lust for money brings trouble and nothing but trouble. Going down that path, some lose their footing in the faith completely and live to regret it bitterly ever after." (1 Timothy 6:2-10 from THE MESSAGE)*

Pray: Lord come temper all my desires with the honesty of heaven. Lie is enough of a Pantomime without measuring myself on a temporal scale of passing stuff. Deliver me form this I pray, in Jesus name, amen and let it be so.

| Vol 01 | Q4 | NW00363 | December 28th |

Night-Whisper | **PERSEVERE**

Die Hard 48 – applying newness

Luke 11:24-26

"When an unclean spirit goes out of a man, he goes through dry places, seeking rest; and finding none, he says, 'I will return to my house from which I came.' And when he comes, he finds it swept and put in order. Then he goes and takes with him seven other spirits more wicked than himself, and they enter and dwell there; and the last state of that man is worse than the first."
NKJV

Will you allow me tonight to take a practical principle from the spiritual reality that our text places before us tonight for in England, these are the dog days of the Holiday season, those quiet few hours, the darkest and quietest of all maybe, between the passing of the night and the coming of the dawn. Christmas is over and everyone is waiting expectantly for the celebration of the coming New Year. Plans and preparations are afoot!

I love new beginnings! Every Lord's day for me is the beginning of a brand new week! So, you can imagine how excited I get about the coming of a brand New Year and all the New Year's Resolutions, New Year plans, and New Year actions I have lined up. However, I am sure you will agree with me when I say that often, it is only a very few days into the New Year, when the old habits so completely take over our life once more, that disappointment, disillusion and settled acceptance and sameness, take up their residence in the house they were so determinedly thrown out of just a few days previously. Why does this happen?

Well it is a true saying that "old habits die hard!" In other words, habits are so linked to ways of thinking, so rooted to heart attitudes, so entrenched in the groove of our life, that resolution alone will not break them! No, it takes nothing short of mental, emotional and physical annihilation to get rid of them! If you're going to be a pussycat about your New Year's resolutions then in a few days, they will have vanished like the morning mist. Some things in you have to die this New Year and friend, it is you that is going to have to kill them!

So tonight, here are just six short thoughts for you to consider, to ruminate on and to hopefully, put into action.

Identify those things which have to go. Identify those things which are perpetuating the existence of those things you wish to eliminate. Consider: What location do they thrive in – then change the location. Consider: What thought processes feeds them – modify the process. Consider: What heart desires attract them – kill those desires.

"Old habits die hard!" In other words, habits are so linked to ways of thinking, so rooted to heart attitudes, so entrenched in the groove of our life, that resolution alone will not break them!

Identify, change, modify and kill are, however, not enough. At best they will leave a yawning vacuum which will be filled and usually by things nastier than you tried to get rid of. No honest, this is a terrible spiritual principle. A vacuum of vacant badness, will attract more of the same! So, it is absolutely necessary and life giving to yourself, that once you've created a space, you must fill it with good things!

So then, Change: Get some different friends, catch a different train, get up at a different time, read some different books, watch some different movies, etc. etc. Change = different.

Modify your thought patterns. Open the Scriptures. Memorize a verse per day, a promise to make yours. Read it out loud. Read it aloud some seven times per day!

Kill your sinful, unhealthy, death laden desires. Show no mercy to them, do not heed their pleading screams Kill them!

Substitute the old and bad desires with new and better ones. Yes, go and court some more desires, no really, stir up the good desires this time, in whatever righteous way you can. Think about how to do that! What *gives you life?*

Yes, old habits die hard, so the last thing I want to say to you tonight is get ready for the long, long haul. For you must consistently apply the newness. Indeed I would say to you tonight that the main key to opening the newness of the coming year is *consistency*.

This year, if you follow my advice, you shall see the Lord Jesus like never before, and others still mourning will not believe your fresh new vision and the change wrought in you! Identify, change, modify, kill, substitute and continue. Six things for you to consider in the dog days of the Holidays as you await a fresh year from God.

Listen: *"Now when He rose early on the first day of the week, He appeared first to Mary Magdalene, out of whom He had cast seven demons. She went and told those who had been with Him, as they mourned and wept. And when they heard that He was alive and had been seen by her, they did not believe." Mark 16:9-11 NKJV*

Pray: Lord, help me to prepare to throw these scabby things out of my life! Lord, heal me, help me and fill me with a passionate and merciless consistency that this coming year, I might see You as I have never seen You before. Amen Lord, amen and let it be so!

| Vol 01 | Q4 | NW00364 | December 29th |

Night-Whisper | **PERSEVERE**

He's a good! He's a good! He's a good! He's Ebeneezer good!

Standing some 600 feet above the plane of Gibeon, Mizpah, The Watchtower, at the time of the prophet Samuel, had become the religious and political center in times of national emergencies. Here Samuel called the whole nation together for a time of repentance and revival, in that, he was calling them back to their vows and thus back to their first love! At this time of year I can think of no better call to send out through Whispering Word, no better call to be sent out from God the Holy Spirit within you, no better call than this deepest of all God's calls, which is, "Come back to your first love and come back now, in all your faithful fullness!"

1 Samuel 7:3-5

"Then Samuel spoke to all the house of Israel, saying, 'If you return to the Lord with all your hearts, then put away the foreign gods and the Ashtoreths from among you, and prepare your hearts for the Lord, and serve Him only; and He will deliver you from the hand of the Philistines.' So the children of Israel put away the Baals and the Ashtoreths, and served the Lord only. And Samuel said, 'Gather all Israel to Mizpah, and I will pray to the Lord for you.'"
NKJV

You might be saying, "I can't Robert. You don't know how much I have lost this year of my love for God, of respect for myself, of my devotion to Jesus, of my passion for His work and church. I can't Robert, because you don't know what precious things once given to me by the Lord of love, are now out of my hands and in the possession of my enemies. I can't come back."

May I tell you tonight, that in this very area of The Watch Tower just some twenty years previous, the Israelites suffered two catastrophic defeats at the hands of the philistines and in the last battle with them, the Israelites had lost the very Ark of God to their enemies. The support of the mercy seat was gone! The very place where the manifest presence of God once touched down and illuminated a gathered nation, was gone! In comparison to this, what have you lost?

Maybe indeed something as precious. Yes, maybe indeed. Nevertheless, Samuel calls Israel to repentance and recommitment and tonight dear friends, I do the same and in so doing, would like to point out just three things to you.

> *Be prepared for a fight then, for any recommitment will be resisted and that by the mightiest of evil manifestations.*

First, that when Samuel called the people together for national repentance their enemies heard of it, the same enemies that had routed them some twenty years before and had robbed them of their preciousness, heard of it and in the hearing, came up to the Watchtower to trounce them once again! Be prepared for a fight then, for any recommitment will be resisted and that by the mightiest of evil manifestations.

Secondly that the Israelites were not a little perplexed when this happened and cried out to God for help, indeed, they had Samuel cry out to God on their behalf. So, pray dear friends and then get people who have power with God to also pray for you! Pray for help!

Thirdly and finally tonight, that when on the back of a blooded sacrificial lamb they prayed for help and deliverance, God thundered against their enemies and Israel rode on this shockwave of the Most High and thoroughly routed their enemies, even the enemy that had slaughtered them not once, but twice some twenty years before and had robbed them of all their preciousness. He shall do the same for you.

In these dog days of the year's end, go to Watch Tower of your heart and repent and recommit yourself to your first love and have the honor of restored victory made your portion once more. When you have done this, set up your own stone of help, so as you consider and look down the past years of your life, you shall be able to say, "Despite it all, up to now, the good Lord has helped me. He's very good. Indeed, He's Ebenezer good!"

Listen: *"And Samuel took a suckling lamb and offered it as a whole burnt offering to the Lord. Then Samuel cried out to the Lord for Israel, and the Lord answered him. Now as Samuel was offering up the burnt offering, the Philistines drew near to battle against Israel. But the Lord thundered with a loud thunder upon the Philistines that day, and so confused them that they were overcome before Israel. And the men of Israel went out of Mizpah and pursued the Philistines, and drove them back as far as below*

Beth Car. Then Samuel took a stone and set it up between Mizpah and Shen, and called its name Ebenezer, saying, 'Thus far the Lord has helped us.' So the Philistines were subdued, and they did not come anymore into the territory of Israel. And the hand of the Lord was against the Philistines all the days of Samuel." 1 Samuel 7:9-13 NKJV

Pray: Lord, tonight I gather myself at the Watchtower of my heart and survey all my battlefields of defeat and places of victory. Father, I recommit myself to You. Jesus, I willingly turn my heart in love to You and tell You that with Your help and only with Your help, I shall love You more, and with that shall also love You more with greater passion. Thunder O God against my foes, put a sword in my hand and an unrelenting swing in my arms until I have pursued them and lain them dead and bloodied at my victorious feet. Help me to gather up the stones at the end of this old year and write in blood upon the rocks that 'up to now, the Lord Himself has been my helper.' In Jesus name I ask it, amen and let it be so!

| Vol 01 | Q4 | NW00365 | December 30th |

Night-Whisper | **PASSION**

Jewels in the crown

Malachi 3:17

" 'They shall be Mine,' says the Lord of hosts, 'On the day that I make them My jewels...' "
NKJV

Any kind of repentance leads to jewels and crowns and a whole lot more! In our text for tonight, the nation of Israel had been lamenting the poor results they had been experiencing in following the Lord. "It's been a waste of time," they said, "Because the proud are still blessed, still wallowing in health and wealth and the wicked are still in power!"

God replied to their complaint by telling them that they had judged Him too harshly here and frankly, He wasn't well pleased. God's hurt indignation to His children's charge was both heard and felt by those who loved Him and they consequently got together and encouraged one another in His faithfulness and goodness, and then, imagine this, they encouraged God in His faithfulness and goodness by meditating on His Name and writing their own names in a book of remembrance before Him! God's response was one of righteous covetousness! God of the angels' armies says, "They are mine, all mine! Jewels in my Crown! The glory of My head, the colors of My rule! They are My kids and I will have compassion on them, I will prefer them above all others!" God was well pleased with their encouragement of Him. Do you see that!

Now the eschatological application of this verse is at the end of days. However, the implication of these verses are both profound and very near to you. I would suggest that anyone who woos the Lord with dedication and wows Him with repentance, will be regarded as precious, granted the gift of discernment, the power of His protection and the covering of His provision.

Now, if that's not encouragement enough to repentance and recommitment at this time of year, then friends, I don't know what is. Do you want to be a jewel in His crown? Well this coming year, get wooing and get wowing God alone! God is a person that needs pursuing.

Listen: *"'On the day that I make them My jewels. And I will spare them As a man spares his own son who serves him.' Then you shall again discern Between the righteous and the wicked, between one who serves God and one who does not serve Him. 'For behold, the day is coming, burning like an oven, and all the proud, yes, all who do wickedly will be stubble. And the day which is coming shall burn them up,' says the Lord of hosts, 'That will leave them neither root nor branch. But to you who fear My name The Sun of Righteousness shall arise With healing in His wings; and you shall go out and grow fat like stall-fed calves. You shall trample the wicked, for they shall be ashes under the soles of your feet on the day that I do this,' says the Lord of hosts. 'Remember the Law of Moses, My servant, Which I commanded him in Horeb for all Israel, with the statutes and judgments. Behold, I will send you Elijah the prophet before the coming of the great and dreadful day of the Lord. And he will turn the hearts of the fathers to the children, and the hearts of the children to their fathers, lest I come and strike the earth with a curse.'" Malachi 3:17-4:6 NKJV*

Pray: Lord, at the end of this year, I choose to rest in Your goodness. Yes Lord, despite all indications to the contrary, I acknowledge Your majesty, I bow down to Your omnipotence, and I tremble at Your justice and rejoice in Your mercy. Lord, with great respect I say to You now, 'Watch out! For this year I am pursuing You with all my heart!

Night-Whisper | **POWER**

The drinking songs of the spirit

Dylan Thomas, the Welsh bard who killed himself with booze at just 39 years of age, wrote which is for me for me, one of the most influential pieces of prose ever to touch my ears and my heart. *'Under Milk Wood, A play written for voices'* is a most remarkable verbal wonder and the beauty of the opening words always, I mean always, moves me tears. It took Thomas some ten years to write it and indeed, it was the last thing he ever wrote, his Magnum Opus if you will. Tonight, on this last night of the year, I refer to this play by Thomas and quote you an opening paragraph.

Psalms 90:12

"So teach us to number our days, That we may gain a heart of wisdom."
NKJV

Listen. It is night moving in the streets, the processional salt slow musical wind in Coronation Street and Cockle Row, it is the grass growing on Llareggub Hill, dew fall, star fall, the sleep of birds in Milk Wood. Listen. It is night in the chill, squat chapel, hymning, in bonnet and brooch and bombazine black, butterfly choker and bootlace bow, coughing like nannygoats, sucking mintoes, fortywinking hallelujah; night in the four-ale, quiet as a domino; in Ocky Milkman's loft like a mouse with gloves; in Dai Bread's bakery flying like black flour. It is tonight in Donkey Street, trotting silent, with seaweed on its hooves, along the cockled cobbles, past curtained fernpot, text and trinket, harmonium, holy dresser, watercolours done by hand, china dog and rosy tin teacaddy. It is night neddying among the snuggeries of babies. Look. It is night, dumbly, royally winding through the Coronation cherry trees; going through the graveyard of Bethesda with winds gloved and folded, and dew doffed; tumbling by the Sailors Arms. Time passes. Listen. Time passes.

At the end of this year, on this night of old endings and new beginnings, I call you to listen! Time passes. Listen! Time passes. Now let me ask you, "What have you done with your time this year, these last years of your life?"

Do you believe the Gospel? Is Christ your lover? Do you take His passionate and sacrificial claims seriously? Or have you been just messing around with God? Have you been conning others and just kidding yourself with your Christianity? Have you been half dead rather than fully alive to God, for God? Listen! Time passes. Listen! Time passes. Enough of this plastic pudding! Enough of this sham and shameful shallowness of a life. You had better get real this year else you shall end up with nothing, yes with nothing at all!

Dylan Thomas, created *Under Milk Wood* and all its exciting cast of characters around a fictitious Welsh town called Llarregub. The town didn't exist, it doesn't exist and it never shall exist. The town is pure fiction! I need to ask some of you tonight, indeed, I must ask some of you tonight this burning question: "Is 'pure fiction' the description of your Christianity?"

> *Enough of this plastic pudding! Enough of this sham and shameful shallowness of a life. You had better get real with God and yourself this year else you shall end up with nothing, yes with bugger all!*

The fictional town of "Llarregub" is, of course, "Bugger all" spelt backwards, and I tell you at the end of this year, that is exactly what any fake Christianity will get you when you come to stand before the Judgement seat of Christ!

Forgive me for being a little rough with you tonight, but the day is far spent and I greatly fear that in the furious wind to come, many who profess life will not stand and many will end up with Llarregub. So, it's time to get real with yourself friend for your sake and for God's sake, for time passes. Listen. Time passes. Tell me then tonight, have you got life? Are you living life? Are you truly alive? Or are in fact, you tucked up in your coffin tonight? Are you passionately seeking God, pursuing Him, preparing for the trouble to shortly come upon you! Friend, above all this year, BE REAL about your relationship with God. Pursue him with all of your heart. If you do not, then you just might end up with Bugger all.

Listen: *"Wake up from your sleep, climb out of your coffins; Christ will show you the light! So watch your step. Use your head. Make the most of every chance you get. These are desperate times! Don't live carelessly, unthinkingly. Make sure you understand what the Master wants. Don't drink too much wine. That cheapens your life. Drink the Spirit of God, huge draughts of him. Sing hymns instead of drinking songs! Sing songs* *from your heart to Christ. Sing praises over everything, any excuse for a song to God the Father in the name of our Master, Jesus Christ." (Ephesians 5:14-20 from THE MESSAGE)*

Pray: O Lord, from the loneliness of Llarregub may all the "dickybird watching pictures of the dead" come visit me in my dreams tonight and talk to me of the redemption of my time. Haunt me Lord with the Ghosts of Christmas past, present and future. Wake me up O God to time given, time spent, time often wasted. May their desperate words and calls to action come upon me like wild waves so that my ship would so tilt and ride, that it might split the hawsers tying me steadfast to my sorry, safe but fictional little harbor. Tomorrow O Lord, suck me out to sea and show to me the big seas of Your dreams, that I might see the Wonders of the Lord. So fill my empty hands with treasure from on high that I might at last begin to live! In Jesus name I pray, amen and let it be so.

DID YOU REMEMBER?

DON'T FORGET TO ORDER YOUR NEXT QUARTER OF NIGHT WHISPERS.

Check us out more at WWW.NightWhispers.com

Buy at Www.WhisperingWord.com

THE MISSION STATEMENT OF THE 66 BOOKS MINISTRY

WWW.66Books.tv | Our Mission is:

1. "To proclaim Jesus, the Savior of the whole world, from the whole Bible, because He is wonderful!"

2. Indeed, we are constrained by the love of God, to communicate the rawness of the Bible to real people, in real ways, and our driving and major project of '66Cities' shall take us to the 66 most influential cities of the 250 nations of the world in the next 25 years. That's 16,500 cities!

3. We are aiming to build relationships with grass roots, real people, that is, ordinary people, who, in their own countries and cities, want to do extraordinary things for Jesus and the Kingdom of God, to bring a Biblical Gospel message that is relevant to now, in a world that has come to believe that Jesus is irrelevant to their lives.

If you would like to partner with us in this great task. Then we want to hear from you! Contact me today on vr@66books.tv

MORE ABOUT 'THE 66 BOOKS MINISTRY'

WWW.66Cities.com | By the year 2047, by the grace of God and according to His will and favor, The 66 Books Ministry shall be preaching consecutively from each of the 66 Books of the Holy Bible, the Gospel of the Lord Jesus Christ in 16,500 of the most influential cities of the world on an annual and ongoing basis!

We do not underestimate the quality teams of trained people that this will take, together with the need for vast amount of materials and finances which will also have to be raised. However, as most futurists indicate that the growing global population will be gathered mostly in major world cities in the coming years, there is a necessity laid upon the church to present and proclaim the God of the whole Bible, through the primacy of preaching in these cities. We are convinced that this is a paramount and pressing concern.

"For since, in the wisdom of God, the world through wisdom did not know God, it pleased God through the foolishness of the message preached to save those who believe" 1 Corinthians 1:21NKJV

"Preach the Word! Be ready in season and out of season. Convince, rebuke, exhort, with all longsuffering and teaching." 2 Timothy 4:2NKJV

The church is looking for a revival. The 66 Books Ministry, however, is trying to start a revolution of a return to the preached Word, from the whole of the Bible as a precursor to any and all coming revival.

For "whoever calls on the name of the Lord shall be saved." How then shall they call on Him in whom they have not believed? And how shall they believe in Him of whom they have not heard? And how shall they hear without a preacher? And how shall they preach unless they are sent? As it is written: "How beautiful are the feet of those who preach the gospel of peace, Who bring glad tidings of good things!" Romans 10:13-15 NKJV

We are unashamedly looking for and seeking to foster a massive, huge, releasing, transformative, and exceptionally disruptive reversal and revolutionary change, both within the church and then in the world. We are not just another mission trying to do the same as every other mission. We are intent on revolution!

To this revolutionary end, we have no fear of seeming failure and will cultivate that audacious atmosphere within our ministry. We want to attract grass roots people who are people of faith risk takers, for we believe it is people of such life hazarding attitudes that are used by God to make breakthroughs in the world for the Kingdom of God. Hanging back for fear of seeming failure, hanging back and waiting for the trained professionals, both wastes the time of the church time and kills the spirit of victory.

In that spirit then, we therefore are believing that this task can be accomplished by such people within the time frame we have given ourselves.

Fully assured then, that we are in full obedience with the great commission of our great God and Savior Jesus Christ, we do, with great confidence in Him, turn ourselves happily to this so great a task in the hope that, like a happy hound straining at the leash to be let loose, we believe that many other people will smile along with us and be part of this brand new grass roots 21st Century Global City Mission.

If you want to know more and want to be part of what we are doing then go to www.The66BooksMinistry.com or call us in the USA on **855 662 6657**, or email V.R. directly on vr@66Books.TV

AUTHOR BIO | PURPLE ROBERT

It won't take too much investigation for you to find out that Purple Robert is in fact, Victor Robert Farrell (Born 1960 and alive until now and still kicking) was born in Chesterfield England to Scottish parents with Irish grandparents, which is an obvious recipe both for writing and emotional disaster if ever there was one!

He grew up a culturally excluded Roman Catholic (his parents were divorced,) which is one of the reasons why he hates religion with a passion, and that's an interesting enough fact by itself, because he is also an ordained protestant minister to boot.

Purple Robert. became a Christian whilst serving on board a Polaris Submarine at the end of the cold war. He has gone on to do many things, including being a broadcaster, App developer, performance poet, and the long-time author of 'Night Whispers,' which is read in over 100 counties and is also translated into Spanish (see www.Night Whispers.com)

Currently, Purple Robert is also President of The 66 Books Ministry: a grass roots global city mission endeavor. I suppose it is this concoction of background and experience which means Purple Robert's communication is always raw and emotive. After all, and as he says, *"If Christianity can be relevant on a Monday morning, several hundred feet underneath an unknown ocean, in a pornographic sewer pipe carrying enough nuclear weapons to destroy a continent whilst hiding from the Russians, then it can be relevant anywhere and everywhere!"*

Purple Robert sees himself as a servant of the 'Word of the Lord' to tasked communicate the God of the whole Bible. His proclamation of the same is done in very raw terms to very real people, is both his burden and his passion.

| May 26th | Reading 147 of 366 |

MORNING → | HISTORICAL BOOKS

- BOOK 11 of 66 → | 1 KINGS 16,17

Signpost Words → | "AN ANSWER"

Highlight Verses → | 1 Kings 16:31-34

And it came to pass, as though it had been a trivial thing for him to walk in the sins of Jeroboam the son of Nebat, that he took as wife Jezebel the daughter of Ethbaal, king of the Sidonians; and he went and served Baal and worshiped him. Then he set up an altar for Baal in the temple of Baal, which he had built in Samaria. And Ahab made a wooden image. Ahab did more to provoke the Lord God of Israel to anger than all the kings of Israel who were before him. In his days Hiel of Bethel built Jericho. He laid its foundation with Abiram his firstborn, and with his youngest son Segub he set up its gates, according to the word of the Lord, which He had spoken through Joshua the son of Nun. NKJV

Some Observations → |

This is nothing but an extended killing time, and it is God who is slaughtering His wayward nation. Decade after decade the decadent mobster kings steer the people more and more out of the way of the Lord. Dogs lick up the blood from slaughtered corpses, birds peck the watery eyeballs out of the maggot eaten heads. Death and destruction stalk the land, yet still the people rise up to pray to an idle and engage in sexual sin. The mercy of God is seen on two legs and heard from one mouth, even the prophets of the Lord. Now, dropped from heaven, out of nowhere, in answer to the madness of Ahab the loon, a prophet like no other arrives on the scene. Elijah the Tishbite!

A Call To Action → |

Fine pulpits and finer churches, are rarely the abode of the prophet.

EVENING → | PAULINE EPISTLES

- BOOK 46 of 66 → | 1 CORINTHIANS 15

Signpost Words → | "ASSURANCE OF SALVATION"

Highlight Verses → | 1 Corinthians 15:1-11

Moreover, brethren, I declare to you the gospel which I preached to you, which also you received and in which you stand, by which also you are saved, if you hold fast that word which I preached to you — unless you believed in vain. For I delivered to you first of all that which I also received: that Christ died for our sins according to the Scriptures, and that He was buried, and that He rose again the third day according to the Scriptures, and that He was seen by Cephas, then by the twelve. After that He was seen by over five hundred brethren at once, of whom the greater part remain to the present, but some have fallen asleep. After that He was seen by James, then by all the apostles. Then last of all He was seen by me also, as by one born out of due time. For I am the least of the apostles, who am not worthy to be called an apostle, because I persecuted the church of God. But by the grace of God I am what I am, and His grace toward me was not in vain; but I labored more abundantly than they all, yet not I, but the grace of God which was with me.... NKJV

Some Observations → |

The two 'wee' words we Evangelicals dislike to discourse upon are 'if' and 'unless.' I believe that once we are saved we are always saved, 'IF' we continue on receiving, believing and standing. I believe that once we are saved we are always saved, 'UNLESS' we prove ourselves to be unfaithful and reprobate in forsaking the Christ of the Scriptures. Paul did not believe he was saved by our works, yet by grace he worked his little heine off!

A Call To Action → |

Continuance in the work of grace is the key to your own assurance.

JOIN THE FELLOWSHIP OF THE BOOK

WWW.TheFellowShipofTheBook.com

The Fellowship of The Book is a Daily Bible Reading Fellowship. It is a morning and evening devotional of four books available each quarter of the year. It includes

Signpost Words
Highlight Verses
Some Observations
Call To Action

Consecutively, Chronologically and in many other ways, Read The Bible Thru in 1 just one year, with both Morning and Evening reading to keep your mind focused on the Lord of the Word and the Word of The Lord. Buy this and several other ways to 'Read the Bible Thru in a Year Books' at www.whisperingword.com

ANOTHER BOOK BY THE AUTHOR, VR

Habakkuk A Prophecy For Our Time

As the Church in the West is found to be mostly dead and covered with Laodicean lukewarm vomit, as The Lord, slips the dead things silently over the side of the storm tossed ship into the dark oblivion of the waves of secular humanism and rising Islam, what remains will need to be fortified with steel to live in a quickly changing anti-Christian world of persecution. There is no better prophecy more equipped to speak to such a remnant who shall be so very besieged. Welcome to Habakkuk, 35 of 66, a prophecy for our time.

Buy at www.whisperingword.com

ANOTHER BOOK BY THE AUTHOR, VR

The 66-Minute Bible

I am told that there are 788,258 words in the King James Bible and of these 14,565 are unique. That's a lot of words! I have been reading the Bible for nearly forty years on an almost daily basis. It still remains to me the most exciting book on the planet, however, it never gets any easier. Bible reading is a spiritual discipline and for me the emphasis is on discipline. I created this resource to aid you in your Bible reading, it gives your brain a sixty second overview of the Bible, a loose enclosure to herd the narrative of the book into something that can be seen as a whole. It was never created to be a substitute, but an aid. Just saying…… Friends, welcome to the most exciting book on the planet! V.R.

Buy at www.whisperingword.com

AN INTRODUCTION TO 'PURPLE ROBERT'

Some Dangerously Different Devotionals!

Now, before I go any further, this guy comes with warning shots! The opening parts of his currently seven volumes pf poetic works says quite clearly, *"If you are easily offended by low level expletives...**Go no further. Do not read this book!** If you are prudish in any way ...**Go no further. Do not read this book!** If you do not want to be challenged...**Go no further. Do not read this book!** If you want to be stroked into unchanging sleep and into the stupor of remaining as you are...**Go no further. Do not read this book!** If you hide under the respectable covers of a comfortable religion...**Go no further. Do not read this book!** If you are frail in faith and dishonest about life under this sun...**Go no further**. If you have no real integrity regarding the state of your own heart,* **then do not read this book!** *If however, you are grown up, honest and have a basic human integrity,   **ENJOY!**"* So, there you go, you have been warned!

Purple Robert is a Performance Poet and a Metaphysical Biblical Realist. If you want to hear some of his work and get hold of the 66 Poems each of the Seven volumes contain, then go to www.PurpleRobert.com and purchase them today.

Also Buy at Buy at www.WhisperingWord.com

www.ingramcontent.com/pod-product-compliance
Lightning Source LLC
Chambersburg PA
CBHW031942080426
42735CB00007B/232